SLM 2218504
$45⁰⁰

Beginning ASP.NET 4.5 Databases

Databases

Third Edition

D1519323

Sandeep Chanda

Damien Foggon

Apress·

SEP 18 2013

Beginning ASP.NET 4.5 Databases

Copyright © 2013 by Sandeep Chanda and Damien Foggon

This work is subject to copyright. All rights are reserved by the Publisher, whether the whole or part of the material is concerned, specifically the rights of translation, reprinting, reuse of illustrations, recitation, broadcasting, reproduction on microfilms or in any other physical way, and transmission or information storage and retrieval, electronic adaptation, computer software, or by similar or dissimilar methodology now known or hereafter developed. Exempted from this legal reservation are brief excerpts in connection with reviews or scholarly analysis or material supplied specifically for the purpose of being entered and executed on a computer system, for exclusive use by the purchaser of the work. Duplication of this publication or parts thereof is permitted only under the provisions of the Copyright Law of the Publisher's location, in its current version, and permission for use must always be obtained from Springer. Permissions for use may be obtained through RightsLink at the Copyright Clearance Center. Violations are liable to prosecution under the respective Copyright Law.

ISBN 978-1-4302-4380-9

ISBN 978-1-4302-4381-6 (eBook)

Trademarked names, logos, and images may appear in this book. Rather than use a trademark symbol with every occurrence of a trademarked name, logo, or image we use the names, logos, and images only in an editorial fashion and to the benefit of the trademark owner, with no intention of infringement of the trademark.

The use in this publication of trade names, trademarks, service marks, and similar terms, even if they are not identified as such, is not to be taken as an expression of opinion as to whether or not they are subject to proprietary rights.

While the advice and information in this book are believed to be true and accurate at the date of publication, neither the authors nor the editors nor the publisher can accept any legal responsibility for any errors or omissions that may be made. The publisher makes no warranty, express or implied, with respect to the material contained herein.

President and Publisher: Paul Manning
Lead Editor: Jonathan Hassell
Technical Reviewer: Michael Mayberry
Editorial Board: Steve Anglin, Ewan Buckingham, Gary Cornell, Louise Corrigan, Morgan Ertel,
    Jonathan Gennick, Jonathan Hassell, Robert Hutchinson, Michelle Lowman, James Markham,
    Matthew Moodie, Jeff Olson, Jeffrey Pepper, Douglas Pundick, Ben Renow-Clarke, Dominic Shakeshaft,
    Gwenan Spearing, Matt Wade, Tom Welsh
Coordinating Editor: Kevin Shea
Copy Editor: Brendan Frost
Compositor: SPi Global
Indexer: SPi Global
Artist: SPi Global
Cover Designer: Anna Ishchenko

Distributed to the book trade worldwide by Springer Science+Business Media New York, 233 Spring Street, 6th Floor, New York, NY 10013. Phone 1-800-SPRINGER, fax (201) 348-4505, e-mail orders-ny@springer-sbm.com, or visit www.springeronline.com.

For information on translations, please e-mail rights@apress.com, or visit www.apress.com.

Apress and friends of ED books may be purchased in bulk for academic, corporate, or promotional use. eBook versions and licenses are also available for most titles. For more information, reference our Special Bulk Sales–eBook Licensing web page at www.apress.com/bulk-sales.

Any source code or other supplementary materials referenced by the author in this text is available to readers www.apress.com. For detailed information about how to locate your book's source code, go to www.apress.com/source-code/.

Dedicated to the three most important women in my life: my mom Reba, wife Sarita, and daughter Aayushi.

—Sandeep Chanda

Contents at a Glance

Contents at a Glance

Contents

About the Author

Sandeep Chanda is a Director of Solutions at Neudesic, a Microsoft National Systems Integrator and Gold Certified Partner. He has been working on several Microsoft technologies (including but not limited to .NET, Azure, BizTalk, SharePoint, and Dynamics CRM) for the past ten years, building large-scale enterprise applications spanning many industries. He is a technology enthusiast and has been a speaker at various corporate events and public webinars. He has authored several articles on Microsoft Dynamics CRM 4.0 in a popular online developer magazine, and he is the author of the book *Microsoft Windows Identity Foundation Cookbook* (Packt Publishing, 2012). Most recently, he has been involved in evangelizing aspects of Application Lifecycle Management (ALM) and developer collaboration using Team Foundation Server 2012 and served as speaker on this topic at the Great Indian Developer Summit 2012. He also spends quite a bit of time traveling and training different teams on the new features of .NET Framework 4.5 and Windows 8 Metro application development. Sandeep holds an M.S. degree in Software Systems from BITS, Pilani. His areas of interest include Service Oriented Computing, Pervasive Computing, and Haptic Devices. He occasionally blogs at http://vstslive.wordpress.com and he can be reached by email at sandeep.chanda@neudesic.com.

About the Technical Reviewer

Michael Mayberry has been developing software using Microsoft technologies for over 13 years. Over that time period, he has consistently adopted new solutions and tools to solve increasingly larger problems.

Michael currently serves as a software architect for a nonprofit organization in the Dallas–Fort Worth area. He has become an expert in integration, providing solutions that allow new software to interact with existing systems. His experiences ranges from content management systems to data warehouses to CRM systems.

Michael has always valued team building and sharing his knowledge with others. Recently, he has expanded his focus to include writing and reviewing.

When he is not working, Michael enjoys spending time with his beautiful wife and four children.

For questions and comments, contact Michael at michaelmayberry@hotmail.com.

Acknowledgments

The entire editorial team, especially Jonathan Hassell, Kevin Shea, and Gary Schwartz.
A special thanks to Michael Mayberry for the review and insightful feedback.

—Sandeep Chanda

Introduction

Welcome to this book. It is much more than a revision of its predecessor, *Beginning ASP.NET 2.0 Databases*. The concepts involved in building data-driven applications have radically evolved over multiple releases of .NET Framework. With the introduction of Entity Framework 5, WCF Data Services, and new features in ASP.NET 4.5 like Strongly Typed Controls and model binding, there is a greater choice among developers to build Web applications fetching data from a wide variety of data sources. The book will seek to get you started building data-driven websites using the new features in .NET Framework 4.5. It will also introduce you to ASP.NET MVC 4 as a leading technology in modern Web application development.

Who This Book Is For

The book is an excellent choice for developers who are still working on .NET Framework 2.0, and who are looking forward to learning the new data access features in .NET Framework 4.5. For the first-timer, this book is a very useful guide to get into the world of data-driven website development using ASP.NET 4.5. The book not only introduces you to the new ways of building a data access layer but also presents the best practices while doing so.

How This Book Is Structured

The book is divided into 13 chapters:

Chapter 1 is an introductory chapter that provides an overview of the new data access paradigms. It also discusses the different data sources that can be used in ASP.NET 4.5. In addition, it provides an introduction to the new features in ADO.NET.

Chapter 2 explores the future of relational databases. SQL Server 2012 is introduced, and some of the data visualization features are discussed.

Chapter 3 describes the concept of non-relational databases and why they are relevant for building data-driven applications in .NET. You will learn NoSQL concepts with MongoDB.

Chapter 4 provides a detailed overview of ADO.NET and performing database operations using it. An important new feature discussed in this chapter is asynchronous CRUD operations.

Chapter 5 provides an overview of LINQ features that will be used throughout the course of the book.

Chapter 6 provides an overview of Entity Data Model. The underlying concept is used by third-party ORM tools, and it is also used by Entity Framework. Conceptual Schema Definition Language features are also discussed in detail.

Chapter 7 explores the ways Entity Framework uses the underlying Entity Data Model concepts to generate data models. It also describes different ways of querying the model using LINQ and Entity SQL and explores a couple of data providers.

Chapter 8 puts to use the data access paradigms discussed in the first chapter with Entity Framework. It also presents an overview of Data Annotations to perform validations in ASP.NET Web Forms.

Chapter 9 provides a detailed overview of how REST-style architecture is used to fetch data using WCF Data Services and Web API. The underlying OData protocol is also discussed.

Chapter 10 shows the new data binding features in ASP.NET 4.5 and ASP.NET MVC 4. It also discusses the enhancements in data presentation.

Chapter 11 discusses the Dynamic Data concept in ASP.NET 4.5 and how you can use it to quickly build a prototype for manipulating data in a repository.

Chapter 12 explores the best practices in building a decoupled data access layer and provides useful tips to real-world issues you will encounter while building data-driven web sites.

Chapter 13 will help you become more productive as a developer building data-driven applications. Some useful ways to use Visual Studio 2012 are discussed augmented by the capabilities of Team Foundation Server (TFS) 2012.

CHAPTER 1

■ ■ ■

ASP.NET 4.5 Data Sources

The last decade has witnessed an extraordinary evolution in the way that computing devices have affected our lives. They are far more pervasive and context driven than we could have ever imagined. The World Wide Web has been transformed from being a humble collection of linked pages to one displaying dynamic behavior based on context and user actions. Web sites today are capable of displaying responsive design, changing layouts based on the resolution of the target device, delivering content based on the location of the user, showcasing media without having the user download and install any media-specific plug-in, and the list goes on. The next decade will be the one where an immersive and fluidic experience for the client will drive innovation.

ASP.NET was a big leap forward in the way dynamic web sites could be rapidly built using Visual Studio as the tool of choice for rapid application development. We are pretty sure that you still like the way you can drag and drop ready-to-go controls on the web application design surface and bind them to data sources in just a few clicks. The evolution of ASP.NET since its inception has also been phenomenal, and to keep pace ADO.NET has seen quite a few changes as well. Today it supports a multitude of data access paradigms including *WCF (Windows Communication Foundation)* Data Services for *REST (Representational State Transfer)*-style *Create, Read, Update, and Delete CRUD* operations.

In this chapter, you will get a glimpse at the modern data access paradigms that will help you learn the ways in which the data access components are designed and, in turn, use them to suit your application requirements. This will be at a very high level without getting into any last-mile implementation details. The concepts discussed here will be used throughout the rest of the book to help you gain an understanding of how the different components of the paradigm come together to build data-driven web sites.

■ **Note**   Data access paradigms are discussed at length in Chapter 8.

Given the overview, here is what we are going to cover:

- What are the new data access paradigms?
- What are the different data sources that you can use with ASP.NET 4.5 web sites?
- What are the enhancements to ADO.NET?
- How to create your first data-driven page in ASP.NET 4.5 and ASP.NET MVC 4.

If you are unsure if data-driven web sites are a good idea, then we would strongly recommend reading the book *Beginning ASP.NET 2.0 Databases: From Novice to Professional* by Damien Foggon (Apress, 2006). It is a nice precursor to the material discussed in this book, and you will easily be able to relate to the newer concepts discussed here.

The New Data Access Paradigms

How do you decide the approach you want to take to building a data access layer in your development workflow? Fortunately, the decision is fairly simple at a very high level in the design process, and it is driven by only a couple of possible scenarios:

>**The database already exists:** In this case you can choose to generate an Entity Model from the existing database and then use the Entity Model to create the data access layer.

■ **Note** *Entity Model* is an Entity Relationship Diagram generated from the database schema typically with the help of a conceptual model generator. Microsoft .NET Framework 4.5 features a built-in model generator in the ADO.NET Entity Framework.

>**The database is newly created:** In this case, there are again a couple of options. You could start by creating the Entity Model first and then use it to drive the steps to create the database. You could also create the database first and then autogenerate the Entity Model as described before.

■ **Tip** It is a good idea to start with the Entity Model–First approach. This way you have an opportunity to play with the conceptual model until it is frozen without having to change the database schema every time and avoid annoying the DBA in your team.

The preceding scenarios are driven by a design-centric approach to application development. You also have the choice of a code-centric approach, and a lot of developers prefer that since it is easy to manipulate in code than to modify the model on the design surface. Another argument in favor of the code-centric approach is the ease of deployment; however, you need to be careful since you may end up writing a lot of code!

For a new database, the code-centric approach is simpler than it is for an existing database. There are tools to generate code for an existing database; however, it is error prone and you could lose the flexibility of having the code structured in the fashion you want.

■ **Note** The code-centric approach is gaining popularity in developer communities as it provides a greater degree of flexibility and control. Developers feel empowered, and it is often easier for multitargeted deployment in scenarios where the database (or a subset of it) could be a part of an isolated storage in a handheld device in addition to the database server.

To summarize, the three paradigms of data access in modern-day application development are illustrated in the following:

>**Database First:** Reverse engineer the Entity Model from the database schema. Generate the entity classes automatically from the Entity Model using tools. Figure 1-1 demonstrates this data access paradigm.

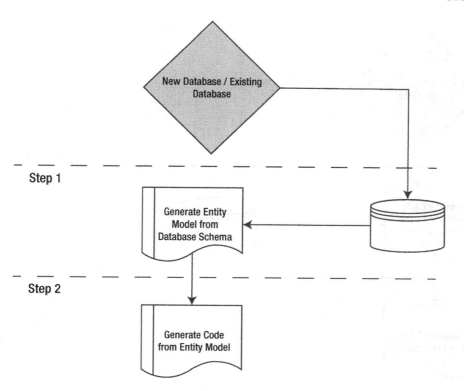

Figure 1-1. *Developer workflow for a Database-First data access paradigm*

Model First: Create the Entity Model in the designer. Generate the database schema and entity classes from the Entity Model. Figure 1-2 demonstrates this paradigm.

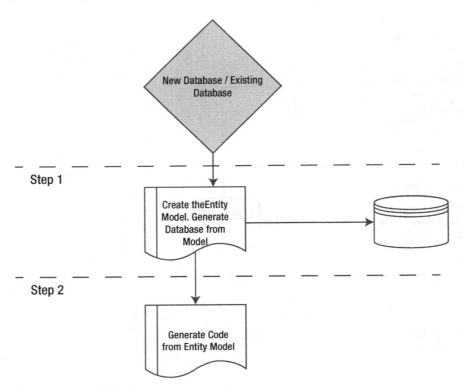

Figure 1-2. *Developer workflow for a Model-First data access paradigm*

⬛ **Note**   For an existing database, the Model-First approach is more complicated than for a new database. The illustration in Figure 1-2 ignores the additional details for simplicity's sake. You will learn further about it in Chapter 8.

Code First: Define the model and relationships in code. For a new database scenario, automatically create it at runtime. Figure 1-3 demonstrates this data access paradigm.

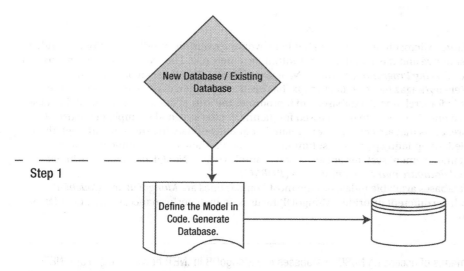

Figure 1-3. *Developer workflow for a Code-First data access paradigm*

Data Sources in ASP.NET 4.5

There has been a remarkable evolution in the support for a multitude of data sources in ASP.NET all the way from standard relational databases to services and feeds.

For a very long time, relational databases ruled the world of data sources with ADO.NET and its predecessor ADO. While ADO.NET is still dominant, newer sources like NoSQL databases, feeds, and services are gaining a very strong foothold. Let's explore some of the very popular data sources in modern web application development scenarios.

ADO.NET Data Sources

ADO.NET continues to reign in the world of .NET. Its popularity is often attributed to its ability to separate data access and manipulation cleanly into discrete components that could be used in isolation.

ADO.NET classes are available as part of the .NET Framework 4.5 under the System.Data namespace, and there are three distinct tasks that they carry out:

- Connect to a database using .NET Framework 4.5 data providers
- Execute commands
- Retrieve results

The list of data sources for ADO.NET is fairly exhaustive, and it includes relational databases like Microsoft SQL Server and Oracle, data sources that can be accessed using ODBC and OLE DB drivers, and conceptual models like the *Entity Data Model (EDM)*. EDM is new, and it is discussed in detail in Chapter 6.

The results retrieved from an ADO.NET data source can either be processed directly or stored in a DataSet for further manipulation. ADO.NET DataSet is very popular for its data manipulation capabilities like fetching data from multiple sources and aggregating them before display.

NoSQL

The developer community at large (Microsoft or otherwise) has been working overtime building solutions to bridge the gap between off-the-shelf software and the actual demand within the enterprise. The "NoSQL movement," as Ted Neward calls in his article *"The Working Programmer – Going NoSQL with MongoDB"* that can be found at `http://msdn.microsoft.com/en-us/magazine/ee310029.aspx`, has been a revolution of sorts. It challenges the theory that all types of data are fit for a relational database, and it promotes the idea of document-oriented databases to store data that is unstructured and that needs to be accessed frequently. A blog is a good example of the use of NoSQL databases as a data store. Posts that are completely unrelated frequently update the site, and although there are concurrency controls needed for updating posts and submitting comments, there are no atomic transactional requirements as such. Content management systems are also good examples where NoSQL databases are better suited than traditional *relational database management systems (RDBMS)*.

There are many NoSQL databases available today, but the most popular ones are *MongoDB* and *CouchDB*. Although they are similar, they have different priorities. MongoDB focuses on high performance, while CouchDB is geared toward high concurrency.

■ **Note**   There are no native means of accessing NoSQL databases like MongoDB in .NET; however, there are .NET Framework drivers available from the community.

Web Services

Web services allow access to data stored in a remote server over HTTP. In the world in which we live today, the term "web services" has become synonymous for exchange of data using the *SOAP (Simple Object Access Protocol)* specifications over HTTP. They have their own share of the evolution story. Having lived through various cycles of standardization, web services are now part of any modern-day application architecture. In fact, a whole layer of architecture has just emerged in the form of *Service-Oriented Architecture (SOA)* formulated from the patterns of implementing services over the years. In .NET, services have transformed from *web service enhancements (WSE)* that leveraged the WS* specifications to a full-fledged framework feature in the form of WCF, first introduced in .NET Framework 3.0.

ASP.NET 4.5 web applications can be configured to consume web services using proxies, or they can access data using the WCF *Rich Internet Application (RIA)* Services domain service. WCF RIA Services domain service will automatically generate methods for CRUD operations.

WCF Data Services

WCF Data Services enables CRUD operations on data using the *Open Data Protocol (OData)*. Microsoft has inserted OData deep into its data access strategy. OData support is now available in all its new-generation platforms including SQL Server 2008 R2, SQL Server 2012, Windows Azure Storage, SharePoint 2013, and PowerPivot.

Data Services will allow REST-style access to data models with flexible querying and association traversal capabilities. This will allow natural integration with web platforms like ASP.NET. Data Services allow data to be represented in well-known formats such as JSON and ATOM.

■ **Note**   In a RESTful service, HTTP verbs like GET, POST, PUT, and DELETE are used as actions for CRUD operations. REST-style data access has become popular due to the widespread awareness of the HTTP protocol among applications including web browsers. The openness of the protocol also makes it easy to use across heterogeneous platforms.

Syndication Services

A natural extension to using services as a source of data is to allow access to Syndication Feeds like RSS and ATOM. ASP.NET is capable of reading and parsing Syndication Feeds and displaying appropriate results.

Azure Storage

Windows Azure provides storage capabilities in the form of Tables, Blobs, and Queues at no extra cost. ASP.NET applications can leverage Azure Storage as a data store and perform data access operations using the Open Data Protocol.

HTML 5 Local Storage

This is relatively new, and it emphasizes the shift in focus on building applications that utilize the power of clients. Local Storage is used to store structured data in web clients in a way that is similar to HTTP cookies, but with robust support for storing session data across multiple windows of the client.

Figure 1-4 illustrates the different sources of data for building data-driven web sites using ASP.NET 4.5:

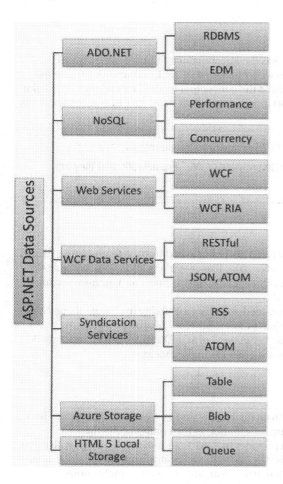

Figure 1-4. *ASP.NET 4.5 data sources*

> ▓ **Note**   In addition, files like XML, Text, PDF, CSV, and Office Documents also serve as a source of data for ASP.NET web sites. The .NET Framework has standard support for XML documents in the System.Xml namespace, and XML files can directly be transformed into a DataSet. For file types like CSV and Excel, standard ODBC and OLE DB drivers are available for direct access via ADO.NET.

Introduction to ADO.NET in .NET Framework 4.5

ADO.NET has been around for a while now. It continues to be the preferred means for accessing data from a variety of sources and serving them up for data-driven ASP.NET web sites. When ADO.NET first arrived, it was a paradigm shift from its predecessor, ADO. Although the core features of ADO.NET (acting as a consistent source of data for relational database and data sources supported by OLE DB and ODBC drivers) have remained unchanged over several .NET Framework revision cycles, a lot of work has gone into improving performance and adding new features like Entity Framework. The introduction of Entity Framework is a significant change that allows applications to work against a conceptual model and provides for a higher degree of abstraction.

What Is New in ADO.NET?

As we mentioned before, the most significant change in ADO.NET was the introduction of Entity Framework in .NET Framework 3.5 SP1. Subsequently, Entity Framework features were enhanced in .NET Framework 4.0 (like the introduction of the Model-First approach, allowing developers to build the conceptual model first and then create the supporting database) and then in .NET Framework 4.5 (like support for enum and new data types in SQL Server 2012).

> ▓ **Note**   Not all versions of Entity Framework are part of the core .NET Framework. Certain releases like Entity Framework 4.1, 4.1 Update, 4.2, and 5 are built on top of the associated release of .NET Framework, and they are generally available as the Entity Framework NuGet Package.

Entity Framework 5.0

Entity Framework 5.0 is built on top of .NET Framework 4.5, and it has a host of new additions. A few additions worth mentioning are support for the new data types in Microsoft SQL Server 2012, like geography and geometry spatial; support for table-valued functions; improvements in query performance; and robust support for batch-importing stored procedures with the Entity Model Wizard.

In addition, support for multiple diagrams for a model is introduced as well as the ability to change shape colors in the Entity Designer surface. One more enhancement worth noting is the support for LocalDb database server. By default, Visual Studio 2012 uses a reference to LocalDb database server instead of SQLEXPRESS. Entity Framework registers LocalDb as the default database server if SQLEXPRESS is not available in the machine.

SqlClient Data Provider

The SqlClient data provider allows the opening of a connection to an instance of an SQL Server database. You have probably seen it a zillion times showing up in the connection string information in the configuration file.

Several new features have been added to the SqlClient data provider in .NET Framework 4.5. The provider now supports the new features introduced in the next version of SQL Server like high availability, support for streaming, and the newer spatial data types. It also supports LocalDb, extended protection, and it allows asynchronous programming for data access. We will explore a few of these new features in the forthcoming chapters.

ADO.NET and LINQ

Not every application programmer is comfortable writing SQL queries. LINQ was introduced with the purpose of allowing developers to write set-based queries against enumerable data in their application. A logical extension was to provide for support in ADO.NET. Several flavors of LINQ are in place for ADO.NET:

- LINQ to DataSet: Optimized querying of a DataSet
- LINQ to SQL: Direct query on an SQL Server database schema
- LINQ to Entities: Querying a conceptual model

Data Providers

Data providers are lightweight native interfaces for accessing data from a variety of sources like relational databases (SQL, Oracle), ODBC and OLEDB data sources (like MS-Access, MS-Excel), and Entity Data Model. The EntityClient provider for Entity Data Model is relatively new, and it was introduced with Entity Framework in .NET Framework 3.5.

■ **Note**   Unlike the other data providers, the EntityClient provider does not interact with a data source directly. It acts as a bridge between other native providers like SqlClient and OracleClient using Entity SQL.

The EntityClient API (System.Data.EntityClient) is similar to the rest of the data providers and provides equivalents for connection (EntityConnection) and command (EntityCommand) objects. The following code demonstrates querying a conceptual model using Entity SQL:

```
string connectionString =
    "Metadata=.\\<specify the entity here>.csdl|.\\< specify the entity here >.ssdl|.\\< specify the
entity here >.msl;" +
    "Provider=System.Data.SqlClient;Provider Connection String=\"" +
    "Data Source=localhost;Initial Catalog=<specify the database name>;Integrated Security=True\"";
```

■ **Note**   The connection string information for EntityClient is different from a regular connection string. You need to specify the <entity> conceptual model information in the Metadata attribute and the actual provider information is set in the Provider attribute.

```
try
{
    using (EntityConnection connection =
        new EntityConnection(connectionString))
    {
        connection.Open();
        EntityCommand command = new EntityCommand(
            "<Specify your SQL Select Statement here>",
            connection);
        // Entity command requires SequentialAccess
        DbDataReader reader = command.ExecuteReader(
            CommandBehavior.SequentialAccess);
```

```
        while (reader.Read())
        {
            Console.WriteLine("{0}\t{1}",
                reader[0], reader[1]);
        }
    }
}
catch(QueryException ex)
{
    Console.WriteLine(ex.ToString());
}
```

The introduction of EntityClient data provider has given developers abstract native provider information from the business services, facilitating the development of pluggable data access layers that can be replaced on demand. This is very crucial to building provider-agnostic data-driven ASP.NET web sites.

Asynchronous Data Access

Prior to .NET Framework 4.5, orchestrating an asynchronous operation was clumsy at best. A lot of developers found it very difficult to program against the asynchronous interfaces exposed by the .NET Framework. This is no longer the case with .NET Framework 4.5. It introduces an overly simplified async programming model where you can perform asynchronous calls without using callbacks. The async and await modifiers in .NET Framework 4.5 are used for this purpose.

Database operations are often time-consuming, and it is prudent to perform them asynchronously to keep the UI relatively free for the user to continue working without freezing up. In the earlier versions of .NET Framework, the data providers exposed SqlCommand methods like BeginExecuteNonQuery that allowed the asynchronous execution of a T-SQL statement or a stored procedure. The implementation returns an IAsyncResult type that could be used to poll or wait for results. An IAsyncResult type of implementation requires methods to be exposed in pairs of Begin Operation and End Operation. The SqlCommand also exposes an EndExecuteNonQuery pair for the asynchronous operation to complete. IAsyncResult is required while invoking the EndExecuteNonQuery method, which will block unless the process of executing the command is complete.

```
using (var connection = new SqlConnection("..."))
    {
        try
        {
            var command = new SqlCommand(commandText, connection);
            connection.Open();
            var callBack = new AsyncCallback(CallBack);

            var result = command.BeginExecuteNonQuery(callBack, command);
            while (!result.IsCompleted)
            {
                //TODO: Continue to perform your other operations here
            }

        }
        catch (SqlException)
        {
            //Log Exception
        }
```

```
catch (Exception)
{
    //Log Exception
}

}
```

You will notice that the main thread is not blocked, and you can continue to see the results inside the while loop that checks for the IAsyncResult IsCompleted property. A simple callback handler will look like the following:

```
private static void CallBack(IAsyncResult result)
{
    try
    {
        var command = (SqlCommand)result.AsyncState;
        command.EndExecuteNonQuery(result);
    }
    catch (Exception)
    {
        //Log Exception
    }
}
```

For a simple asynchronous execution of the command, this is lot of code. You will find out how this is simplified in .NET Framework 4.5.

■ **Note**   In order for the asynchronous operation to work, the attribute "Asynchronous Processing=true" needs to be set on the connection string element of your configuration file.

Async Programming Model in .NET Framework 4.5

The asynchronous programming model just discussed has not been deprecated in .NET Framework 4.5. It continues to be supported; however, the preferred approach is to use the new model leveraging a task-based parallel programming pattern along with async and await modifiers. It is very important that you implement the modifiers appropriately. The implementation can become synchronous unless one follows an async call by one or more await modifiers. The async modifier indicates an asynchronous operation, and when the program execution encounters the await modifier, it exits the current method. When the forked task finishes, execution resumes in the method.

■ **Caution**   Asynchronous operations are not supported if the attribute "Context Connection" is set to "true" in the connection string.

The ADO.NET Async programming model in .NET Framework 4.5 exposes an equivalent asynchronous method for every synchronous method exposed by the data providers. Continuing with the previous example, the SqlCommand ExecuteNonQuery command has an equivalent asynchronous method named ExecuteNonQueryAsync. It accepts a CancellationToken as a parameter allowing the operation to be aborted before the command timeout elapses.

Now let's take a look at how the programming model significantly reduces the lines of code you have to write for the same operation.

```
private static async Task<int> ExecuteCommandAsync(SqlConnection connection, SqlCommand command) {
    await conn.OpenAsync();
    await cmd.ExecuteNonQueryAsync();
    return 1;
}
```

A caller method can pass the connection and command instances to call this method and execute the T-SQL statement or procedure.

```
using (var connection = new SqlConnection("..."))
        {
            try
            {
                var command = new SqlCommand(commandText, connection);
                int result = ExecuteCommandAsync(connection, command).Result;
            }
            catch (SqlException)
            {
                //Log Exception
            }
            catch (Exception)
            {
                //Log Exception
            }

        }
```

The async programming model is extremely robust, and it allows you to execute a task-based chain of commands. You could potentially use the new async pattern along with your existing asynchronous implementation using the older model. Here is an example using the code bits used previously:

```
using (var connection = new SqlConnection("..."))
        {
            try
            {
                AsyncCallback callBack = new AsyncCallback(CallBack);
                connection.OpenAsync().ContinueWith((task) =>
                {
                    SqlCommand cmd = new SqlCommand("...", connection);
                    IAsyncResult ia = cmd.BeginExecuteNonQuery(callBack, cmd);
                }, TaskContinuationOptions.OnlyOnRanToCompletion);

            }
            catch (SqlException)
            {
                //Log Exception
            }
            catch (Exception)
            {
                //Log Exception
            }

        }
```

Notice the `ContinueWith` method. It allows you to delegate anonymously a task-based operation. You can use the `ContinueWith` option to execute a chain of commands. In addition, the async programming model also provides support for transactions:

```
transaction = await Task.Run<SqlTransaction>(
            () => connection.BeginTransaction("Transaction")
            );
......

await Task.Run(() => transaction.Commit());
```

Developing Your First Example

Let's now put our theories into practice and explore the steps to create data-driven web sites using ASP.NET 4.5.

For the purpose of this exercise, you will use Visual Studio 2012 Ultimate Edition with .NET Framework 4.5. Also, you will be running the example inside of a Windows 8 System running Internet Explorer 10. You can, however, run this sample from your machine running Windows 7 or above using Visual Studio 2012 Express Edition. The application should run fine on IE 8 or above.

The editions of Visual Studio 2012 includes a lightweight web server in IIS Express, so if you don't have access to a full-fledged version of IIS, you can use the Express edition to test your deployment.

■ **Caution**   Some of the features discussed in this exercise are specific to Visual Studio 2012. The exercise may not work correctly if you are trying to run it with .NET Framework 4.5 in Visual Studio 2010.

Various editions of Visual Studio 2012 and .NET Framework 4.5 can be downloaded from `http://www.microsoft.com/visualstudio/eng#downloads`.

In addition, for data access you will use the SQL Server Express LocalDB database that ships with Visual Studio 2012. However, the example should work fine with SQL Server 2008 R2, SQL Server 2012, and SQL Azure.

Try It Out: First Data-Driven Page in ASP.NET 4.5

In this example, you will create a simple data-driven page in ASP.NET 4.5 using the Entity Model concepts I discussed thus far. For this example, you will use the SQL Server Express LocalDB Gadgets database, which stores information about different gadgets and the available quantity. In the end, the result will display the name of the gadget, followed by its type and quantity.

Let's first create the database. Follow these steps:

1. If you are using Windows 8 to create this example, then Visual Studio can be launched from the Start screen. Go to the Start screen and click the Visual Studio tile, as shown in Figure 1-5. This will take you to Desktop and launch the *integrated development environment (IDE)*.

Figure 1-5. Launching Visual Studio 2012 from Windows 8 Start screen

   2.   In the Visual Studio 2012 IDE, open SQL Server Object Explorer and click the Add SQL
        Server option, as shown in Figure 1-6.

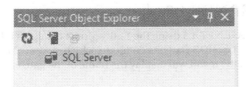

   Figure 1-6. Connecting to an SQL Server database

■ **Note**   Options like Schema Compare and Transact-SQL Editor, which were part of the Database menu in Visual Studio
2010, are now available under the SQL menu in Visual Studio 2012.

You will be prompted to connect to an instance of SQL Server. In the Server name option specify

`(LocalDb)\v11.0`

and connect with the Windows Authentication option selected. You will be connected to your instance of SQL Server Express LocalDB.

3. From the SQL Server Object Explorer, create the database Gadgets.

4. Under the Gadgets database, right-click the Tables folder and click Create Table. Specify the name of the table as GadgetStore.

5. Create the fields `Name (nvarchar(50))`, `Type (nvarchar(50))`, and `Quantity (bigint)`.

6. Once finished, click the Update button in the Create Table Design Surface. The script will run and create the table under the Gadgets database as shown in Figure 1-7. The SQL Server Object Explorer should look like the one shown in Figure 1-8.

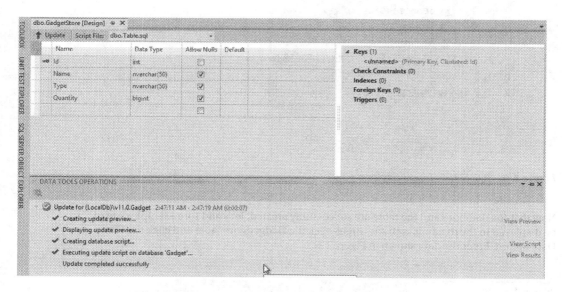

Figure 1-7. Creating the Gadgets database and the GadgetStore table

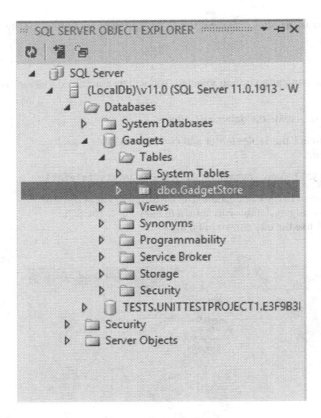

Figure 1-8. *SQL Server Object Explorer*

7. Now that the database and the table are successfully created, let's add some sample data to be displayed in the dynamic web site. Right-click the GadgetStore table and click the View Data option. Enter the data shown in Figure 1-9.

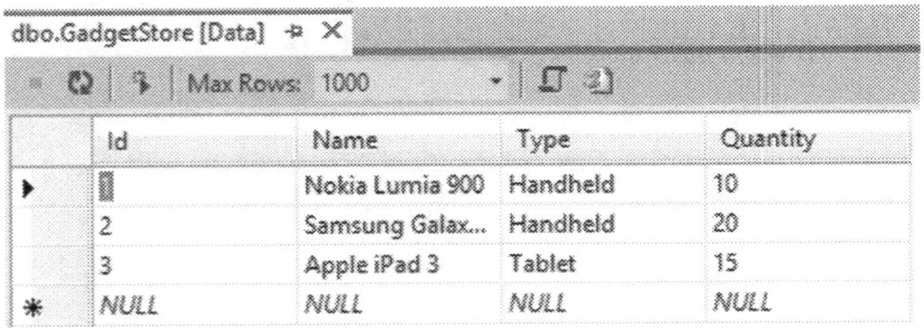

Id	Name	Type	Quantity
1	Nokia Lumia 900	Handheld	10
2	Samsung Galax...	Handheld	20
3	Apple iPad 3	Tablet	15
* NULL	NULL	NULL	NULL

Figure 1-9. *Sample data for the GadgetStore table*

8. Now that the source of data is ready, you will create the ASP.NET 4.5 web site next to consume the data in a data-driven ASPX page. In the VS 2012 IDE, Create a New Visual C# ASP.NET Web Forms Application project and specify the name FirstDataDrivenWebsite as shown in Figure 1-10.

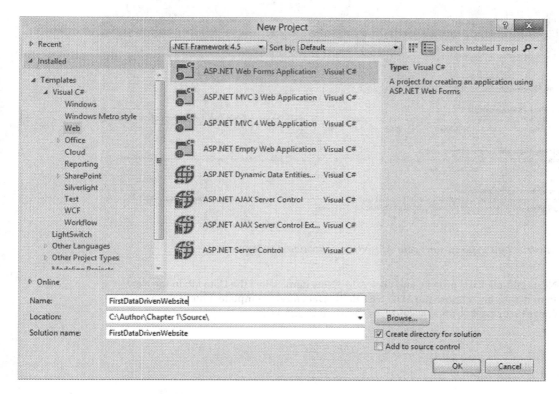

Figure 1-10. *Creating new ASP.NET Web Forms Application project*

9. Open Solution Explorer. Compile the solution and run the FirstDataDrivenWebsite project. Notice that the site launched in your browser is running from IIS Express. The ASP.NET Web Forms Application template comes with a few default implementations. The Default page that is launched in your browser provides a few jump-start instructions as shown in Figure 1-11. Also notice that it provides an implementation of the membership provider feature of .NET Framework, and you can customize it.

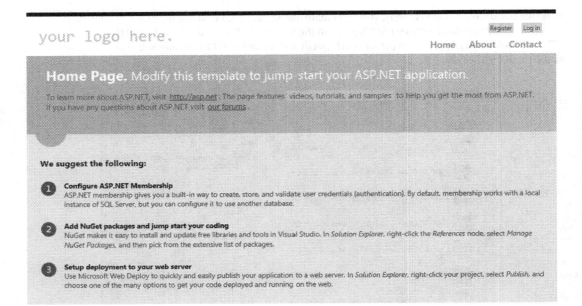

Figure 1-11. *Instructions to jump-start your ASP.NET application development*

10. Next right-click the project, and click Add || New Item. Select the Data tab in the New Item dialog, and choose the ADO.NET Entity Data Model template. Enter the name GadgetStore.edmx, and click Add, as shown in Figure 1-12.

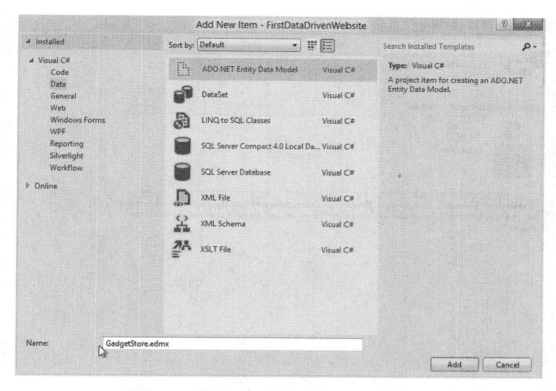

Figure 1-12. *Adding ADO.NET Entity Data Model*

11. Adding the ADO.NET Entity Data Model template launches the Entity Data Model wizard. In the first step, you decide whether to start with the Model (Model-First paradigm) or generate it from an existing Database Schema (Database-First paradigm). In this example, since you already have the database created, you will start with the Database-First option. We will explore the Model-First approach in the forthcoming chapters.

12. In the Choose Model Contents step, select the Generate from database option, as shown in Figure 1-13.

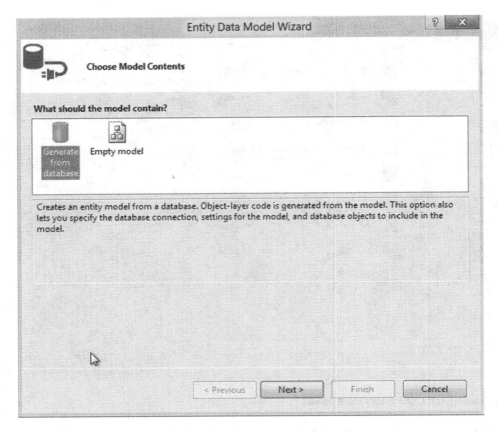

Figure 1-13. *Generating Entity Data Model from an existing database schema*

13. In the Choose Your Data Connection step, click the New Connection button to create a new connection to your instance of SQL Server Express LocalDB. Save the connection string information in the Web.config file under the name Entities as shown in Figure 1-14.

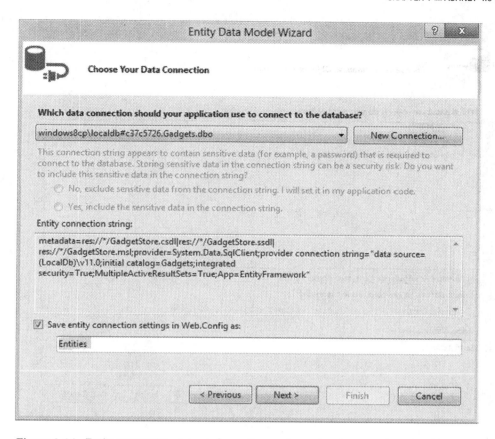

Figure 1-14. *Entity connection string information*

14. Next, as shown in Figure 1-15, choose the Database Objects that you want to be part of your Entity Model, including tables, views, and procedures. You also have the option of selecting each individual artifact from the list of database objects. For the generated entities, you can choose singular or pluralized object names and specify if you want to include foreign key columns.

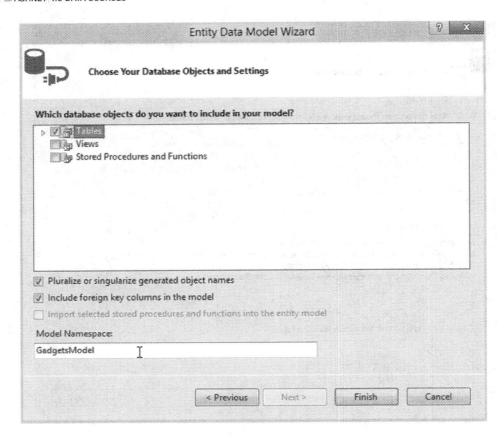

Figure 1-15. *Choosing your database objects and settings*

15. Click Finish to complete running the wizard and to create the Entity Model. Now you are ready to consume the conceptual model in your web site. There is a nice view-scoping feature in the Solution Explorer. Right-click the GadgetStore.edmx file and click "Scope to This," as shown in Figure 1-16. This will collapse all the other artifacts from the Solution Explorer and will show only elements related to the GadgetStore.edmx file.

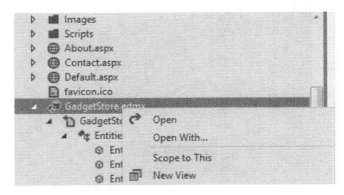

Figure 1-16. *Scoping the solution structure to show only the GadgetStore.edmx entities and related objects*

Visual Studio 2012 has a number of enhancements for developers. Most of these changes may seem minor at first glance, but they add up to save time and effort and help enhance the overall productivity of the developers. One such change is the ability to navigate through the code from within the Solution Explorer. Once you are in the scope of the file GadgetStore.edmx, expand the GadgetStore.edmx.designer.cs file and you will see the methods and properties exposed for creating a database context as shown in Figure 1-17.

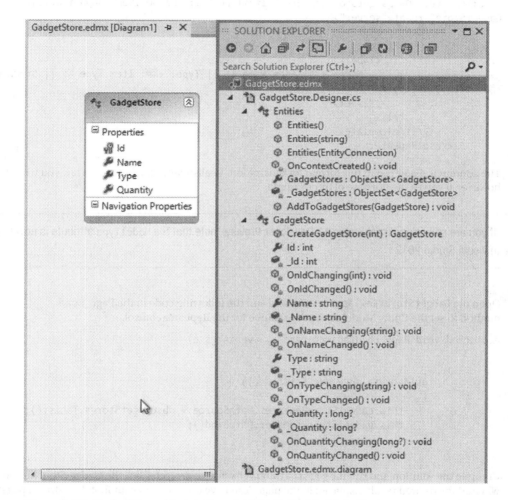

Figure 1-17. *GadgetStore object explorer and the Entity Model designer*

In addition, you can also click the GadgetStore.edmx file to preview the Entity Model in the designer.

1. There are a couple of things you need to do before using the Entity Model to display data. First add a new web form to the FirstDataDrivenWebsite project and name it GadgetStoreView.aspx.

2. Next, modify the Site.Master master page to include a link to the GadgetStoreView.aspx page. Double-click the GadgetStoreView.aspx page, to pin it to the IDE.

3. In the GadgetStoreView.aspx page source view, add an ASP.NET Repeater control and set the ItemType property to the namespace containing the conceptual model entities. Notice that once the ItemType property is set, IntelliSense will be available for you to explore and build the Repeater control template with the Entity Model properties. The final code to display the gadget store should look like the following:

```
<asp:Repeater ID="gadgetStoreRepeater" ItemType="FirstDataDrivenWebApplication.
GadgetStore" runat="server">
        <ItemTemplate>
            <li>
                <label>
                    Name: <%#: Item.Name %> || Type: <%#: Item.Type %> || Stock Count:
<%#: Item.Quantity %>
                </label>
            </li>
        </ItemTemplate>
    </asp:Repeater>
```

The content is displayed in this format for illustration. Realistically, this is not the view you would want; however, it serves the purpose of our example.

⬛ **Caution**   If you are still using Visual Studio 11 Developer Preview, note that the ModelType attribute is now renamed to ItemType in Visual Studio 2012.

4. Open the GadgetStoreView.aspx.cs file, and add the following code in the Page_Load method to set the Entity Model as the data source for the Repeater control.

```
protected void Page_Load(object sender, EventArgs e)

    {
        using (var db = new Entities())
        {
            this.gadgetStoreRepeater.DataSource = db.GadgetStores.ToList();
            this.gadgetStoreRepeater.DataBind();
        }
    }
```

Compile the solution and run the FirstDataDrivenWebsite project. Click the GadgetStore link, and you will find the desired result displayed in the page. You have now created your first data-driven page!

This style of data binding is new to the ASP.NET 4.5 Web Forms Application. Don't worry yet about how it is working; we will explore the model-binding features of ASP.NET 4.5 in detail in the forthcoming chapters.

⬛ **Note**   In addition to using strongly typed models, you can also use an EntityDataSource control to act as a source of data for the view, as shown in Figure 1-18. We will leave that for you to try to figure out.

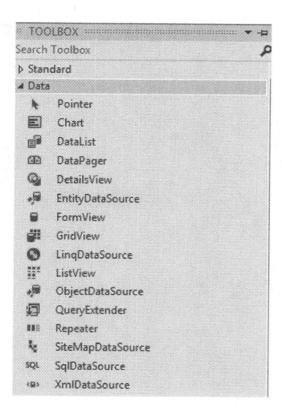

Figure 1-18. *The EntityDataSource control*

How It Works

In this chapter's example, you saw how to create a Conceptual Entity Model from an existing database and use it to create a strongly typed Repeater control with the Entity Model acting as a source of data. Your implementation created a layer of abstraction over the physical data source, thereby facilitating the use of any standard database behind the scenes. In addition, you also saw some of the new IDE features in Visual Studio 2012.

Summary

In this chapter, you explored the new data access paradigms at a very high level. You learned about some of the enhancements in ADO.NET in .NET Framework 4.5, specifically around the new set of data sources that can be used to build data-driven web sites. You learned the following:

- There are many new data sources in ASP.NET 4.5 available as part of ADO.NET or otherwise.

- ADO.NET has evolved along with the .NET Framework, and it has recently introduced support for the Conceptual Entity Model.

- ADO.NET supports a robust programming model for asynchronous operations.

- Finally, you created your first data-driven web site using the Visual Studio 2012 IDE, leveraging the Entity Model– and Database-First design concepts.

In the next chapter, you will learn more about the future of relational databases with SQL Server 2012.

CHAPTER 2

■ ■ ■

The Future of Relational Databases

In Chapter 1, you learned that modern data-driven web sites built using ASP.NET 4.5 are capable of consuming data from a variety of sources. That being said, relational databases are leading in terms of their use in the enterprise and are the most widely used source of data for dynamic web sites. Relational databases make most sense in web applications that act as an interface for transactions waiting to happen within or outside the enterprise. The transactions could be between users or between users and systems. For web sites that are more like content-driven blogs, forums, and social sites, another category of databases is gaining prominence over relational databases. They are popularly known as *NoSQL databases*, and they are discussed in detail in Chapter 3.

You could ask why we are dedicating a complete chapter on the future of relational databases. We are doing so because it is important for you to understand that the majority of data-driven web sites today rely completely on relational databases for serving up relevant information to their customers. Getting the database design right is as, if not more, important than the design of the application itself. Relational databases can become incredibly complex and, while you may have written a lot of code to bridge a capability that didn't exist in the relational database you use today, understanding some of the newer capabilities in the latest release of any popular relational database will help you make the right choices in terms of distributing the responsibilities appropriately between the application and the database. Moreover, some of the newer capabilities will also help you provision a data source and perform CRUD operations from the application far more quickly and easily than you could have imagined beforehand.

This chapter does not attempt to introduce you to relational database management system concepts such as normalization. To a certain degree, we assume that you have a fair amount of knowledge of RDBMS concepts and that you have worked on leveraging any one of the relational databases (Microsoft SQL Server, Oracle, MySQL, and so forth) in the past while building data-driven web sites. We will instead focus on the new features introduced in Microsoft SQL Server 2012 and how they can help speed up your database and application development activities. Being part of the same ecosystem, Microsoft SQL Server 2012 is an obvious choice for this exercise.

In particular, here is what we are going to cover:

- An overview of the future of relational databases.

- The new features in Microsoft SQL Server 2012.

- An introduction to a very special data type called *spatial data*.

- Enhancements in core and T-SQL features.

- Data visualization enhancements.

- Migrating your enterprise database to the cloud.

■ **Note**   The book *Beginning ASP.NET 2.0 Databases: From Novice to Professiona* by Damien Foggon (Apress, 2006) provides a great introduction to relational databases from the perspective of building data-driven web sites.

The Evolution of Relational Databases

Over the last 30 years, several data store paradigms have threatened to challenge the existence of relational databases. During three decades of evolution, not only have relational databases thwarted every challenge posed to them, but they have also grown stronger in the process. They hold a major foothold in every large or small enterprise today, and they lead all other data store and access mechanisms. That being said, they are not without their share of problems. Let's take a look at some of the major reasons why application developers and administrators have been frustrated with relational databases time and time again.

The Drawbacks of Relational Databases

There are two major drawbacks to relational databases, despite their simplicity in organizing and decomposing data:

1. RDBMS are not very intuitive for dictionary-type data structures.

2. RDBMS are difficult to scale out.

In dictionary-type data structures, records are stored in key/value pairs. This is not very natural for relational databases, which are used for storing data in different normalized domains. Dictionary-type data structures are easier to program in code and ensure that data integrity becomes a responsibility of the application consuming the data. Another implication of using dictionary-type data structures in relational databases is that reporting on such data becomes a complex task. Traditionally, such data structures (often referred to as *unstructured data*) were often forced to be part of the relational model simply to leverage the transactional benefits that the relational databases offered, and they were not available for general access via the file system. The NoSQL movement produced a slew of data stores targeted at storing and accessing unstructured data. Often, these are highly available and distributed key/value stores allowing storage volumes in petabytes or greater, and they support superior scaling.

How Microsoft SQL Server Is Overcoming the Limitations

FileTables

We will discuss the NoSQL movement further in Chapter 3, but guess what? Microsoft SQL Server isn't behind in its ability to store unstructured data. Although primarily a relational data store, it is extending its capabilities to store unstructured data in the form of *FileTables* in Microsoft SQL Server 2012. How is this beneficial given that you could choose a cheaper alternative in one of the NoSQL stores or just use the file system for that matter?

FileTables are an exciting new addition to SQL Server primarily because they offer the best of both worlds. FileTables extend into the file system allowing access to data in the form of files and folders. They also account for data integrity at the lowest levels, and they provide the transactional benefits of a relational database management system. FileTables also make it possible to scale out to support large volumes of data. We will explore FileTables more in upcoming sections.

░ **Note**   There are multiple editions of Microsoft SQL Server 2012, and for the purposes of this book all references to Microsoft SQL Server 2012 will mean the Enterprise Edition.

SQL Azure

Complexities in horizontal scaling were one of the issues often cited by NoSQL enthusiasts for gaining an edge over relational databases in storing large volumes of unstructured data. SQL Azure provides *scale on demand*, meaning that you pay for only what you use and, if needed, you can scale out through sharding. SQL Azure databases are highly available and have built-in support for failover and redundancy. They support horizontal scaling through *Federations*. A Federation is a collection of database partitions in which tables within the database are split by row. Federations are supported by a distributed scheme that determines the distribution of data within the federation. You will learn more about SQL Azure later in this chapter.

■ **Note**   *Sharding* is a database architecture where horizontal partitioning is achieved by holding rows of data separately. This is different from normalization or vertical splitting. Each partition can be stored in a different physical machine.

Introducing Microsoft SQL Server 2012

The concepts of relational database management systems have barely changed since they were first introduced; however, proprietary databases based on RDBMS concepts like Microsoft SQL Server and Oracle release new versions every few years, which add impressive capabilities and improve performance. Both Microsoft and Oracle stand tall in their claims to be better RDBMS and, although the choice is debatable, we have chosen to use Microsoft SQL Server 2012 to demonstrate ways of building data-driven web sites in this book. In this section, we will explore some of the new features introduced in Microsoft SQL Server 2012.

What Is New?

While there are several new features introduced in multiple service areas of Microsoft SQL Server, the new features that you will learn about in this section are the ones of greatest significance in terms of their overall impact.

AlwaysOn: SQL Server 2012 *AlwaysOn* delivers the SLA of required 9's. It is an enterprise alternative to mirroring that ensures high availability. The AlwaysOn feature provides support for Availability Groups, which is a failover platform for a set of databases that failover together. It allows customers access to a set of corresponding secondary databases that can be made available for read/write or backup operations. SQL Server 2012 takes advantage of the *Windows Server Failover Clustering (WSFC)* infrastructure to support AlwaysOn Availability Groups. You can create a new Availability Group using SQL Server PowerShell or T-SQL scripts or by using the Create Availability Group Wizard in Management Studio. You can monitor the status using the AlwaysOn Dashboard, which is launched from Management Studio, as shown in Figure 2-1.

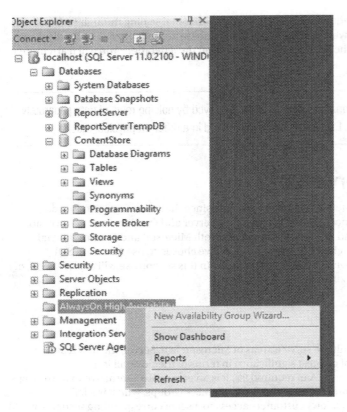

Figure 2-1. AlwaysOn High Availability Dashboard

Superior Performance: Not only does SQL Server 2012 have features for better performance, but it also has numerous enhancements in performance governance. SQL Server 2012 introduces a feature called *Columnstore indexes.* These provide blazing performance in conjunction with enhanced query-processing features and reduce the need to depend on aggregates that were prebuilt for performance in earlier versions. Columnstore is a new index for improving warehouse query processing performance. It is based on the idea of indexing columns and, instead of storing them in a single row in a page, storing them in in their own set of pages.

■ **Caution**   Columnstore indexes are not applicable everywhere. As a matter of fact, they can lower the performance of certain types of queries like outer joins.

In addition, SQL Server 2012 also introduces a number of enhancements to the *Resource Governance* feature, which allows you to perform better resource management in hybrid platforms that provide multitenant support, such as private cloud. Resource Governor now supports 64 resource pools, provides for better CPU usage, and supports resource allocation in a more predictable fashion.

■ **Note**   Resource Governance is available only in the Enterprise Edition of Microsoft SQL Server 2012.

You can create resource pools with default Resource Governance settings to handle workloads using the following T-SQL command:

```
CREATE RESOURCE POOL TransactionLoadPool
GO
ALTER RESOURCE GOVERNOR RECONFIGURE;
GO
```

Alternatively, you can override the default settings by specifying different properties associated with the pool like MIN_CPU_PERCENT, MAX_CPU_PERCENT, CAP_CPU_PERCENT, AFFINITY, and so on. You can also use Management Studio to configure and manage resource pools, as shown in Figure 2-2.

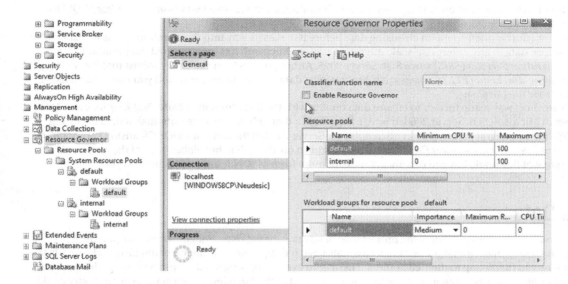

Figure 2-2. *Creating and managing resource pools*

Data Exploration and Visualization: There have been several enhancements with a new feature called *Power View for SQL Server Reporting Services (SSRS)*, which immensely improves the way end users can interact with reports. We will discuss this further in upcoming sections.

Self-Contained Databases: Often, DBAs are tasked with the complex job of migrating databases from one environment to another. Until recently, SQL Server databases were tightly coupled with their server instances. Moving a database from one server instance to another required you to make sure that the target instance had the appropriate logins present. As a DBA, you would also spend quite a bit of time solving collation problems.

In Microsoft SQL Server 2012, the concept of *Contained Database* has been introduced. In a Contained Database, most of the database metadata information is stored as part of the database itself (instead of storing it in master), so that you can avoid some of the hassle during migration. In addition, all the metadata is defined using the same collation, eliminating the need to solve collation issues.

In SQL Server 2012, all databases are created with containment set to NONE. You can create a partially contained database by setting containment to PARTIAL during creation as follows:

```
CREATE DATABASE [Asset] SET CONTAINMENT = PARTIAL
```

■ **Note**   The Contained Database option must be enabled on the database server instance before you can create contained databases. Use the `sp_configure` procedure to enable the Contained Database option.

For existing databases, you can run the alter script to enable partial containment or use Management Studio to open the database properties and set the `Containment` type to `Partial` on the `Options` page.

Enhanced Developer Productivity: There are several new enhancements targeted toward a better database development experience, which you will learn about throughout this book. A significant addition is the new SQL Express database called *LocalDB*. LocalDB has all the programmatic capabilities of Express, yet is lightweight and runs in user mode with a zero-configurations install.

Consistent Data Quality: Microsoft SQL Server 2012 introduced services like *Data Quality Services (DQS)* for ensuring consistent data quality.

A significant effort is often spent on cleansing data before it makes its way into the warehouse. It is an exhaustive exercise to cleanse data in any enterprise-scale migration project. Microsoft has incorporated the popular ETL tool *SQL Server Integration Services (SSIS)* since SQL Server 2005. Although SSIS is an extremely robust tool for creating *Extract, Transform, and Load (ETL)* packages, it is limited in its data-cleansing function, and you may end up using additional tools for the purpose.

Though an effort was made further to ensure data quality with the introduction of *Data Profiling Task* and *Data Profile Viewer* in Microsoft SQL Server 2008, it is SQL Server 2012 that fully realizes the potential of data cleansing through *DQS*. It is an integral part of SSIS in Microsoft SQL Server 2012 in the form of a DQS Cleansing component, and it is a part of *Master Data Services (MDS)* in the MDS Add-in for Excel. Further elaboration of these topics is beyond the scope of this book, but you can always find out more from MSDN if such topics interest you.

Spatial Data

If you work in real estate, then you know the importance of location-based data. Imagine producing a report showcasing a heat map of desirable properties across states. Such *geospatial* information could be used by real-estate agents to do targeted marketing to their customers. There is an ever-increasing need for processing spatial data, not just in industries like real estate, but also in engineering areas and in the life sciences. Virtually every industry could use such information in one way or another.

Traditional relational databases are not suitable for processing spatial data like finding the distance between two points in space, calculating the area of an ellipse, or finding all dealers of a car manufacturer located within a 25-mile radius around a particular ZIP code. You could do some processing by storing the latitude and longitude information, but there are no out-of-the-box functions to perform such operations.

■ **Note**   A spatial database is optimized for storage and retrieval of geospatial data. It uses spatial indices for optimized spatial queries. PostGIS is an example of a geospatial database.

Spatial Data and SQL Server

Microsoft first provided support for spatial data in SQL Server 2008 in the form of the *geometry* and *geography* data types. However, there are several new enhancements in Microsoft SQL Server 2012.

Spatial Data Types

There are two kinds of data that you can store and process in a geospatial context:

1. Euclidean or planar data, such as points and polygons supported by the geometry data type in SQL Server.

2. Ellipsoidal or round-earth data, such as latitude and longitude coordinates supported by the geography data type in SQL Server,

---

■ **Note**   The geometry data type is based on the Open Geospatial Consortium standards, and the geography data type is based on WGS 84 coordinate system.

The spatial data types in SQL Server 2012 expose several simple and collection instance types as illustrated in Figure 2-3.

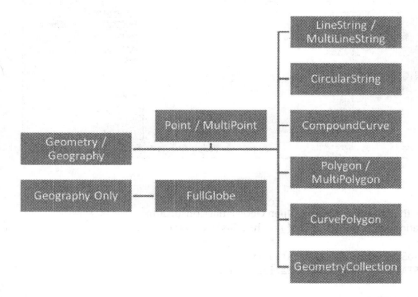

Figure 2-3. *Spatial instance types*

Let's create our first spatial table in Microsoft SQL Server 2012. Follow these steps:

1. Log in to your SQL Server 2012 Management Studio and open a New Query editor for an existing database that you will use for the exercise.

2. First, create a table with columns to store spatial data.

```
CREATE TABLE GeospatialStore (SpatialId INT IDENTITY (1,1), GeographicalData
GEOGRAPHY, GeometricalData GEOMETRY)
GO
```

Execute this statement to create the table.

3. Then, insert some sample spatial data to test the output.

```
INSERT INTO GeospatialStore (GeographicalData, GeometricalData)
VALUES (geography::Point(33.6694, 117.8222, 4326),
geometry::STGeomFromText('POLYGON((0 0, 150 0, 150 150, 0 150, 0 0))', 0));
```

■ **Note** Spatial Data Type instances use a *Spatial Reference Identifier (SRID)*. The SRID represents the spatial reference system in use for planar or ellipsoidal mapping.

---

4. To view the results, run a SELECT query on the table. Microsoft SQL Server 2012 introduces a new result window called *spatial results*. You can use the spatial results to see the output plotted in the spatial graph, as shown in Figure 2-4.

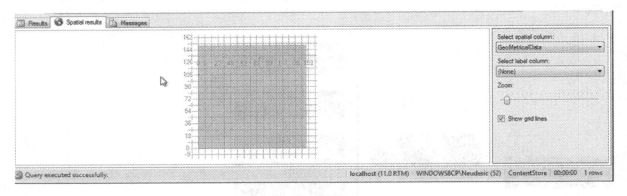

Figure 2-4. *Spatial results*

5. In addition, you can also see the output in string or Open Geospatial Consortium Well-Known Text representation using the ToString() or the STAsText() methods.

```
SELECT GeometricalData.ToString() FROM GeospatialStore
SELECT GeometricalData.STAsText () FROM GeospatialStore
```

Both of these statements will produce similar results.

Full Globe Support

In SQL Server 2008, you were limited by the fact that geography-type instances could be only as large as a logical hemisphere. This limitation has been removed in SQL Server 2012, and it now supports a *Full Globe*, meaning virtually the entire earth is now in scope.

The following query will display the result as the area of earth in sqare meters, confirming the support.

```
DECLARE @globe geography = 'FULLGLOBE'
SELECT @globe.STArea()
```

Spatial Index

As is clear from the definition, spatial index allows you to index a spatial column. You can create a spatial index on columns that store both geometry and geography types.

■ **Caution**   Applying a spatial index on a nongeospatial column will produce an exception.

You can specify the geometry/geography tessellation schemes while creating the index.

```
CREATE SPATIAL INDEX SIndx_GeospatialStore_geometry_GeometricalData
ON GeospatialStore (GeometricalData)
USING GEOMETRY_GRID
```

There are four tessellation schemes that you can specify—GEOMETRY_GRID, GEOMETRY_AUTO_GRID, GEOGRAPHY_GRID, and GEOGRAPHY_AUTO_GRID.

The AUTO tessellation schemes are new to SQL Server 2012, and with the AUTO scheme you cannot specify additional options like GRID to specify the grid density at each level of a scheme.

■ **Note**   A spatial index can be applied only on a table with a clustered primary key.

You can also create a spatial index using Table Designer in SQL Server 2012 Management Studio, as shown in Figure 2-5.

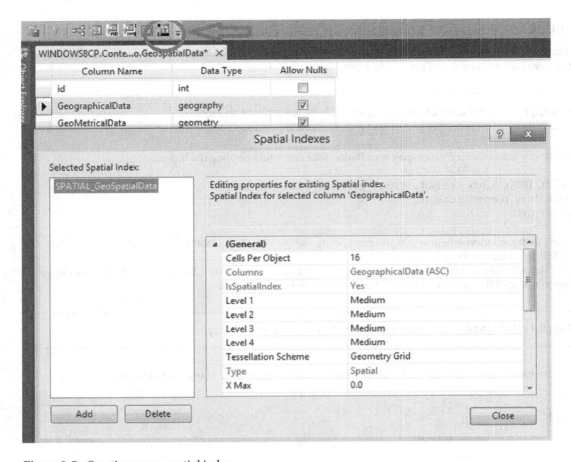

Figure 2-5. *Creating a new spatial index*

Spatial Aggregates

There are four spatial aggregate operations available in SQL Server 2012:

1. Union

2. Envelope

3. Collection

4. Convex Hull

The aggregate operations are applicable to both geometry and geography types.

■ **Note**   Spatial aggregate operations are not available to client libraries.

The envelope aggregate operation is different from other aggregate operations in the way that it applies differently to geometry and geography types. For geometry types, it returns a rectangular polygon object, whereas for geography types, it returns a CurvePolygon.

You can read more about spatial aggregates in the MSDN blog at: http://blogs.msdn.com/b/edkatibah/archive/2011/04/27/spatial-aggregates-in-sql-server-denali.aspx. We will limit our discussion on aggregates, since it is beyond the scope of this book.

Circular Arc Segment

Circular Arc Segment is new to SQL Server 2012. A Circular Arc Segment is represented by three points in a two-dimensional plane. There are three instance types—CircularString, CurvePolygon, and CompoundCurve. There are some interesting exercises that you can build using circular and line string instances. We will leave that for you to explore further.

Database Engine and T-SQL Enhancements

If T-SQL is unfamiliar territory for you, then you should grab a book on T-SQL before reading further in this section. Several chapters in this book rely heavily on your experience with T-SQL, since it is one thing used exhaustively in conjunction with ADO.NET to build queries for data-driven web sites. There are several core enhancements in SQL Server 2012; however, we will discuss only those that are most relevant.

Support for Pagination

Pagination represents the ability of the system to display a fixed number of records to the user requesting the data and then allowing the user to navigate to the next set of records in the set. This is an extremely useful and widely used technique in web sites where end users can consume sizeable amounts of data instead of scrolling down through a vast list of records dumped into the page. Traditionally, support for pagination was a shared responsibility between the data access technology and the database, due to a lack of direct pagination support in the database being used.

In SQL Server 2012, the T-SQL ORDER BY clause has been enhanced to support two additional arguments: OFFSET and FETCH. The ORDER BY statement is used in T-SQL query expressions to sort data. The OFFSET argument specifies the number of rows to be skipped before fetching the next record set from the expression, whereas the FETCH argument specifies the number of rows to be returned after OFFSET has been processed. The following expression illustrates this concept:

```
SELECT * FROM SYS.ALL_COLUMNS ORDER BY NAME
SELECT * FROM SYS.ALL_COLUMNS ORDER BY NAME OFFSET 5 ROWS FETCH NEXT 10 ROWS ONLY
```

The output shown in Figure 2-6 compares the results of the query expressions.

| 100 % ▾ ◄ | | | | | | |

	object_id	name	column_id	system_type_id	user_type_id	max_length
1	-367613366	abort_state	5	231	231	256
2	-205	accdate	5	61	61	8
3	-544912451	access_type	8	231	231	120
4	-118208564	acquire_time	8	61	61	8
5	-136	actadd	4	52	52	2
6	-137	action	3	48	48	1
7	-647968877	action_id	3	167	167	4
8	-686562332	action_id	1	167	167	4

	object_id	name	column_id	system_type_id	user_type_id	max_length	precision
1	-137	action	3	48	48	1	3
2	-686562332	action_id	1	167	167	4	0
3	-647968877	action_id	3	167	167	4	0
4	-686562332	action_...	9	104	104	1	1
5	-132597256	action_...	2	231	231	512	0
6	-132597256	action_...	3	36	36	16	0
7	-1040075...	action_...	6	56	56	4	10
8	-1040075...	action_...	3	231	231	120	0
9	-132	actions	6	56	56	4	10
10	-421	activati...	14	231	231	1552	0

Figure 2-6. *T-SQL query expression demonstrating pagination*

Inspecting the result of the second T-SQL query expression reveals that the first five records are skipped and the next ten records are displayed.

Sequence

For years, IDENTITY has been a safe way of generating running numbers, and it is probably the most widely used mechanism for uniquely identifying a row within a table in SQL Server. However, there was previously no simple way to maintain a global sequence that could be used across the database. With SQL Server 2012, this constraint is eliminated through the SEQUENCE object. A *sequence object* is capable of generating a numeric sequence based on the attributes defined, and it is bound to a user-defined schema.

■ **Note** Unlike IDENTITY, which generates the next value only when a row is inserted, a SEQUENCE can be used to prefetch the next value without inserting any data.

Let's look at a very simple example of SEQUENCE:

```
CREATE SEQUENCE dbo.IncrementByFive
START WITH 1
INCREMENT BY 5;
```

The statement will create a sequence that starts with 1 and increments by 5. To fetch the next ten sequences, execute the following query expression:

```
SELECT seq = NEXT VALUE FOR dbo.IncrementByFive
GO 10
```

The result displays the numbers 1, 6, 11, 16, 21 . . .

■ **Note**   You cannot create a sequence prefixed with any particular database name. It has to be created on a schema. You can grant/revoke permissions to create a sequence on a particular schema.

In addition to START and INCREMENT, there are additional attributes that you can specify with the sequence object. Execute the following query expression to see the attributes and the default values associated with them.

```
SELECT * FROM sys.sequences WHERE name = 'IncrementByFive'
```

Figure 2-7 displays the output.

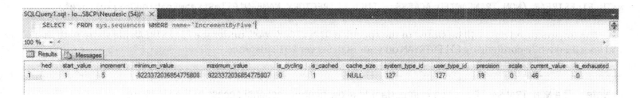

Figure 2-7. *Displaying the sequence object attributes*

■ **Caution**   If you are using the CACHE option, you can expect better performance. However, in case of an abrupt database failure, cache values could be lost and you may end up having a broken sequence.

Sequence for Specific Data Types

You can create a sequence with specific numeric data types like SMALLINT and DECIMAL. The following expression demonstrates the process of creating a decimal sequence:

```
CREATE SEQUENCE dbo.DecimalIncrement
AS decimal (3, 0)
START WITH 1
INCREMENT BY 5
NO CYCLE
```

■ **Note**   The NO CYCLE option will prevent a restart once the maximum value is reached.

Range of Sequences

The natural extension of using a global sequence is to generate a range of sequence values. The `sp_sequence_get_range` stored procedure can be used for this purpose.

Execute with Result Sets

The `EXEC` command in SQL Server now has an additional set of attributes. The `WITH RESULT SET` attribute can be used to provide an alias to the returned columns and also to change the data types of the returning result set. This provides a lot of maneuverability for SQL developers to return different results from the same stored procedure or query expression.

FileTable

We discussed FileTables in the section "How Microsoft SQL Server Is Overcoming the Limitations." Since you now know the purpose of FileTables, let's discuss how they are created and used.

A database must be `FILESTREAM` enabled before you can create FileTables in it. `FILESTREAM` allows SQL Server applications to store unstructured data such as documents on the file system. To enable `FILESTREAM`, execute the following command in the query editor in your Management Studio:

```
CREATE DATABASE dbo.FileStreamEnabledDb
WITH FILESTREAM (NON_TRANSACTED_ACCESS = FULL, DIRECTORY_NAME=N'FileStreamEnabledDbFileStore')
```

The unstructured data will be stored in the specified `DIRECTORY_NAME` under the `FILESTREAM` file share path that you specified while configuring `FILESTREAM` on your SQL Server 2012 instance.

■ **Note**   The `NON_TRANSACTED` option is important to allow nontransactional access to the file share.

For an existing database, you can run the `ALTER` command to enable `FILESTREAM`. At this stage, you have a couple of options. You can use the `FILESTREAM` data type directly on a table column to get the best of both worlds, leveraging the transactional capabilities of storing structured data and storing the unstructured data on the physical disk with nontransactional access, or you could create a FileTable. FileTables have a predefined schema. You can create a FileTable with the `CREATE TABLE` command.

```
CREATE TABLE UnstructuredDataStore AS FileTable
```

You can specify attributes for collation and directory name where the unstructured data will be stored.

Data Visualization

This is one particular area where all the leading databases are racing against each other to capture a bigger piece of the market. Some would even call it the "future of business intelligence." Every major database in the enterprise today provides support for data visualization through tools and guidance, and yet there are hundreds of tools available on the market focused only on data visualization. Data visualization is highly appreciated for its ability to unlock the potential that is locked in an enterprise data warehouse and its facility to communicate information clearly and effectively through graphical means.

Microsoft is up to date in this arena. SQL Server 2012 includes an in-memory data visualization component called *Power View*. Previously code named "Crescent," Microsoft's Power View is a huge step forward in the world of big data visualization.

Power View and Power Pivot

Power View is an interactive data exploration and visualization tool that is available as an *SSRS* add-in for Microsoft SharePoint Server 2010 Enterprise Edition. Power View reports are built on data models in SharePoint Server 2010 Document Libraries. Power View is tightly integrated with SharePoint 2010, and in order to leverage its capabilities, you must install the *Power Pivot* add-in for Excel in addition to activating the feature in SharePoint. You can create Power View visualizations from a Power Pivot data source in the PowerPivotGallery library in your SharePoint 2010 Business Intelligence web site. Figure 2-8 shows the Power View Designer.

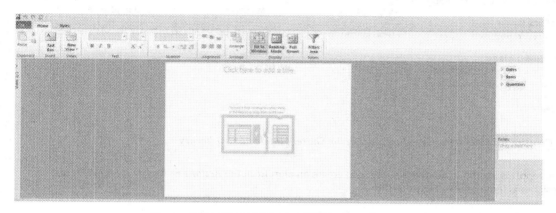

Figure 2-8. *The Power View Designer*

You can use the Designer to build your data visualizations by dragging items from the right onto the design surface. You also have the option to save the report as a PowerPoint slide deck from the File menu.

■ **Note**   Power View is not designed to replace Report Builder. It coexists with Report Builder, and it is primarily meant for power users looking to build reports on demand with no intervention from the DBA or the developer.

Self-Service Alerting

SQL Server 2012 Reporting Services features data-driven alerts that can be delivered via e-mail. This is quite interesting, since it allows the right information to be sent automatically at the right time. Data alerts can be defined against a series of rules. Microsoft SQL Server Reporting Services feature a Data Alert Designer that can be used to configure rules for data alerts.

■ **Note**   The Data Alert Designer option is available only when you install Reporting Services in SharePoint Integration Mode.

Before you can set up the alerts, create or upload the report in your SharePoint 2010 Business Intelligence Site document library, as shown in Figure 2-9. The report can be designed using the SQL Server 2012 Report Builder 3.0.

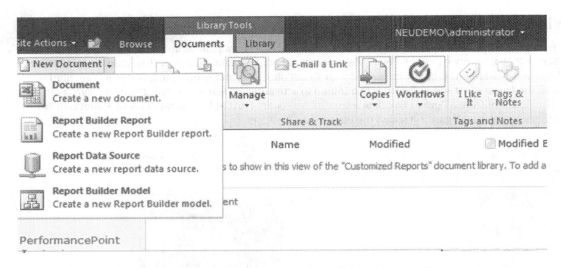

Figure 2-9. *Creating an SSRS report and hosting it in the SharePoint document library*

Once the report is hosted in SharePoint, you can create an alert from the *Actions* → *New Data* Alert menu. The Alert Designer is illustrated in Figure 2-10.

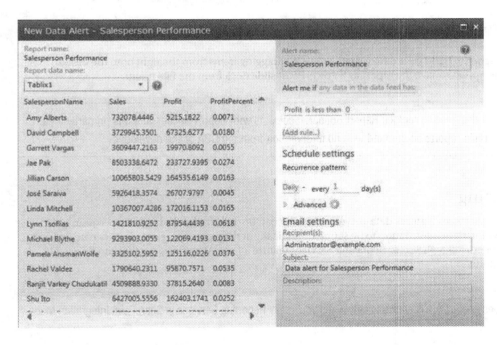

Figure 2-10. *Self-service Alert Designer*

SQL Server 2012 Cloud

Microsoft SQL Server 2012 is a cloud-ready platform. It provides capacity and scale on demand with public and private cloud offerings. Microsoft SQL Server also allows the database design to be abstracted from the instance, thus allowing seamless migration between private and public clouds. Migration to SQL Azure (a public cloud) is now a built-in feature in Management Studio. As illustrated in Figure 2-11, you can right-click a database, and you will find the migration wizard right under the *Tasks* menu.

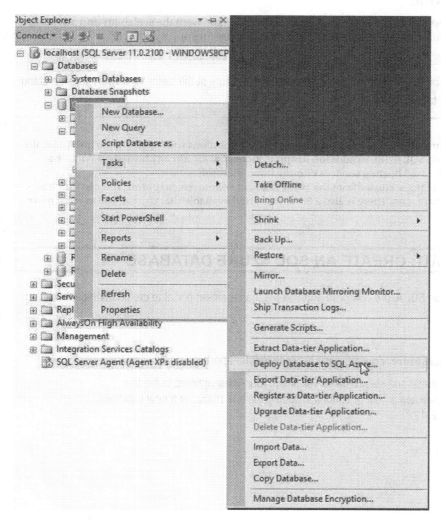

Figure 2-11. *Deploying database to SQL Azure*

Private Cloud

With the infrastructure virtualization guidance provided by Microsoft, you can build your own private cloud. There is however a "*Microsoft HP Database Consolidation Appliance*" that has the necessary setup preconfigured for a private cloud. If you are not interested in the appliance, you can still use the HP Database Consolidation Solution Architecture to build your own.

SQL Azure – Public Cloud

If you are weary of doing physical administration of your enterprise database and want the scalability and metering benefits of having a cloud-based database, then SQL Azure is the right solution for you.

▓ **Caution**   Not every operation of an on-premise version is possible in SQL Azure at this point. Make sure to understand the limitations well before you move to SQL Azure.

SQL Azure is loaded with features that allow you to implement hybrid solutions with applications hosted locally having the ability to access data from SQL Azure in addition to applications that are already hosted on Windows Azure. Windows Azure is the cloud-based hosting services offering from Microsoft.

You can create an SQL Azure database cluster from the *Windows Azure management portal*. You can purchase a subscription from www.windowsazure.com. There is also a 90-day free trial available that you can use to learn more about the features.

TRY IT OUT: CREATE AN SQL AZURE DATABASE

In this example, you will create an SQL Azure database and use the management portal to create additional artifacts within the database.

Follow these steps:

1. Log in to www.windowsazure.com to access the management portal.

2. Click the Database menu and select the server under your subscriptions. In the top navigation bar, you will see a host of options including the one to create a new database, as shown in Figure 2-12.

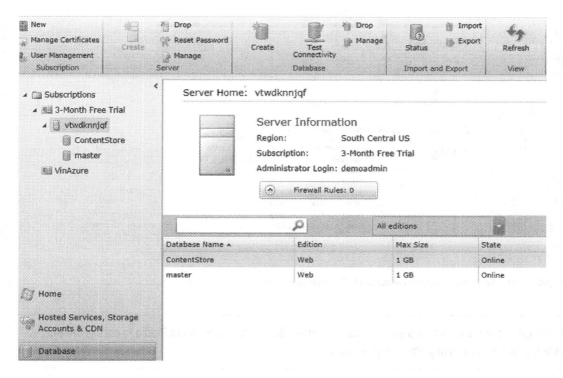

Figure 2-12. *SQL Azure server instance*

3. Click Create to create a new database.

4. Select the created database from the left navigation pane and click Manage. It will launch the management portal.

■ **Caution** In order to log in to the SQL Azure instance, make sure that you add your IP address under the Azure Server firewall rules.

5. After successfully signing into the portal, you can start creating the artifacts for the database. Also, use the query editor to run T-SQL queries. Figure 2-13 illustrates managing the SQL Azure database through the management portal.

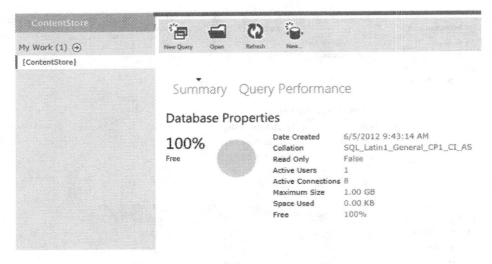

Figure 2-13. *Managing SQL Azure database through the management portal*

▓ **Note**   In addition to the management portal, you can also use SQL Server Management Studio to access the SQL Azure database just as you access any other on-premise database.

---

6. The connection string information to log in to the database is available under the Connection Strings property under the Properties pane on the right side of the portal.

7. You are now ready to use the SQL Azure database as a source of data for your web sites.

SQL Azure Data Sync

While enterprises are getting ready to move their IT to the cloud, many challenges remain before the industry can meet the huge task of optimizing for this proposition. Not all applications or databases are ready to move to cloud. Enterprise architects around the world are engaged in assessing the cloud-readiness of different enterprises, and they are proposing *Hybrid IT* solutions for a majority of them. One of the pitfalls of having a Hybrid IT solution is the need to keep data synchronized across multiple on-premise and cloud-based databases. This could be one of many reasons why you would need data synchronization, but nevertheless it is an important feature of SQL Azure. Some of the benefits of data sync include the following:

1. There is no need for complex logic for synchronization. It is configuration-driven, and it can be set up quickly.

2. Data sync allows synchronization between on-premise and the cloud and between databases hosted in the cloud.

3. It provides the ability to specify fine-grained rules for synchronization.

You can provision data sync first by enabling it in your Windows Azure management portal and then creating synchronization groups either for an on-premise–cloud synchronization or for a cloud-to-cloud synchronization. Figure 2-14 shows the data sync configuration for an on-premise–cloud synchronization operation.

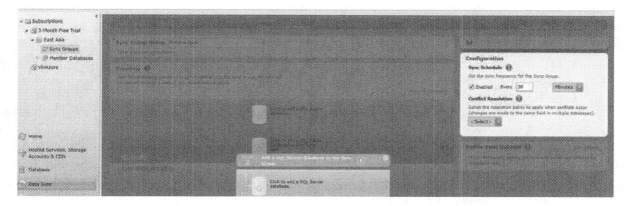

Figure 2-14. *Synchronization group for an on-premise-to-cloud synchronization*

Summary

In this chapter, you learned about the continuing importance of relational databases, and you experienced a quick overview of some of the very interesting enhancements in Microsoft SQL Server 2012. Here's a recap of what you learned:

- Relational databases are extending their capabilities to support the storage and retrieval of unstructured data.

- There is a host of new features in Microsoft SQL Server 2012. Microsoft SQL Server 2012 is now a highly scalable and highly available database with features for enhanced performance. A new spatial data type has been introduced specifically to store and operate on geospatial information.

- T-SQL features in SQL Server have been enhanced to include support for pagination, the ability to create a global sequence, and support for storing and retrieving unstructured data-like documents.

- SQL Server now has support for advanced and on-demand data visualization using Power View. It is also cloud-ready with versions for private and public clouds.

In Chapter 3, you will learn more about the NoSQL movement and why it is gaining popularity within large enterprises across the globe. You will look specifically at MongoDB, a popular NoSQL database, and how you can use it as a data store for content-driven web sites.

■ ■ ■

Introducing Non-Relational Databases

NoSQL databases have quickly become immensely popular, so much so that their popularity has earned them the distinction of been tagged as a movement! What are NoSQL databases and why have they become so popular? Let's find out.

Relational databases have been a way of life for most application developers over the decades of building data-driven applications. However, there is a relatively new breed of individuals who want to break free from the rules of storing data in relational databases. They firmly believe that not all data is fit for relational databases. The belief is more profound when large volumes of unstructured data are stored. How is this data generated?

Most web sites today are driven by their social influence, letting millions of users congregate and generate large volumes of content. Such mass content cannot be fit into a model, and thus we have the category of "unstructured data." You may try to store such content in relational databases by attempting to create a model out of it, but that's not natural according to the believers in the NoSQL movement. You don't have to use a relational database just for the sake of doing so!

The NoSQL movement has given rise to a new group of database paradigms. A fairly popular one is document-oriented databases. The purpose of a document-oriented database is to store "documents" and not "relationships." Documents are closely-knit collections, which are disconnected from other data elements. Document-oriented databases are designed for high performance and concurrency. In the previous chapter, you learned how Microsoft SQL Server 2012 is extending its capabilities to support the storage of unstructured data in a high-performance environment. In this chapter, we will focus on NoSQL and explore a popular document-oriented database called *MongoDB*. You will learn more about the following:

- Different technologies under the NoSQL umbrella

- Introduction to document-oriented databases

- Setting up and configuring MongoDB

- Storing and retrieving data from MongoDB using C#

Understanding NoSQL Databases

A lot of businesses today are driven by their social presence on the Web. Facebook, for example, is an institution that pioneered social networking, with millions of visitors logging in on a regular basis. Such web presences require the storage of petabytes of data with intelligible analytics to make some sense out of the volumes generated. A simple relational database would not be sufficient. What is needed is a data platform that can do the following:

- Offer high availability

- Scale out through partitioning

- Scale in an elastic fashion, growing and changing rapidly

- Provide a flexible schema to allow for storage of unstructured data

NoSQL technologies have evolved to provide for such a platform, making availability a bit more of a higher priority than global data consistency.

■ **Note**   NoSQL doesn't represent any one technology. It covers a range of architectures and priorities.

Overview

NoSQL stands for "Not only SQL." This is the definition that the people behind this movement have settled upon. At this point, it covers a broad range of technologies and theories. It is possible, however, that sometime in the future, it will get split into individual focus areas, as the movement gathers steam and gains attention from the industry at large.

From the standpoint of an enterprise, there is an important question to answer. Should you choose a NoSQL database over the traditional relational databases? The answer is not simple,. Enterprise architects today have the choice of modern relational databases that extend to support NoSQL features and provide them with a lot of flexibility in terms of storing both structured and unstructured data.

One benefit that definitely stands out in favor of NoSQL technologies is that most of them are open sourced. This directly translates into savings in CAPEX and OPEX costs for an enterprise. Let's explore some of the key benefits.

Key Benefits

- **Open-source stores with community support.** For example, MongoDB is extremely popular and it is used by some large enterprises.

- **High availability, performance, and scalability.** You must have heard this several times by now. NoSQL databases specifiy the ability to allow scalable replication for failover scenarios and provide for scale on demand. This is another area where the proprietary relational databases are extending their capabilities to compete with the open-source NoSQL technologies.

- **Flexible schema.** NoSQL databases support the ability to allow modifications to the schema without any downtime.

- **Developer friendly.** NoSQL databases have a flexible open-data model that let developers build the schema over a period of time based on need, rather than forcing a schema. This approach also facilitates an easier deployment model.

Popular NoSQL Technologies

There are quite a few NoSQL data stores available in the market today depending on the data model paradigm. Most of them are open source driven by the community.

Key/Value Pair Stores

Key/value pair stores are optimized for faster storage and retrieval of high volumes of data, offering limited functionality beyond fast lookups. Such stores are very useful for content caching; for example, storing order items in a shopping cart. Some popular examples of distributed key/value stores are Voldermort, Redis, Memcache, Oracle BDB (proprietary), and Windows Azure Distributed Cache (proprietary).

Distributed Table Stores

Such data stores are generally based on distributed file system implementations. Big Table, for example, is a high-performance data store based on proprietary Google technologies like the Google File System. Microsoft makes its own contribution in the form of Windows Azure Tables and SQL Server Sparse Columns. HBASE and Cassandra are popular open-source distributed table stores.

Document-Oriented Databases

This is the most popular category in the league of NoSQL stores. We will discuss these in detail in the next section.

Graph Databases

GraphDB, Neo4J, and Intellidimension are some examples of graph databases. These data stores use different graph algorithms to look up data, and they are extremely well suited for social networking applications. However, they are not easy to cluster.

Extended Relational Databases

The majority of the existing proprietary relational databases, like Microsoft SQL Server, Oracle, and IBM DB2, are extending their capabilities to support NoSQL features. You learned in the previous chapter how Microsoft SQL Server is using FileTables to store unstructured data.

Document-Oriented Databases

Unlike relational databases, document-oriented databases or document databases store data in the form of a series of self-contained documents. There are no tables, columns, rows, or relations. There is no strict schema. A good example of where such a database could be useful would be a web site for technical articles. Each article could be a self-contained document with all the necessary attributes. Any additional attributes needed could be added to the specific document without impacting other documents. So how are document databases better than SQL in such scenarios? Here's how:

- Complex objects can be stored as is in their current state. There are no repeated insert statements and no translation to a schema. Objects (for example, *JSON [JavaScript Object Notation]* data) can be serialized as documents.

- Better performance with reduced side effects of concurrency.

- No need for data restructuring with new attributes, as the changes are contained within the document.

- Persistent view states; that is, there is no need to re-create view states from scratch. The entire view state can be made persistent instead of separating the values from the model and storing in a relational data store.

- Store dynamic data with end-user–customizable entities and flexible schema.

■ **Note** Document Databases allow concurrent updates to objects; however, they forego *ACID (Atomicity, Consistency, Isolation, Durability)* properties in favor of a Highly Available, Soft State, and Eventual Consistency model, meaning that there could be a window of time where the transactional characteristics are compromised.

In this chapter, we have chosen to explore a very popular document database called MongoDB. It is designed for high-performance scenarios, and it is very useful in applications where data needs to be accessed often and quickly. In the following section, you will learn about the steps to set up MongoDB and program it using the official MongoDB C# driver from 10gen.

■ **Caution** Document databases like MongoDB are not designed to replace your enterprise relational database in transactional operations with mission-critical data. In such cases, they best augment the relational database as a highly available cache store.

Programming with MongoDB

MongoDB was created by *10gen* (www.10gen.com) primarily to bridge the gap between key/value pair stores and relational databases. It retains some of the nice features of relational databases like indexes; however, it changes the data model from relational to document oriented to facilitate scalability and promote developer agility.

How to Set Up MongoDB

Setting up MongoDB is very easy. Download the relevant zip package from www.mongodb.org/downloads, and extract the package into a folder on your physical drive. Go to the bin folder under the extracted package. You will find several binaries and executables. The most important one is the mongod.exe—the MongoDB database process.

■ **Note** There is a 2GB data limit if you are using the 32-bit version for Windows.

You can start the MongoDB process simply by firing up the command prompt and running the mongod.exe command. Depending on your OS, you may get a prompt to loosen up the application port (which is 27017 by default). Figure 3-1 shows the prompt for the Windows 7 OS.

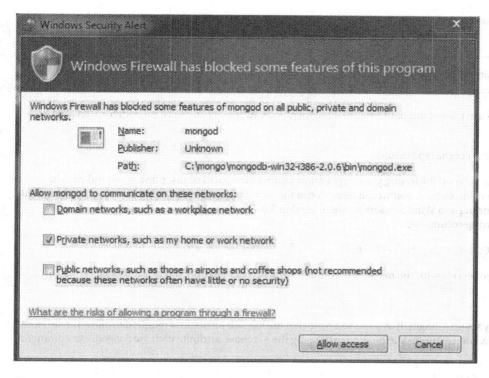

Figure 3-1. *Open MongoDB ports in Windows Firewall*

By default, MongoDB will use the C:\Data\db path to store data. You must create the folder manually, or else the process will throw an exception. Once the folder is created and the port is open for access, mongod will start listening for requests on the listed port, as shown in Figure 3-2.

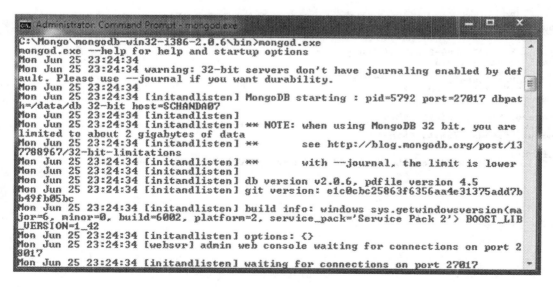

Figure 3-2. *MongoDB set up and ready for use*

You have now successfully set up MongoDB. You can use the client shell (mongo.exe) to test the connection with the server.

■ **Note**   The version of MongoDB used in this book is 2.1.1.

If you do not want to use the default path to store data, then you can specify an alternate path for \data\db with the dbpath setting:

```
mongod.exe --dbpath d:\alternatepath\data
```

The command shells are good for testing your application against MongoDB or just playing around with it. However, in a production environment, you would want to run the mongod process as a Windows service. MongoDB has added support for running as a Windows service since version 2.0. To run the MongoDB server process as a service, execute the following command:

```
mongod.exe --logpath C:\Data\Log.txt --install
```

You can then start the service with the net start command:

```
net start mongodb
```

You have successfully set up MongoDB as a service! Note that the logpath attribute is required to allow the service to log the status in the log file. You can uninstall the service by using the --remove attribute with the mongod.exe command.

Using the MongoDB Client

MongoDB also comes with a default client shell that you can use to connect to the server. You can use this client to connect to a database (*test* is the default database in MongoDB) and start storing JSON content. You can use the Save and Find functions to store and retrieve content, as illustrated in Figure 3-3.

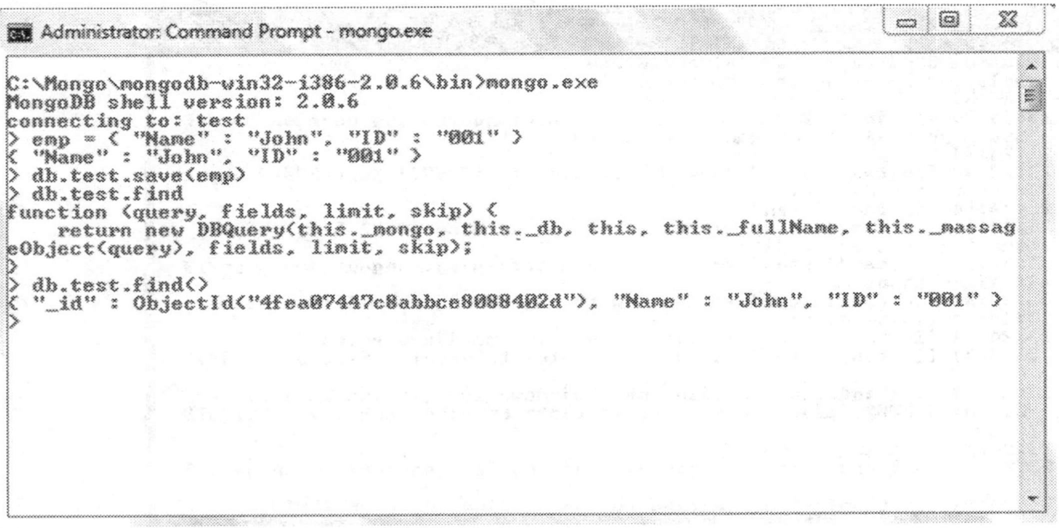

Figure 3-3. *Storing and retrieving JSON data in MongoDB*

▓ **Note**   Although MongoDB uses JSON as the data notation, it stores data internally as Binary JSON (BSON).

Familiarity with JSON will be very useful in operating MongoDB. If you are not familiar with JSON, you can learn more about it at www.json.org.

Programming MongoDB Using C#

MongoDB is written in C++, so programming in it using C# requires a driver. There are quite a few community-driven drivers available on the Internet. Sam Corder wrote a popular one, and it can be downloaded at www.github.com/samus/mongodb-csharp. However, we recommend that you use the official driver available from 10gen. You can download the driver from the github site located at https://github.com/mongodb/mongo-csharp-driver. From the Downloads tab, you can choose to download the MSI and then install it.

▓ **Note**   If you downloaded the source instead of the dll, then compile the CSharpDriver-2010 solution and pick the MongoDB.Driver.dll from the Driver project.

Follow these steps to create your first MongoDB project using .NET Framework 4.0 and Visual Studio 2010:

1. Create a new Visual Studio 2010 C# Console Application project. Add a reference to the MongoDB.Driver.dll assembly.

2. Open the Program.cs file and write the following code to make a connection to the MongoDB database server instance.

```csharp
using System;
using MongoDB.Driver;

namespace FirstMongoDbProject
{
    class Program
    {
        static void Main(string[] args)
        {
            MongoServer dbServer = MongoServer.Create();
            dbServer.Connect();

            Console.WriteLine("Connected");

            Console.ReadLine();
            dbServer.Disconnect();
        }
    }
}
```

■ **Note** You must fire up the MongoDB server console or start the service if you have installed MongoDB as a service.

3. To get the record that you inserted earlier during the console client exercise, update the code inside the Main method to search for the record in the default "test" database. The following code snippet illustrates this:

```
using System;
using MongoDB.Driver;
using MongoDB.Bson;

namespace FirstMongoDbProject
{
    class Program
    {
        static void Main(string[] args)
        {
            MongoServer dbServer = MongoServer.Create();
            dbServer.Connect();

            MongoDatabase database = dbServer.GetDatabase("test");
            foreach (var doc in database["test"].FindAll())
            {
                Console.WriteLine(doc);
            }

            Console.ReadLine();
            dbServer.Disconnect();
        }
    }
}
```

While creating the record, no collection was mentioned, so the record got inserted in the default "test" collection. The variable doc represents a BSON document that gets printed in the console. In our example, you should see the record that you inserted earlier now displayed in the console. You have now successfully queried the MongoDB database for the records that you inserted. Next we will run through a "try it yourself"-type of exercise to help you gain a better understanding of the capabilities of MongoDB.

TRY IT OUT: QUERY A MONGODB DATABASE COLLECTION

Data in MongoDB is grouped by collections (a group of BSON documents). Collections can be organized by namespaces for reference and can be programmatically accessed in two different ways—the dot notation, where they are separated by dots, and the named notation.

■ **Caution** Maximum length for a collection name is 128 characters.

In this exercise, you will first learn to create a collection and add a document to the collection, and then you will learn how to query the collection to fetch documents. Follow these steps:

1. Add reference to the driver assemblies in a new Visual Studio C# Console Application project. From the previous exercise, use the code to connect to a MongoDB server instance.

2. Use the `CreateCollection` method of the MongoDatabase object to create the collection called "items."

3. Create an instance of BsonDocument and fill it with sample data. Insert the document into the collection. The following code snippet shows this implementation:

```
using System;
using MongoDB.Driver;
using MongoDB.Bson;

namespace QueryCollections
{
    class Program
    {
        static void Main(string[] args)
        {
            MongoServer dbServer = MongoServer.Create();
            dbServer.Connect();

            MongoDatabase db = dbServer.GetDatabase("test");
            if (db.GetCollection("items") == null)
            {
                db.CreateCollection("items");
                BsonDocument document = new BsonDocument
                {
                    {"SKU", "I001"},
                    {"Variant", "Tubes"},
                    {"Quantity", "10"},
                    {"Cost", "150.50"}
                };

                db["items"].Insert<BsonDocument>(document);
            }
            Console.WriteLine(db["items"].FindOne());
            dbServer.Disconnect();
            Console.ReadLine();
        }
    }
}
```

In the output, you will see the record printed with the object id, which is the key to identifying the document in the collection. You could also insert an array of documents or even create nested documents. Now that we have created the record, you can query it in a number of ways.

The first and the preferred option is to use the query builder. The `MongoDB.Drivers.Builders` namespace exposes appropriate classes and methods to build your query. The following code illustrates this:

```
var query = Query.EQ("Variant", "Tubes");
        var results = db["items"].Find(query);
```

This returns a collection of `BsonDocument` that matches the query expression. Another option is to use the `QueryDocument` object:

```
var query = new QueryDocument("Variant", "Tubes");
        var results = db["items"].Find(query);
```

The Query class exposes quite a few different methods for creating query expressions that you must explore. You have now successfully created and searched for documents in a MongoDB database collection!

LINQ Support in MongoDB

LINQ is a very powerful feature for querying objects in .NET. If you haven't explored beyond .NET Framework 2.0, chances are that you may not be familiar with LINQ. Chapter 5 in this book focuses solely on LINQ, so read that chapter before proceeding further with this section.

The MongoDB C# Driver provides LINQ support for querying MongoDB Collections. The `MongoDB.Driver.Linq` namespace contains the necessary artifacts to use LINQ with MongoDB Collections. The moment that you add this namespace, you will notice that the extension methods for LINQ support are available to the collection classes. The following code returns the same result as the previous example using the `FindOne` method, however this time using LINQ.

```
using System;
using System.Linq;
using MongoDB.Driver;
using MongoDB.Bson;
using MongoDB.Driver.Linq;

namespace QueryCollectionsWithLinq
{
    class Program
    {
        static void Main(string[] args)
        {
            MongoServer dbServer = MongoServer.Create();
            dbServer.Connect();

            MongoDatabase db = dbServer.GetDatabase("test");
            var collection = db.GetCollection("items").AsQueryable();

            var result = collection.FirstOrDefault();
            Console.WriteLine(result);
            dbServer.Disconnect();
            Console.ReadLine();
        }
    }
}
```

The most important thing to note in the example is the AsQueryable method. The Driver allows the queryable extension on the collection, and the rest is straightforward LINQ. You can use LINQ queries as well as Lambda Expressions to query results.

How Does MongoDB Work?

The primary database component in MongoDB is the mongod.exe process. By default, MongoDB is configured for a lazy write. This allows frequent and faster updates to data and minimizes flush-to-disk operations. By default, the process flushes to disk every 60 seconds and commits journal every 100 seconds. This can, however, be configured based on the needs of the environment.

▓ **Note** There is no complex transaction with rollback support in MongoDB. It supports atomicity only at the document level. This allows for faster performance even in the case of partitioned databases.

In addition, MongoDB supports auto-sharding using the mongos.exe process. The auto-sharding feature is interesting, since it allows an application to outgrow a single database instance and automatically converts into a cluster. The sharding architecture allows data to be partitioned horizontally across multiple machines, preserving the order. In addition to sharding, MongoDB also supports replication for high availability. Figure 3-4 illustrates this architecture.

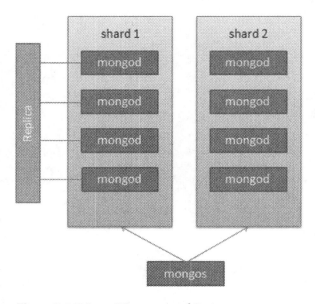

Figure 3-4. MongoDB process architecture

Summary

This chapter introduced you to the world of NoSQL databases. You learned why they are important for modern socially influenced web sites. You also learned about the different NoSQL technologies that are gaining popularity among developers around the world, especially document-oriented databases. Finally, you learned how to program the MongoDB database using the official C# driver. You may explore further programming MongoDB with JavaScript, given that it is the language of choice for client side programming, and it is also gaining attention on the server side of web application development.

CHAPTER 4

■ ■ ■

Accessing Data Using ADO.NET

ADO.NET and its predecessor ADO have a long history of facilitating direct data access for a variety of applications built using Microsoft technologies. ADO.NET has evolved tremendously since it was first introduced almost a decade ago. The biggest change in ADO.NET, however, was the addition of *Entity Framework*. The ability to work with a conceptual model against the native providers has captured the imagination of developers who want to use the .NET Framework for application development. Interacting with the conceptual model provided the abstraction level that programmers always wanted in their applications. In addition, this also reduced the number of lines of code that programmers had to write to fetch data from different sources, which made the technology extremely popular.

In Chapter 1, you were briefly introduced to the latest additions to ADO.NET. In this chapter, we will dive more deeply into the features of ADO.NET, but we will refrain from discussing Entity Framework, since it is covered in detail in Chapter 7. Specifically, we will talk about the following:

- How to read and modify a database using core ADO.NET concepts.

- How DataSource Controls are used to abstract the process of querying a database and perform manipulations using DataSet and DataReader in a declarative fashion.

- The different data type mappings between .NET Framework types and the native database.

- How to design a secure data access layer using ADO.NET.

ADO.NET Architecture

Traditionally, ADO.NET served as a platform that let applications connect to data stores and perform data queries and manipulations. That hasn't changed much. However, a significant investment has gone into making ADO.NET more intelligent and to perform better with a variety of options to allow data manipulation in a disconnected fashion. As DataSets were the only available option previously, with Entity Framework you now have quite a few choices. Figure 4-1 illustrates the different components of ADO.NET and how they relate. You read an overview of these components in Chapter 1.

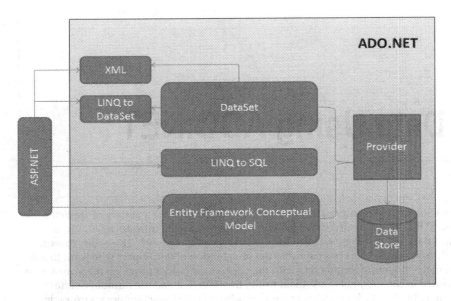

Figure 4-1. *ADO.NET components*

Although there have been significant changes to ADO.NET since it was first released with .NET Framework 1.0, the database providers have seen subtle changes mostly involving performance and security. The book *Beginning ASP.NET 2.0 Databases: From Novice to Professional* by Damien Foggon (Apress, 2006) covers the database providers in great detail for .NET Framework 2.0. In this chapter, we will first start by exploring ADO.NET for reading and modifying a database and then we will discuss what's new in the .NET Framework 4.5 release.

Reading and Modifying a Database Using ADO.NET Data Providers

The data providers in ADO.NET are designed for fast forward-only read-only access to the data, and they perform manipulations in the form of inserts, updates, and deletes. Generally, these are referred to as *CRUD* (Create, Read, Update, and Delete) operations. CRUD operations can be performed via inline queries or stored procedures.

■ **Note**   For reasonably complex queries, it is a good idea to use stored procedures for CRUD operations for performance and security benefits. By using stored procedures, you can help prevent SQL injection attacks, and since they are precompiled after the first run, there would be a boost in performance on subsequent data access operations.

There are native providers based on the database drivers you are using to access data. However, they all follow a common architecture. Figure 4-2 illustrates this.

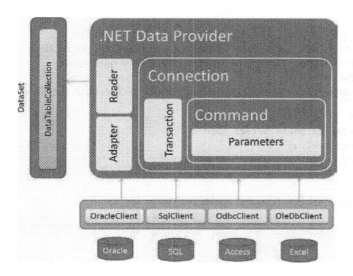

Figure 4-2. *ADO.NET provider architecture*

The provider exposes Connection, Command, DataReader, and DataAdapter to let you perform CRUD operations on the database. The DataSet is a way to store the data in memory in a provider-agnostic fashion. Using DataSet, you can manipulate the data in memory and then use the providers to push the changes to the database.

DataSet vs. DataReader

Since a DataReader is part of the provider, it is faster than DataSet for accessing data in a forward-only, read-only fashion. DataSet, on the other hand, is a powerful means of holding data in memory and performing manipulations on it. DataSet is a good choice for applications where you are expecting data from multiple heterogeneous sources and to perform updates to the set via interactions from a user interface. It is also a good choice if you are looking for a mechanism to cache large snapshots of data in the application. Figure 4-3 shows how data from multiple sources can be populated in a DataSet and then displayed in the presentation layer using data-bound controls.

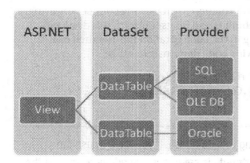

Figure 4-3. *DataSet populated with data from multiple sources of data*

Connecting to a Database

The first step in accessing data using the providers is to create a connection. Connections are provider specific. Each provider has an implementation of the DbConnection object exposed by the System.Data.Common namespace. SqlConnection is an implementation for the SQL client provider.

To establish a connection with SQL Server, you can create an instance of the SqlConnection object that specifies the connection string parameter.

```
readonly string ConnectionString = "Data Source=<database server name /
address>;Initial Catalog=Store;Integrated Security=True";
        protected void Page_Load(object sender, EventArgs e)
        {

            using (SqlConnection con = new SqlConnection(ConnectionString))
            {
                con.Open();
            }
        }
```

■ **Note**   Connection Strings are specific to providers.

The connection string information is typically stored in a configuration file like the Application Configuration file or the Web Configuration file. The standard Application/Web Configuration file schema supports storing connection strings of different providers.

```
<configuration>
  <connectionStrings>
    <add name="ApplicationServices"
        connectionString="data source=<database server name /
address>;Integrated Security=SSPI;AttachDBFilename=|DataDirectory|\<database file
name>.mdf;User Instance=true"
        providerName="System.Data.SqlClient" />
  </connectionStrings>
```

The connection information can also be built using the SqlConnectionStringBuilder class under the System.Data.SqlClient namespace. It can add additional connection information to an existing connection string. The connection string builder is a good idea if a connection needs to be built based on user inputs. It is designed to safeguard against injection. You could store a partial connection string in the configuration file and then use the builder to set additional properties based on the provider. The following code demonstrates this:

```
SqlConnectionStringBuilder builder = new SqlConnectionStringBuilder(
ConfigurationManager.ConnectionStrings["ApplicationServices"].ConnectionString);
        builder.DataSource = ".";
```

■ **Caution**   Integrated authentication is the preferred means of connecting to a database. If you have to use the database credentials, then make sure that the Persist Security Info attribute is set to false. In addition, encrypt the sensitive credential information in the configuration file. You can use the ASPNET_REGIIS command with the -pe switch in the Visual Studio Tools Command Prompt to encrypt specific configuration sections. This is explained later in this chapter in the "Encrypting Web Configuration" section.

Connecting to a Database with SQL Credentials

The SqlCredential class is newly introduced in .NET Framework 4.5. It is designed to provide the SQL Server Authentication credentials with a SqlConnection instance in a more secure way. The credentials can now be specified outside of the connection string. This is a secure way of using a connection string in an application in case you have no choice other than to use SQL authentication.

```
using (SqlConnection con = new SqlConnection(ConnectionString))
{
SecureString password = txtPassword.SecurePassword;
password.MakeReadOnly();
SqlCredential credential = new SqlCredential(txtUserName.Text, password);
con.Credential = credential;
con.Open();
}
```

The SqlConnection object supports the Credential property in .NET Framework 4.5. You can use this property to specify the SQL database authentication credentials.

■ **Note**   The password is set as an immutable SecureString.

Asynchronous Connection

ADO.NET extensively supports asynchronous operations. You can asynchronously open a connection to a database, with the new asynchronous features of .NET Framework also being extended to ADO.NET. The SqlConnection object has the OpenAsync method to open a connection asynchronously.

```
readonly string ConnectionString = "Data Source=<database server name /
address>;Initial Catalog=Store;Integrated Security=True";
        protected async void ExecuteCommandAsync()
        {

            using (SqlConnection con = new SqlConnection(ConnectionString))
            {
                await con.OpenAsync();
            }
        }
```

Asynchronous CRUD operations were discussed briefly in Chapter 1.

Logging Connection Failures

ADO.NET has built-in support for Data Tracing for all the native providers. The SqlConnection instance exposes a ClientConnectionId property that can be used to capture diagnostic information about connection failures.

■ **Note**   Connection issues are logged in the Extended Events Log.

Commands for CRUD Operations

A command executes a query and either returns a result set or modifies the database. Each provider has a concrete implementation of the DbCommand class (generic command implementation) that allows execution of parameterized and inline queries. The command could use a select query to return a forward-only, read-only DataReader for iterating through the result set. The ExecuteReader method is used for the purpose.

```
readonly string GetReaderQuery = "SELECT RESULT FROM STORE";
        protected void GetRecords()
        {

            using (SqlConnection con = new SqlConnection(ConnectionString))
            {
                con.Open();
                SqlCommand command = new SqlCommand(GetReaderQuery, con);
                command.CommandType = CommandType.Text;
                var results = command.ExecuteReader();
              //....process results
            }
        }
```

You can use the SqlDataReader object to loop through the results and perform meaningful operations on the data.

```
if (results.HasRows)
            {
                while (results.Read())
                {
                    //Perform operations on data
                }
            }
            else
                results.Close();
```

Manipulating Data with Stored Procedures

Microsoft SQL Server supports stored queries in the form of stored procedures. It is a good idea to use stored procedures for CRUD operations instead of using inline queries for security and performance, as demonstrated in the previous section.

▓ **Caution**   Inline queries are always susceptible to injection attacks, so avoid using them in your code.

Fortunately, using stored procedures is easy. The DbCommand object supports three types of commands. Stored procedure is one of them. In the previous example, all you have to do is replace the command type and use the stored procedure name in the command text.

```
readonly string GetReaderProcedure = "sp_GetResults";
        protected void GetRecords()
        {

            using (SqlConnection con = new SqlConnection(ConnectionString))
            {
                con.Open();
                SqlCommand command = new SqlCommand(GetReaderProcedure, con);
                command.CommandType = CommandType.StoredProcedure;
                var results = command.ExecuteReader();
              //....process results
            }
        }
```

The command execution can be parameterized with the help of SqlParameter. The SqlCommand accepts a collection of parameters. The following insert operation illustrates this usage:

```
readonly string GetNonQueryProcedure = "sp_InsertRecord";
        protected void GetRecords()
        {

            using (SqlConnection con = new SqlConnection(ConnectionString))
            {
                con.Open();
                SqlParameter param = new SqlParameter
                {
                    ParameterName = "@StoreName",
                    SqlDbType = SqlDbType.NVarChar,
                    Direction = ParameterDirection.Input,
                    Value = "Gadgets"
                };

                SqlCommand command = new SqlCommand(GetNonQueryProcedure, con);
                command.CommandType = CommandType.StoredProcedure;
                command.Parameters.Add(param);
                var result = command.ExecuteNonQuery();
            }
        }
```

Another important artifact to note in the code sample is the ExecuteNonQuery method. It allows data manipulation in the form of inserts, updates, and deletes. (You can find the code samples for this chapter in the Source Code/Download area of the Apress web site [www.apress.com].)

■ **Note**   As mentioned previously, asynchronous support is also extended to the DbCommand class. This translates into equivalent asynchronous methods for operations exposed by the DbCommand class. You learned about this in Chapter 1.

Asynchronous Data Streams

In Chapter 1, you learned how CRUD operations can be performed asynchronously using ADO.NET in .NET Framework 4.5. In addition, in Chapter 2 you learned how SQL Server 2012 is extending its capabilities to support storage of large volumes of unstructured data. How can you access these large volumes of data through your .NET application? The answer lies in the new Asynchronous Data Streaming support in .NET Framework 4.5. You can use the streaming support in SqlClient provider to stream documents, media, and images. If you have a table in SQL to capture data of type VARBINARY, then you can use the following command to stream the data asynchronously:

```
public async Task GetResourceStream() {

        using (SqlConnection connection = new SqlConnection(ConnectionString)) {
            await connection.OpenAsync();
            using (SqlCommand command = new SqlCommand("SELECT binaryData FROM ContentStore",
connection)) {
                using (SqlDataReader reader = await
command.ExecuteReaderAsync(CommandBehavior.SequentialAccess)) {
                    if (await reader.ReadAsync()) {
                        if (!(await reader.IsDBNullAsync(0))) {
                            using (Stream data = reader.GetStream(0)) {
                                // await ...perform awaitable operation on data
                            }
                        }
                    }
                }
            }
        }
    }
```

Notice the GetStream method with the DataReader instance that returns a Stream object. It is a new addition to .NET Framework 4.5. In addition, there are methods like GetTextReader and GetXmlReader to retrieve text and XML streams from the SQL Server database.

Provider Factories

The provider factory pattern allows a layer of abstraction when accessing data from different providers, allowing you to create a single *application programming interface (API)* implementation of multiple native providers. The System.Data.Common namespace exposes generic provider class like the DbConnection and DbCommand, which are implemented by each native client provider, such as SqlClient. The DbProviderFactory class in the System.Data.Common namespace also provides the methods for generic implementation of native providers. The SqlCommand example shown in the preceding section "Commands for CRUD Operations," modified using a provider factory implementation, would look like the following:

```
DbProviderFactory provider = DbProviderFactories.GetFactory("System.Data.SqlClient");
        using (DbConnection con = provider.CreateConnection())
        {
                con.ConnectionString = ConnectionString;
                con.Open();
                DbParameter param = provider.CreateParameter();
                param.ParameterName = "@StoreName";
                param.DbType = DbType.String;
```

```
        param.Direction = ParameterDirection.Input;
        param.Value = "Gadgets";

        DbCommand command = provider.CreateCommand();
        command.Connection = con;
        command.CommandText = GetReaderProcedure;
        command.CommandType = CommandType.StoredProcedure;
        command.Parameters.Add(param);
        var result = command.ExecuteReader();
    }
```

The methods that allow creating concrete provider types are the CreateConnection and CreateCommand methods of the DbProviderFactory class. Since SqlClient is the provider used in the example, it would naturally return the SqlConnection and SqlCommand instances.

■ **Note** The connectionStrings configuration section supports a providerName attribute to allow storing provider-specific connection strings. The provider name for SqlClient is System.Data.SqlClient.

Figure 4-4 illustrates the factory implementation.

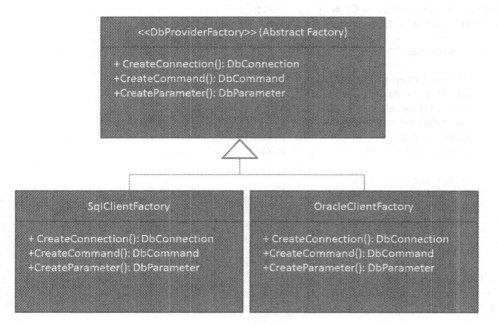

Figure 4-4. *DbProviderFactory asbtract factory and native provider factory implementation*

69

Multiple Active Result Sets

ADO.NET allows batch operations to be performed on a single connection with *Multiple Active Result Sets (MARS)*. Without this feature, developers had to open multiple connections or use cursors to perform batch operations. MARS can be enabled on a connection by setting the `MultipleActiveResultSets` attribute on the connection string to "true." This is extremely useful when you want the results of one particular query to act as parameters for another. The following code illustrates this:

```
readonly string ConnectionString = "Data Source=.;Initial
Catalog=Store;Integrated Security=True;MultipleActiveResultSets=True";
        readonly string GetProducts = "SELECT ProductName FROM Store WHERE StoreName=@StoreName";
        readonly string GetStores = "SELECT StoreName FROM Store";
        protected void GetRecords()
        {

            DbProviderFactory provider = DbProviderFactories.GetFactory("System.Data.SqlClient");
            using (DbConnection con = provider.CreateConnection())
            {
                con.ConnectionString = ConnectionString;
                con.Open();
                DbCommand storeCommand = provider.CreateCommand();
                storeCommand.CommandText = GetStores;
                storeCommand.CommandType = CommandType.Text;
                using (var storeResults = storeCommand.ExecuteReader())
                {
                    while (storeResults.Read())
                    {
                        DbDataAdapter productAdapter = provider.CreateDataAdapter();
                        DbParameter param = provider.CreateParameter();
                        param.ParameterName = "@StoreName";
                        param.DbType = DbType.String;
                        param.Direction = ParameterDirection.Input;
                        param.Value = storeResults["StoreName"].ToString();

                        //This requires MARS
                        DbCommand productCommand = provider.CreateCommand();
                        productCommand.Connection = con;
                        productCommand.CommandText = GetProducts;
                        productCommand.CommandType = CommandType.Text;
                        productCommand.Parameters.Add(param);
                        productAdapter.SelectCommand = productCommand;
                        DataSet products = new DataSet();
                        productAdapter.Fill(products, "products");
                    }
                }
            }
        }
```

The code uses the sample from the provider factories section and manipulates it to feed the result of one query to another. Note that the second command execution requires MARS to be enabled.

DataSets, DataAdapters, and DataSource Controls

DataSets represent in-memory snapshots of data that is independent of the source. This provides the ability for you to fetch data from multiple data sources, perform in-memory operations, and then update them back in the respective data store. This is a very powerful feature of ADO.NET. There are caveats, however, of which you must be aware while using DataSets in your application. Incorrect usage could hurt performance instead of improving on it.

Since DataSets are disconnected and can hold entire sets of tables, constraints, and relationships, there is a performance cost associated with using DataSets. It is advisable to limit the number of records with which you want to populate a DataSet by selectively introducing conditions in your queries.

The ADO.NET DataAdapter controls the interaction between DataSets and their source. For data retrieval, there is the all-important Fill method available with the DataAdapter instance that executes the Select command and populates the DataSet with necessary data. Modifying the GetRecords method used in the preceding code example to use the DataAdapter would look like the following:

```
using (DbConnection con = provider.CreateConnection())
        {
            con.ConnectionString = ConnectionString;
            DbDataAdapter adapter = provider.CreateDataAdapter();
            DbParameter param = provider.CreateParameter();
            param.ParameterName = "@StoreName";
            param.DbType = DbType.String;
            param.Direction = ParameterDirection.Input;
            param.Value = "Gadgets";

            DbCommand command = provider.CreateCommand();
            command.Connection = con;
            command.CommandText = GetReaderProcedure;
            command.CommandType = CommandType.StoredProcedure;
            command.Parameters.Add(param);
            adapter.SelectCommand = command;
            DataSet store = new DataSet();
            adapter.Fill(store, "stores");
```

An important change you might notice here is the absence of con.Open(). The Fill method is implicitly capable of opening and closing a connection.

░ **Note** The SqlDataAdapter Fill method has an overloaded implementation that you can use to page your query result. You can specify the current index and page size (number of records to be fetched per page).

DataSets could be populated with data from multiple sources, each connecting through a different provider. You could build relations among the snapshots of data inside the DataSet and bind to controls for display or for manipulation. DataSets are also serialization friendly, making them a preferred choice among developers.

Now that the data is loaded in the DataSet, you want to display the data to the users and allow them the ability to perform modifications. ASP.NET supports DataSource controls that act as an intermediary between the data-bound controls and the provider and do all the heavy lifting of wiring up the controls with the source for data retrieval and manipulation. With DataSource controls, you do not need write all the plumbing code to fetch data from the source and bind it to the control. With declarative markup syntax, DataSource controls can take care of that.

As shown in Figure 4-5, there are several DataSource controls. One of particular interest in this chapter, however, is the SqlDataSource control. It allows fetching and modifying data from different SQL data providers like SqlClient, OracleClient, and so on.

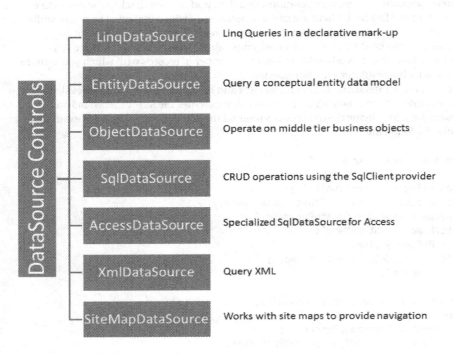

Figure 4-5. *DataSource controls*

■ **Note**   The DataSource controls take care of the much-needed abstraction from different providers without forcing you to write a lot of code.

The following code in an ASPX page illustrates the use of the SqlDataSource control:

```
<form id="form1" runat="server">

    <asp:SqlDataSource
        id="SqlDataSource1"
        runat="server"
        DataSourceMode="DataSet"
        ConnectionString="<%$ ConnectionStrings:ApplicationServices%>"
        SelectCommand="SELECT Content FROM Store"
        UpdateCommand="Update Store SET Content=@Content WHERE StoreId=@StoreId">
    </asp:SqlDataSource>

</form>
```

Although the control can be programmed using code, the declarative syntax makes it extremely intuitive to use. An important attribute to note here is DataSourceMode. It can be set to either DataSet or DataReader, depending on your requirement for data retrieval and modification. The DataSource control is bound to a View control with the DataSourceID attribute on the View control (GridView in our example).

```
<asp:GridView
        id="GridView1"
        runat="server"
        AutoGenerateColumns="False"
        DataKeyNames="StoreId"
        AutoGenerateEditButton="True"
        DataSourceID="SqlDataSource1">
        <columns>
            <asp:BoundField HeaderText="Content" DataField="Content" />
        </columns>
    </asp:GridView>
```

Using stored procedures with the SqlDataSource is also fairly simple. The important attribute to set is the command type. For the SelectCommand attribute, set the SelectCommandType to StoredProcedure. In addition, you can also specify parameters for the stored procedure. An interesting feature with SqlDataSource is that it can accept parameters from different sources like query strings, form variables, sessions, or cookies.

```
<asp:QueryStringParameter
                ConvertEmptyStringToNull="True"
                DefaultValue="string"
                Direction="Input"
                Name="StoreId"
                QueryStringField="StoreId"
                Type="String"
            />
```

In addition to the SqlDataSource control, we will be using the EntityDataSource extensively in due course to connect to a conceptual model using Entity Framework, and we will perform CRUD operations through the data-bound controls.

This concludes a brief discussion of some of the core ADO.NET features. You may have found these topics discussed in several books over multiple versions of .NET. However, there is no harm in having a little refresher before you proceed with some of the more interesting concepts related to ASP.NET and databases. Next, we will look at the various data type mappings in the different providers and how we handle issues generated out of mapping .NET types to native database types.

Data Type Mappings

Data types in .NET are represented by the *Common Type System (CTS)*. The types that CTS exposes don't automatically translate into types that a native database understands, so ADO.NET has to do the mapping either explicitly or implicitly. Each data provider exposes types that represent the database with which they interface. For example, the relevant types for SQL Server are available under the System.Data.SqlTypes namespace. They are faster and safer than the native .NET types, as they safeguard against any conversion issues. Figure 4-6 illustrates some of the important data type mappings between SQL Server and .NET Framework types and their equivalent enumeration in the provider.

SQL Server Types	.NET Framework Type	System.Data.SqlDbTypes
binary	Byte[]	VarBinary
bit	Boolean	Bit
char	String Char[]	Char
datetime	DateTime	DateTime
datetime2		DateTime2
decimal	Decimal	Decimal
FILESTREAM	Byte[]	VarBinary
float	Double	Float
int	Int32	Int
money	Decimal	Money
numeric	Decimal	Decimal
real	Single	Real
rowversion	Byte[]	Timestamp
sql_variant	Object	Variant
varbinary	Byte[]	VarBinary
varchar	String Char[]	VarChar
xml	Xml	Xml

Figure 4-6. *Data type mappings between SQL Server and .NET Framework*

Precision with Floating-Point Numbers

This is probably the only outlier in mapping .NET types to database types, irrespective of the provider. Floating-point numbers could not be represented in true binary form and thus could cause an aberration during conversion from SQL types to .NET and vice versa. Therefore, it is a good idea to use a fixed precision in storing floating-point data like decimals.

Secure Data Access

A badly designed data access layer with security vulnerabilities is the last thing you want for your application. Although ADO.NET has several security measures to protect your data, a good design is absolutely essential in preventing disruptions and even loss the through the theft of your vitally important data. This section elaborates some of the best practices designed to make sure that only users who are authorized for this purpose can securely access data.

Application security is performed at multiple levels, starting from application code (code access security) and going all the way to the databases (secure schemas, role-based access). For the purpose of this book, we will restrict our discussion to securing your ADO.NET implementation for data access.

Permissions for Accessing an SQL Database

Web applications are a little different in the way the database is accessed. The account accessing the database is different from the users using the system. It is a good practice to create a Windows service account and assign it the privileges on the database. This service account should be set as the Application Pool Identity for the web application. Figure 4-7 shows you how to set the Application Pool Identity.

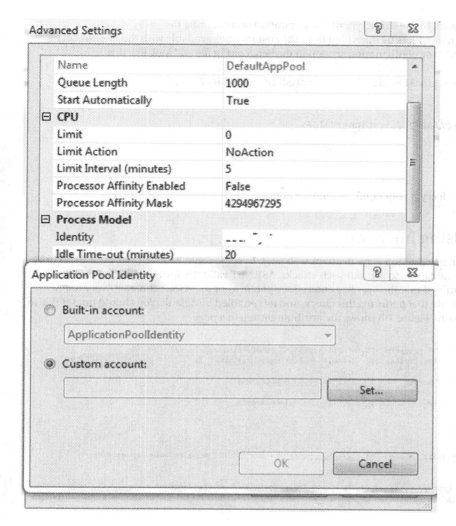

Figure 4-7. *Set Application Pool Identity to a Windows service account*

Your connection string in the Web.config file should be set for Integrated Security. Avoid using SQL credentials for accessing the database. In the worst case, if your web server is compromised, your database will still be safe from attack. However, if you have no option to use Integrated Security, and then consider passing the SQL credentials at runtime using the SqlConnectionStringBuilder class as shown in the preceding section "Reading and Modifying a Database Using ADO.NET Data Providers."

Encrypting Web Configuration

ASP.NET allows you to encrypt configuration sections in the Web.config file to strengthen further the security of your application. You can use the ASPNET_REGIIS command with the -pe switch to encrypt a configuration section. The following code illustrates encrypting the connectionStrings configuration section:

```
aspnet_regiis -pe "connectionStrings" -site "Content Store Site"  -app
"/ContentStore" -prov "RsaProtectedConfigurationProvider"
```

You can specify the provider you want to use to encrypt the configuration section using the –prov switch. It is also possible to write your own providers by inheriting from the custom ones available with the Framework. Postencryption, your connectionString configuration section in the Web.config file will look like this:

```
<connectionStrings configProtectionProvider="RsaProtectedConfigurationProvider">
  <EncryptedData>
    <CipherData>
      <CipherValue>HoAwE/Cl+sBAAAAH2... </CipherValue>
    </CipherData>
  </EncryptedData>
</connectionStrings>
```

You can use the –pd switch to decrypt your configuration section.

Preventing Exploits Using Injection

Script and SQL injection are the most common ways to attack web sites. In some ways, ASP.NET has built-in security mechanisms, such as form input validation, to prevent such attacks. ASP.NET validates form inputs and raises a framework exception if it is determined that the user has entered script blocks or malicious content. Every ASPX page has a ValidateRequest attribute that performs this check, and it is enabled by default. You should not set this to "false" unless you are absolutely sure. Figure 4-8 shows the attribute setting in a page.

```
<%@ Page Title="Home Page" Language="C#" MasterPageFile="~/Site.master" AutoEventWireup="true"
    CodeBehind="Default.aspx.cs" Inherits="InstallWeb._Default" ValidateRequest="true" %>

<asp:Content ID="HeaderContent" runat="server" ContentPlaceHolderID="HeadContent">
</asp:Content>
<asp:Content ID="BodyContent" runat="server" ContentPlaceHolderID="MainContent">
    <h2>
        Welcome to ASP.NET!
    </h2>
    <p>
        To learn more about ASP.NET visit <a href="http://www.asp.net" title="ASP.NET Website">www.asp.net</a>
    </p>
    <p>
        You can also find <a href="http://go.microsoft.com/fwlink/?LinkID=152368&amp;clcid=0x409"
            title="MSDN ASP.NET Docs">documentation on ASP.NET at MSDN</a>.
    </p>
</asp:Content>
```

Figure 4-8. *Validate page input request*

■ **Note** ASP.NET 4.5 has a new feature called *deferred request validation*, which allows you to read unvalidated request data selectively. You can enable this by setting the requestValidationMode attribute of the HTTP runtime to 4.5 <httpRuntime requestValidationMode="4.5" />. This causes the validation to be invoked only for values that are accessed (for example, by using the Request.Form collection). In addition, the HttpRequest object now has an Unvalidated property that can be used to access raw unvalidated request data.

There are some design decisions as well, however, which you must make in order to secure your application. The best practice for preventing SQL injection attacks is to avoid inline queries and use parameterized queries, or even better, use stored procedures. For script exploits, make sure that you are applying appropriate HTML encoding while displaying string content and accepting string data that may contain HTML scripts. You can use the HttpServerUtility HtmlEncode method for this purpose.

```
Server.HtmlEncode(content);
```

In addition, you should also perform appropriate casting operations before transmitting the values to the database captured from an input form. Every .NET Framework type exposes a TryParse method that returns "true" if the casting operation is successful. This is the preferred means over direct casts, which can throw an exception. In your select operations, you should also perform null value checks on key parameters that are used to retrieve unique records.

Exception Handling

Hackers trying to gain access to your database can use exception information to find out more about the source of data. It is therefore very important that you don't expose database-specific errors to the client application. Make sure that SQL exceptions are handled and logged and that only necessary exception information is propagated back to the client application.

Secure String for Processing Sensitive Information in Memory

.NET Framework has a SecureString class implemented from System.String, which is encrypted by default. You can use an instance of the SecureString object to process sensitive information in memory. The example under the preceding section "Connecting to a Database with SQL Credentials" demonstrates the use of SecureString. SecureString also has a MakeReadOnly method that can be used to make the instance immutable.

Microsoft SQL Server 2012 Extended Protection

Extended protection was first featured in Microsoft SQL Server 2008 R2. It protects in scenarios where an attacker acts as a client and authenticates against the database. The attacker could spoof the client into a false sense of connecting to a service while redirecting the client to the DNS and IP set by the attacker. SQL Server achieves extended protection through channel and service binding. In channel binding, a transport layer security is in place to ensure a secure connection between the client and the SQL Server instance. In service binding, the SQL Server instance validates the authenticity of the client using the *service principal name (SPN)* of the client. The SPN cannot be relayed, preventing the attacker from acting on behalf of the client.

Summary

The primary goal of this chapter is to bring back the focus to core ADO.NET concepts, some of which you may already know. The chapter also addresses the enhancements in multiple iterations of the framework.

You started the chapter with an overview of the different components of ADO.NET, and how the core components are involved in performing CRUD operations on a database. You also learned how DataSource controls can minimize the amount of code you need to write for database operations by using simple declarative markup syntax. Finally, you also learned about securing your data access layer.

The next chapter focuses on *Language Integrated Query (LINQ)* and how it has revolutionized the way framework operates on data.

■ ■ ■

CHAPTER 5

Introducing Language-Integrated Query (LINQ)

Emerging from a research project at Microsoft codenamed *Comega* (pronounced "see omega"), **Language-Integrated Query**, or **LINQ** as it's now known, has been an integral part of the .NET Framework since version 3.5. Nothing else has advanced the evolution ADO.NET better than LINQ.

If you are building data-driven applications, you know the pain of fetching data from multiple data sources. At some point, you will need to emerge from your comfort zone and learn the native query languages of the data sources on which you are attempting to operate. This is a phenomenal task for developers given the overwhelming number of data sources from which applications written in .NET can fetch data.

Wouldn't it be great if you could write the queries in .NET itself, and somehow they get magically transformed into the native query languages of the relevant data sources? With LINQ, you can do just that.

In this chapter, we will cover the following:

- How to write queries using LINQ.

- The different sources of data that can be queried using LINQ.

- The difference between enumerable and queryable types.

- How query operators function.

- How you can use LINQ to query ADO.NET data sources.

- How LINQ can leverage hyperthreading concepts to execute queries in parallel.

- How you can query Open Data (OData) Data Services using LINQ.

The ability to query data sources using one language is powerful, and it is used for building data-driven web sites. Hence, the concepts discussed in this chapter are important, and you will be using them moving forward through the remainder of this book.

Writing Queries Using LINQ

A LINQ expression has three basic parts. It is analogically equivalent to a database query expression. A great example is Transact-SQL (T-SQL), used to query and manipulate data in Microsoft SQL Server. If you are familiar with the T-SQL syntax, you know that a query to retrieve information is primarily formed using SELECT followed by the source using FROM, and it is then immediately followed by a condition using WHERE. There are, of course, additional keywords aiding a sort or grouping. The source of data is the table(s) you create, and then you execute the query. In a similar fashion, in LINQ you have the following:

1. Enumerable collections act as the source.

2. You build a query using LINQ Query Syntax (available for multiple languages, including VB and C#).

3. You execute the query by processing the results into a variable.

Let's examine each of these parts in detail.

LINQ Data Sources

A variety of data sources can be queried using LINQ. The sources, however, are broadly categorized into a couple of buckets. The first is in-memory sources, which basically assume that data is already loaded into a .NET enumerable collection that can be read in a forward-only fashion.

■ **Note**   Enumerable collections in .NET typically implement the IEnumerable interface or its generic equivalent IEnumberable<T>. They could also implement the derived IQueryable interface. Collectively, types that implement any of these interfaces are called *queryable types* in LINQ.

In essence, every object that implements IEnumerable in some form (implicitly or explicitly) is available to be queried. This is often referred to as *LINQ to Objects*.

Let's now explore the syntax of LINQ using a List. Imagine that you have a list of sales contacts and that you want a subset of contacts from the state of California. To draw similarities, an equivalent SQL query for fetching this information from the database would look like this:

```
SELECT [Name], [Email] FROM Contacts WHERE [State] = 'CA'
```

If you had preloaded all of the Contacts from the store into a List (List<Contact>), then the LINQ query would appear as follows:

```
var result = from contact in contacts
                    where contact.State == "CA"
                    select contact;
```

To execute, you can loop through the result and perform the necessary operations on the output.

```
foreach (var item in result)
        {
              Console.WriteLine(item.Name);
        }
```

■ **Note**   The query is not executed until the results are processed. You can, however, force the immediate execution by calling aggregate functions like Count on the query result or by caching the result using the ToList or ToArray extension methods.

As you probably observed, the LINQ query resembles an actual SQL query, except that it provides room for little syntactical differences, such as the SELECT that appears at the end. The preceding example represents a very basic query that can be performed on a collection. In the next section, you will explore additional querying capabilities like performing joins, sorting, and grouping.

In addition to support for querying in-memory collections, LINQ supports querying abilities on a variety of different data sources by exposing LINQ providers for each of them. Examples are querying XML types supported by the LINQ to XML provider, SQL supported by the LINQ to SQL provider, and so forth. An full list of providers is available here: http://blogs.msdn.com/b/charlie/archive/2008/02/28/link-to-everything-a-list-of-linq-providers.aspx. In fact, you could potentially create a provider of your own.

Typically, these providers support LINQ capabilities using the powerful IQueryable interface and its generic equivalent IQueryable<T>. IQueryable inherits IEnumerable; hence, by default, it possesses all the features of IEnumerable. So how is it different and, most importantly, useful? Let's explore this in more detail.

Deferred Execution with IQueryable

The variable results in the preceding example will be of type IEnumerable<T>, where T is the Contact class in this case. You can cast it to IQueryable using the AsQueryable extension method as shown here:

```
var resultAsQueryable = (from contact in contacts
                         where contact.State == "CA"
                         select contact).AsQueryable();

        foreach (var item in resultAsQueryable)
        {
            Console.WriteLine(item.Name);
        }
```

So what is the real difference when we execute both queries (the IEnumerable one shown before and the IQueryable in the preceding example) simultaneously? In our example, there is virtually none. Both will print the same output, except that if the data changes before the second foreach loop for the IQueryable executes, then you could see a different result for resultAsQueryable. The reason for this is that both IEnumerable and IQueryable follow a deferred execution pattern, meaning that the query is not executed until the results are evaluated. In our case, this is the foreach loop. The real difference is how the query is executed. For the IEnumerable type, the data is always loaded into memory and the filter is executed on the data in memory. IQueryable, on the other hand, allows the query to be executed on the source itself along with all of the filters. For example, for *LINQ to SQL*, the query is constructed on the provider and executed in the database. This will become even clearer if the results from the select query are filtered as shown in the following code:

```
var resultAsQueryable = (from contact in contacts
                         where contact.State == "CA"
                         select contact).AsQueryable();

var filteredResults = resultAsQueryable.Where(contact => contact.Name != "");

        foreach (var item in filteredResults)
        {
            Console.WriteLine(item.Name);
        }
```

The entire query, along with the filtered condition, would be executed on the source. This could boost performance in several scenarios, since a limited result set will be returned from the source. Subsequent filters will also go back to the source for IQueryable, while the in-memory DataSet is still accessed for IEnumerable.

Figure 5-1 illustrates this difference.

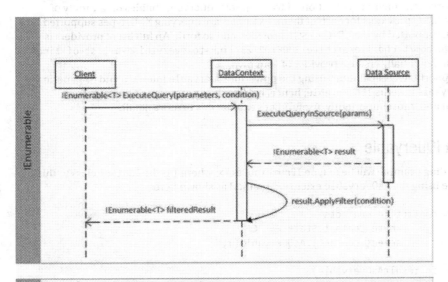

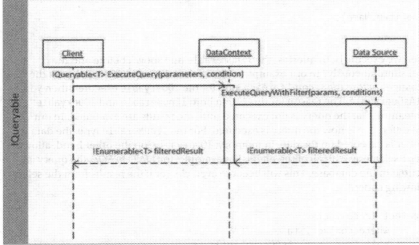

Figure 5-1. *IEnumerable vs. IQueryable execution cycle*

DataContext in Figure 5-1 represents the in-memory collection holding the data from the data source.

▨ **Note** Although both IEnumerable and IQueryable exhibit deferred query execution, IQueryable exhibits it in a true sense. IQueryable is particularly useful in scenarios like data paging and beats IEnumerable in performance for providers other than LINQ to Objects.

IQueryable vs. IEnumerable

Now that you understand why the IQueryable interface is useful, the question of when to use it instead of IEnumerable might be bothering you. Figure 5-2 provides guidance to help you decide when it's best to use each.

Scenario	IEnumerable	IQueryable
Remote Data Access (Web Services, Relational Database, etc.)		✖
Forward Only Operations (in-memory)	✖	
Evaluating Expression Trees (IQueryable has additional methods like CreateQuery<T> and Execute<T>		✖
Moving between items		✖
In-memory filters	✖	
Filters on remote data sources		✖

Figure 5-2. *When to use IQueryable vs. IEnumerable*

Building Queries Using LINQ

The example used in the previous section demonstrated the execution of a simple LINQ expression. Queries can be incredibly complex with a series of joins, unions, filters, sort, and grouping. LINQ also supports transformations, and you can use the querying capabilities to transform data from one form to another. This allows you to create lightweight views of very large and complex objects. The following code illustrates a LINQ join operation:

```
var transformedResult = from contact in contacts
                        join order in orders
                        on contact.ID equals order.ContactID
                        select new { contact.Name, order.Quantity };
```

Notice that transformedResult is a transformed entity with Name and Quantity as its properties.

```
foreach (var item in transformedResult)
    {
        Console.WriteLine(string.Format("{0}:{1}",item.Name, item.Quantity));
    }
```

This is evident when you do a foreach on the result and print the output.

▒ **Note** Observe the data transformation that happened as a result of the join operation. The result produced a new entity altogether, merging the requested properties from two related entities.

If you need multiple results to be stored in a single element, then you could perform a GroupJoin operation.

Projections

The select clause is capable of producing a variety of transformations. When the select clause returns a result other than the source, it is called a *projection*. The preceding code sample is an example of a projection.

■ **Tip** You may have noticed that the examples shown so far demonstrate the ability to allow the compiler to infer the type of result from the query. If you are performing complex projections, the implicitly typed local variable convention allows you to process results without worrying about the type of the transformed result.

Query Expression Identifier

In a complex transformation, you may need an expression to be evaluated as part of the query execution. LINQ syntax has a let identifier that allows you to evaluate expressions. To demonstrate, we tweaked the preceding code sample to introduce a price factor to the Order entity and to create a projection for orders on a price condition. The following code demonstrates this:

```
var transformedResult = from contact in contacts
                        join order in orders
                        on contact.ID equals order.ContactID
                        let effectivePrice = order.Rate * order.Quantity
                        where effectivePrice < 400
                        select new { contact.Name, order.Quantity };
```

With this, we conclude the discussion of building queries using LINQ.

So far, you have gained a fair insight into how LINQ operates, and you also learned about the complex querying and data transformation capabilities of LINQ. However, you have just scratched the surface. In the next section, we will explore the powerful querying capabilities of LINQ in more detail and understand how it works under the hood.

Query Operators

The .NET Framework compiler translates the query expressions into meaningful executable CLR method calls. These methods are called *query operators*, exposed by LINQ to allow you perform queries on sequences. The truth is that the query syntax is merely a syntactic carrot for you to drive an analogy toward SQL-style queries, and the standard query operators ultimately perform the operations themselves. In fact, some operations still do not have equivalent query expressions and need to be performed directly using the operator methods. One example of the method style was shown in the preceding section "*Deferred Execution with IQueryable*," which used the Where operator.

■ **Note** The expression passed inline to a query operator is called a *lambda expression*. The goes to (=>) operator is a lambda operator that allows you to access properties of the entities being evaluated. In the preceding Where example (contact => contact.Name != ""), the lambda expression is used to check if the contact name is empty.

Query Operator Classification

There are a bunch of operators available as extension methods to enumerable and queryable objects. They are categorized under the type of operations they perform. For example, Max, Count, Sum, and so on are categorized as *aggregate operations*. In addition, the query operators are also classified as the ones for enumerable types and queryable types.

Query Operator Execution

The query operators differ in the way they get executed. If you recall the discussion of "*deferred execution*," there are certain query operators that force immediate execution, while others follow the deferred execution mechanism. For example, all aggregate operations force immediate execution, while Filter operations, like Where and Select, follow deferred execution. Similarly, all *quantifier operations* like All, Any, and Contains also force immediate execution.

The following query retrieves the sum of all orders placed in the contacts and orders example:

```
var totalOrder = orders.Sum(order => order.Rate * order.Quantity);
```

The following example shows immediate execution with the All operator fetching results for all orders where quantity is greater than ten:

```
var quantityGreaterThanTen = orders.All(order => order.Quantity > 10)
```

▓ **Tip**   It is possible to use multiple operators on a sequence. For example, you could first run a filter, with Where and then run an aggregate using Sum on the result: <sequence>.Where(<lambda>).Sum(<lambda>).

Now that you have a good understanding of how LINQ works behind the scenes, it's time to learn about accessing data in ADO.NET using some of the popular LINQ providers.

LINQ for ADO.NET Data Access

There is no better time to restate the reason behind immense popularity of LINQ; that is, developers' need for a paradigm that lets them query heterogeneous data sources without having to learn the native query syntaxes for each of them. LINQ provides that abstraction. It brought powerful querying capabilities right inside the languages supported by .NET Framework, such as C# and VB, and it also provided a framework for building native data providers that translate LINQ expressions into native queries. Figure 5-3 illustrates the architecture stack.

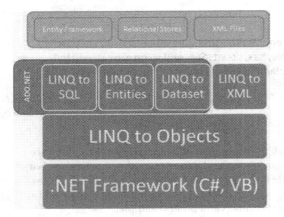

Figure 5-3. *ADO.NET data access using LINQ*

There are several LINQ providers. In this section, we will discuss the ones that are related to ADO.NET.

LINQ to SQL

LINQ to SQL creates an entire infrastructure around relational databases mapping SQL artifacts like tables, stored procedures, and user-defined functions into .NET objects, which can be queried using LINQ. In addition, it also supports the transactional capabilities of relational databases like Microsoft SQL Server. What does this mean for you?

You can now use database tables to create an entity relationship in your data access layer. Then you can use LINQ to query entities as you did in LINQ to Objects. LINQ to SQL will take care of executing the queries in SQL and returning the desired result. Fantastic, isn't it? You don't have to write any SQL statements. If the database developer on your team has created stored procedures, you can also leverage them. Let's try creating a project in Visual Studio to understand the capabilities of LINQ to SQL.

TRY IT OUT: MANIPULATE DATA IN A MICROSOFT SQL SERVER DATABASE USING LINQ

In this exercise, we will create a Visual Studio 2012 C# Console Application project to access data from a Microsoft SQL Server 2012 Express Edition database using LINQ to SQL. Following are the prerequisites:

- The exercise can be created on any edition of Visual Studio beginning with version 2008. In our example, we will be using Visual Studio 2012 Professional.

- Create a database named Store in your Microsoft SQL Server 2012 Express Edition instance, and add two tables, Orders and Customers, with the structure shown in Figure 5-4. Run the following script to add some sample data into the tables.

```
INSERT INTO Contacts (Name, Email, [State]) VALUES ('John Doe', '', 'CA')
INSERT INTO Contacts (Name, Email, [State]) VALUES ('Jane Doe', '', 'AZ')

INSERT INTO Orders (ContactID, Quantity, Rate) VALUES (1, 10, 10)
INSERT INTO Orders (ContactID, Quantity, Rate) VALUES (2, 20, 20)
```

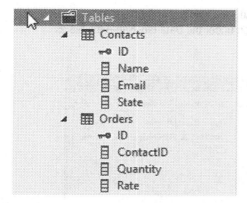

Figure 5-4. *Store database table structure*

Follow these steps to complete the exercise:

1. Create a Visual Studio 2012 C# Console Application project and name it LinqToSqlStore as shown in Figure 5-5.

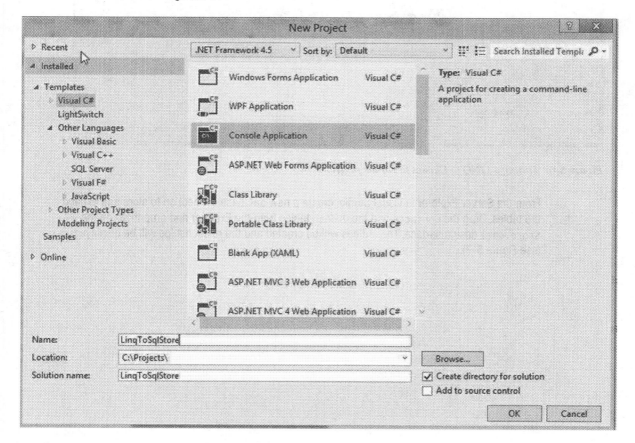

Figure 5-5. *Visual Studio 2012 C# Console Application project*

In the Solution Explorer, right-click the project and click "Add ➤ New Item. . ." to launch the Add New Item dialog. Select the "LINQ to SQL Classes" option under the Data tab. Name the file as Store.dbml, as shown in Figure 5-6.

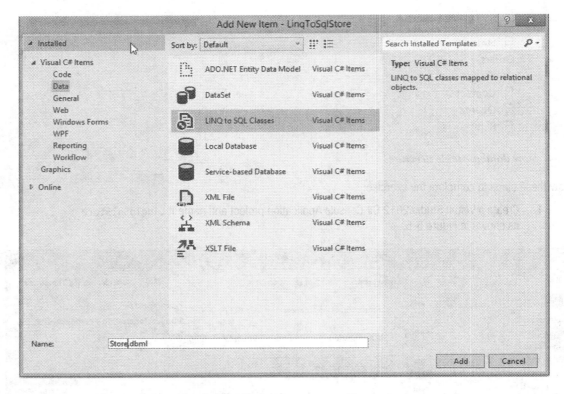

Figure 5-6. *Adding a LINQ to Classes file to the project*

From the Server Explorer in Visual Studio, create a new database connection to store and expand the tables. Drag the Contacts and the Orders tables from the Explorer and drop them on the Store.dbml design surface. The entities will be created and the relationships will be displayed (see Figure 5-7).

Store.dbml* Program.cs

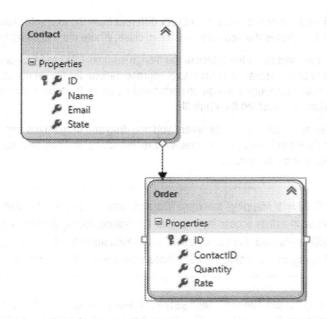

Figure 5-7. *LINQ to SQL Designer displaying entity and relationships between entities*

Open the `Program.cs` file and write the following code in the `Main` method:

```
using (StoreDataContext context = new StoreDataContext())
    {
        var transformedResult = from contact in context.Contacts
                                join order in context.Orders
                                on contact.ID equals order.ContactID
                                select new { contact.Name, order.Quantity };

        foreach (var item in transformedResult)
        {
            Console.WriteLine(string.Format("{0}:{1}", item.Name, item.Quantity));
        }
        Console.ReadLine();
    }
```

Compile and run the application. The results that are output will be same as in the
example shown in the previous section "*Building Queries Using LINQ*" (see Figure 5-8).

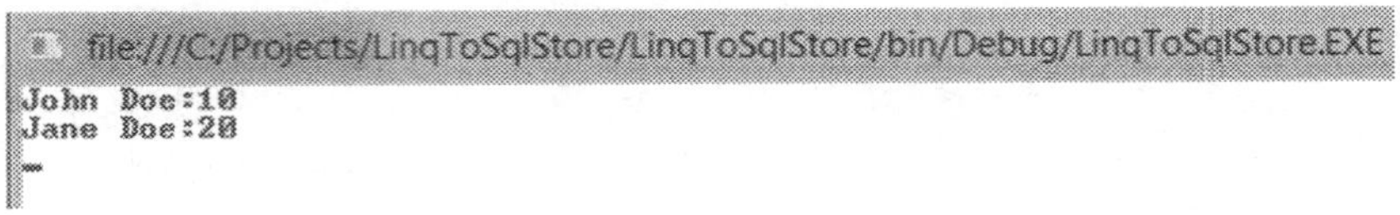

```
file:///C:/Projects/LinqToSqlStore/LinqToSqlStore/bin/Debug/LinqToSqlStore.EXE
John Doe:10
Jane Doe:20
_
```

Figure 5-8. *Output of the Join Query executed*

If you inspect the code block in step 4, you will notice that it is not very different from the example shown in the previous sections. The important thing to notice is the StoreDataContext class. Where did this come from?

When you add the LINQ to SQL Classes file and place the tables in the design surface, LINQ to SQL generates a mapping class under the hood that contains equivalent entity (table) representations for the relational tables, and it also contains methods for the CRUD operations that can be performed on them. By default, it appends a "DataContext" to the file name with which you created the dbml file.

The dbml file has an *O/R (Object Relational) Designer* surface where you can drag and drop tables from the database, and it will automatically create the entity classes and relevant relationships. You can then use the DataContext class to access the entities using LINQ syntax.

■ **Note** LINQ to SQL is an ORM (*Object Relational Mapping*) tool from Microsoft that competes with several other similar tools on the market today. You can use it to build a data access layer in your application, letting it do all the heavy lifting of connecting to a database and running CRUD operations. You could use a Design-First approach by modeling the database in the O/R Designer or follow a Code-First approach by coding the DataContext class from the ground up.

Behind the scenes, LINQ to SQL uses a command-line tool called sqlmetal.exe to perform all the mapping tasks. You can use this tool directly in situations where you need the DataContext to be generated outside of Visual Studio. This is a good candidate for a team build component. You can learn more about the tool in this MSDN article: http://msdn.microsoft.com/en-us/library/bb386987.aspx.

Lazy Loading

If you look at the Association Editor in the O/R Designer, you will notice that an association is already created between the Orders and Contacts entities based on the foreign key relationship defined in the database. Figure 5-9 illustrates this association.

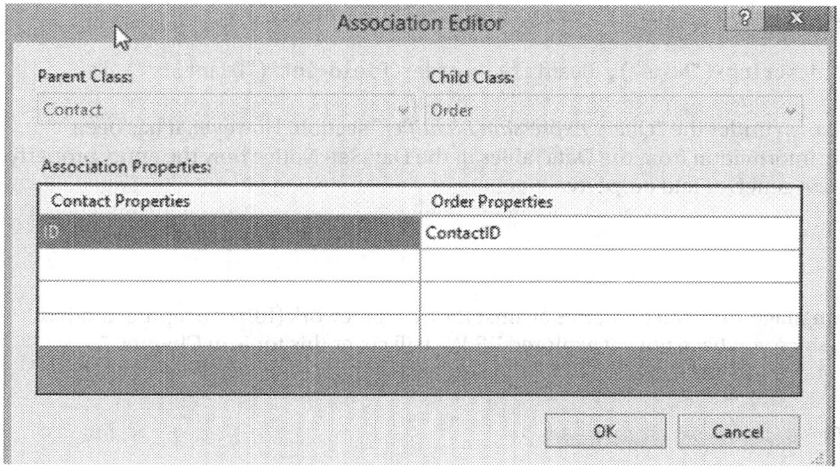

Figure 5-9. Entity associations

Potentially, associations can let you define complex relationships between entities. By default, however, when an entity is loaded with data, child entities are not populated. This is the lazy loading feature that LINQ to SQL supports for performance reasons. For example, in the Store DataContext, whenever an enumerable collection of the Order entity is retrieved, the associated Contact entity values will not be populated by default. You have the option of overriding the default behavior using the DataLoadOptions class. You can create a DataLoadOption instance to eager load child entities. (You can do this selectively and use this feature to optimize performance.) The following code demonstrates this:

```
DataLoadOptions loadOptions = new DataLoadOptions();
            loadOptions.LoadWith<Order>(order => order.Contact);
            context.LoadOptions = loadOptions;
```

Now, when you try to load the Orders, the associated Contact information will be loaded automatically. There are two methods exposed by the DataLoadOptions class: LoadWith and AssociateWith (and their generic equivalents). AssociateWith can be used to filter the eager load options further.

LINQ to DataSet

The language support in the form of LINQ extension methods is applicable to DataTables. DataSets (container for DataTables) themselves act as cached abstractions for provider-independent data access. With LINQ support, you can extend the querying capabilities on multiple data sources from which data is loaded into a DataSet. DataTables support the AsEnumerable and AsDataView extension methods that allow you query the sources and bind data to controls for display and manipulation.

```
EnumerableRowCollection<DataRow> enumerableOrdersDataRow =
aggerateSet.Tables["OrdersTable"].AsEnumerable();
EnumerableRowCollection<DataRow> enumerableContactsDataRow =
aggerateSet.Tables["ContactsTable"].AsEnumerable();

var transformedResultFromDataSet = from contact in enumerableContactsDataRow
                        join order in enumerableOrdersDataRow
                        on contact.Field<int>("ID") equals
                        order. Field<int>("ContactID")
```

```
let effectivePrice = order.Field<decimal>("Rate") * order.Field<int>("Quantity")
where effectivePrice < 400
select new { Name = contact.Field<string>("Name"), Quantity = order.Field<int>("Quantity") };
```

The query is similar to the one shown under the *"Query Expression Identifier"* section. However, it has been modified to collect the entity property information from the DataTables in the DataSet. Notice how the entity property values are fetched using the DataColumn generic Field property.

LINQ to Entities

LINQ to Entities allows you to write language-integrated queries against Entity Framework (EF) conceptual models. It is too early to discuss this in detail, since you have not yet explored EF. We will cover this topic in Chapter 7.

LINQ and Parallelism

True *parallelism* made its way into the world of .NET when the *Task Parallel Library* was introduced in .NET Framework 4.0. It was done to leverage the hyperthreading features introduced by Intel in multicore processors. A logical outreach was to extend the benefits of parallelism to LINQ. Thus *Parallel-LINQ* (PLINQ) was born. With PLINQ, you have the ability to scale queries to leverage the number of cores available in the machine efficiently, thereby improving performance. The framework also provides concurrent data structures to store results occurring out of parallel executions of queries concurrently.

.NET Framework 4.5 has several enhancements in PLINQ, primarily designed to improve performance. Figure 5-10 illustrates how PLINQ functions.

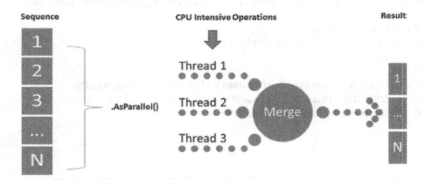

Figure 5-10. *Executing LINQ queries in parallel*

AsParallel Extension

The ParallelEnumerable class has most of the functionality related to PLINQ. It provides the AsParallel extension method, which allows queries to be executed in parallel. The following example illustrates the execution of a LINQ query in parallel utilizing multicore support.

```
var parallelResult = source.AsParallel().Select(x => IntensiveOperation(x));
```

■ **Note**　The source is an enumerable/queryable collection, and each item in it participates in a CPU-intensive operation represented by the `IntensiveOperation` method.

Not all PLINQ queries run parallel by default. The framework is capable of evaluating the performance benefits of running a query in parallel, and if there aren't any, then the query runs sequentially. For example, `ElementAt` operations will always fall back to sequential execution. In .NET Framework 4.5, parallel queries have broadened their reach, and now lesser operations fall back to running sequentially. The following MSDN article provides some details into such operations and the potential risks due to this change:
http://blogs.msdn.com/b/pfxteam/archive/2011/11/11/10235999.aspx.

■ **Caution**　Exercise your right to use PLINQ queries with discretion. In low-CPU-intensity scenarios, they could actually hurt performance due to the overhead involved, and benefits may not be realized. In addition, although the LINQ query may execute in parallel, the `foreach` statement executing it runs sequentially. You have the option of running the `ForAll` operator on the query result variable instead if you are not concerned about preserving the order of the items.

Querying WCF Data Services

WCF Data Services allows you to expose your data as *RESTful* services over the Web using the *Open Data* (*OData*) protocol. You can execute queries against such data services using LINQ. LINQ expressions executed on a data service are transformed into equivalent queries in OData format. The WCF Data Services Client Library facilitates the translation of LINQ into HTTP requests that represent the OData queries. You will learn more about how WCF Data Services function in Chapter 9. In this section, we will focus on querying data services using LINQ syntax. Let's try the steps of querying a data service using the *Netflix OData Catalog*, which allows you to browse through over 100,000 movies and actors.

TRY IT OUT: QUERY THE NETFLIX ODATA CATALOG USING LINQPAD

In this exercise, we will use a popular LINQ editor, LINQPad, to query the Netflix data service: http://odata.netflix.com. You can download LINQPad from here: http://www.linqpad.net/.

Make sure to download the LINQPad version for .NET Framework 4.x. Once you download the zip package, extract it to a folder and then double-click LINQPad.exe to launch the editor. Follow these steps to query the Netflix catalog using LINQ:

1.　In the LINQPad editor, click the *Add connection* link to launch the *Choose Data Context* dialog, as shown in Figure 5-11.

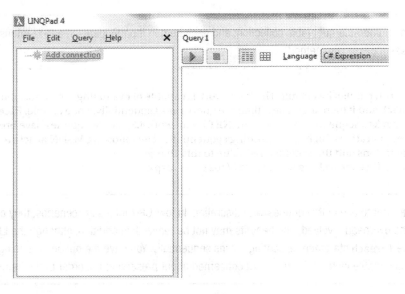

Figure 5-11. *Adding WCF Data Service Connection*

2. In the *Choose Data Context* dialog, select the *"WCF Data Services (OData)"* option under the *"Build data context automatically"* list, as shown in Figure 5-12. Click *Next*.

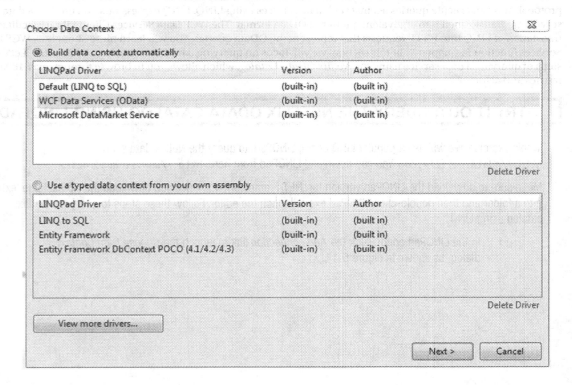

Figure 5-12. *Choose Data Context*

3. In the WCF Data Services (OData) Connection dialog, enter the Netflix Catalog URL,
    `http://odata.netflix.com`, and click the Test button to check if the connection
    succeeds (see Figure 5-13). Click *OK* once the test is successful.

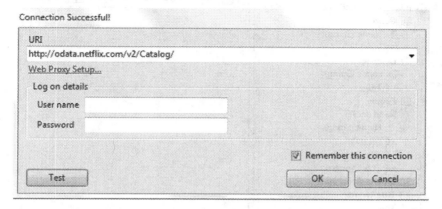

Figure 5-13. *Successful test of the Netflix Catalog connection*

4. Notice that all the available entities are displayed. Expand the entities, and you will notice
    that the relationships with other entities are also visible, as shown in Figure 5-14.

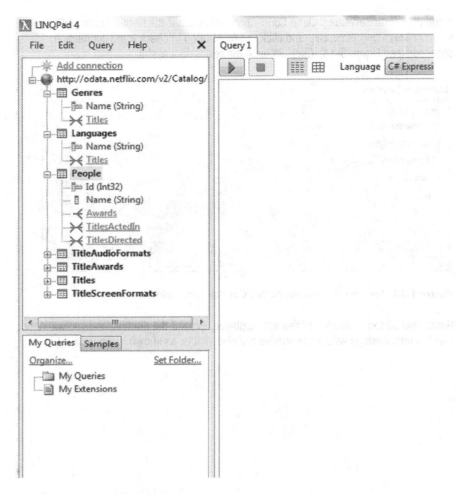

Figure 5-14. *Netflix OData API entities and relationships*

5. Right-click the Genres entity, and you will see templates for a variety of LINQ queries that you can execute on this entity. Click "*from g in Genres where ... select g*" (see Figure 5-15).

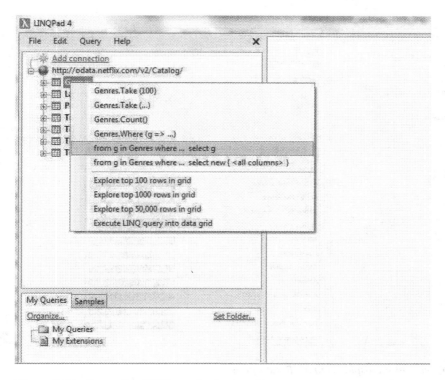

Figure 5-15. *Generating LINQ queries from entities*

6. In the generated query, delete the `where` condition and execute the query to see the results. The list of available genres is displayed in the results pane. You can switch the results view to see the lambda and OData equivalents of the executed query, as shown in Figure 5-16.

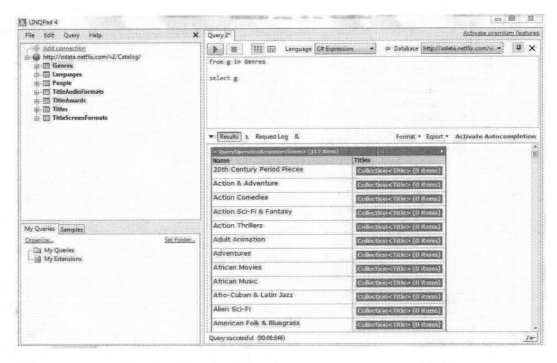

Figure 5-16. *Query output displayed in the Results pane*

You can play with the LINQPad editor and the Netflix data service by executing different queries. The output will be instantly displayed in the results pane. LINQPad is a useful tool for trying out and honing your LINQ skills using different data sources including WCF Data Services. You can also test your queries out before using them in your data and business layers.

Summary

LINQ is a fairly big topic in its entirety. The idea behind this chapter was for you to explore the power of LINQ in querying heterogeneous data sources. The concepts discussed in the chapter were selected for their relevance in the context of this book. You learned how to query objects in memory and remote data sources (including WCF Data Services) using LINQ, and you explored how LINQ augments ADO.NET. In addition, you also learned how LINQ leverages the parallel programming features of .NET Framework to improve the performance of queries. In the next chapter, we will focus on the concept of Entity Data Model being leveraged by several ORM tools in .NET and by Entity Framework.

■ ■ ■

CHAPTER 6

ADO.NET Entity Data Model

Entity Relationship Diagrams (ERD) are very popular for modeling data tiers. They allow architects and developers to create a conceptual model that is totally decoupled from the actual storage schema of any specific database. For data-driven applications, it is challenging, however, to map the conceptual model to a physical database since data is stored and retrieved from a variety of sources containing a mix of relational and object-based stores.

This challenge gave birth to a large number of *Object Relationship Mapping (ORM)* tools to map *Entities* and *Relationships* in code into storage schemas specific to the database. ADO.NET also stood up to the challenge and provided a feature called *Entity Data Model (EDM),* which is a provider-neutral way of defining Entities and Relationships. EDM allows developers to model data in code and use CLR languages to perform operations on the entity classes. Tools such as Entity Framework use EDM specifications behind the scenes to map operations on entity classes to CRUD operations on the physical database. Although EDM is extensively used by Entity Framework, the specifications are not limited to Entity Framework and could be used to build your own ORM tool. EDM specifications are also used by *Open Data (OData)* protocol services in *WCF Data Services.*

In this chapter, we will cover the following topics:

- The architecture of Entity Data Model.

- How EDM functions using the conceptual, storage, and mapping schemas.

- The role of ADO.NET metadata.

- How you can query conceptual models using Entity SQL.

EDM is an important concept for you to learn before you can start using Entity Framework to build data-driven applications.

EDM Architecture

EDM allows you to define Entities and Relationships. You can use EDM to model data in your application in a storage provider–neutral fashion and then program against the model.

EDM is composed of three related concepts:

1. *EDM Schemas*: A set of XML files representing design schemas.

2. *ADO.NET Metadata*: A robust metadata system for structuring data.

3. *Entity SQL*: A query language for querying the conceptual models.

In addition, there are tools that allow you to generate CLR code as programmable objects in your application from the design schemas.

There are three layers in EDM design schema. The three schemas are as follows:

1. The *Conceptual Schema*: This is responsible for defining the conceptual model.

2. The *Store Schema*: This is responsible for defining the storage model.

3. The *Mapping Schema*: This is responsible for mapping the conceptual model to the storage model.

Figure 6-1 illustrates the EDM design schema architecture.

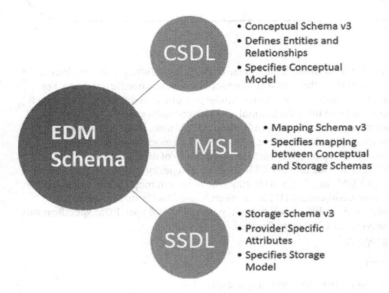

Figure 6-1. EDM design schema layers

ADO.NET components like Entity Framework and WCF Data Services use these schemas to map conceptual models created in code or Designer to a physical data store and then allow CRUD operations to be performed on the mapped models. You will learn more about the components of EDM in detail in forthcoming sections of this chapter.

Conceptual Schema

The conceptual model in Entity Framework is governed by a *Conceptual Schema Definition Language (CSDL)*. At the time of this writing,, CSDL v3 is the most current version. CSDL is an important part of the EDM architecture described in the previous section. It is responsible for defining the Entities and Relationships in their conceptual form, and it is used by the Entity Framework runtime to map the conceptual model to its physical store representation.

Let's take a look at the structure and attributes of CSDL. The following code block illustrates the CSDL for our Store database containing the Contacts and Orders tables:

```
<Schema Namespace="StoreModel" Alias="Self" xmlns:annotation="http://schemas.microsoft.com/
ado/2009/02/edm/annotation" xmlns="http://schemas.microsoft.com/ado/2008/09/edm">
  <EntityContainer Name="StoreEntities" annotation:LazyLoadingEnabled="true">
    <EntitySet Name="Contacts" EntityType="StoreModel.Contact" />
    <EntitySet Name="Orders" EntityType="StoreModel.Order" />
```

```
    <AssociationSet Name="FK_Orders_Contacts" Association="StoreModel.FK_Orders_Contacts">
      <End Role="Contacts" EntitySet="Contacts" />
      <End Role="Orders" EntitySet="Orders" />
    </AssociationSet>
  </EntityContainer>
  <EntityType Name="Contact">
    <Key>
      <PropertyRef Name="ID" />
    </Key>
    <Property Name="ID" Type="Int32" Nullable="false" annotation:StoreGeneratedPattern="Identity" />
    <Property Name="Name" Type="String" Nullable="false" MaxLength="50" Unicode="true"
FixedLength="false" />
    <Property Name="Email" Type="String" MaxLength="50" Unicode="true" FixedLength="false" />
    <Property Name="State" Type="String" Nullable="false" MaxLength="2" Unicode="true"
FixedLength="false" />
    <NavigationProperty Name="Orders" Relationship="StoreModel.FK_Orders_Contacts"
FromRole="Contacts" ToRole="Orders" />
  </EntityType>
  <EntityType Name="Order">
    <Key>
      <PropertyRef Name="ID" />
    </Key>
    <Property Name="ID" Type="Int32" Nullable="false" annotation:StoreGeneratedPattern="Identity" />
    <Property Name="ContactID" Type="Int32" Nullable="false" />
    <Property Name="Quantity" Type="Int32" Nullable="false" />
    <Property Name="Rate" Type="Decimal" Nullable="false" Precision="18" Scale="0" />
    <NavigationProperty Name="Contact" Relationship="StoreModel.FK_Orders_Contacts"
FromRole="Orders" ToRole="Contacts" />
  </EntityType>
  <Association Name="FK_Orders_Contacts">
    <End Role="Contacts" Type="StoreModel.Contact" Multiplicity="1" />
    <End Role="Orders" Type="StoreModel.Order" Multiplicity="*" />
    <ReferentialConstraint>
      <Principal Role="Contacts">
        <PropertyRef Name="ID" />
      </Principal>
      <Dependent Role="Orders">
        <PropertyRef Name="ContactID" />
      </Dependent>
    </ReferentialConstraint>
  </Association>
</Schema>
```

The Schema root element contains the namespace http://schemas.microsoft.com/ado/2008/09/edm representing CSDL v3. The CSDL XML structure contains the EntityContainer element, which acts as a container for grouping Entities and Relationships for our Store model. It is comprised of two EntitySet elements representing the instances of entities (Contact and Order) and one AssociationSet element representing the relationship.

■ **Note** The CSDL specification is becoming the de facto standard for defining conceptual models, and it is also used by the OData protocol. The OData CSDL specification is already in a working draft with the OASIS (Open Specifications Committee).

Annotations

The Conceptual Schema supports annotation attributes to allow you specify additional behavioral instructions. For example, the LazyLoadingEnabled attribute is set by default to let Entity Framework perform lazy loading of entities.

CSDL with WCF Data Services

You will learn about WCF Data Services in Chapter 9. Nevertheless, you should know that EDM is also used by WCF Data Services to define the conceptual model using CSDL. Query a WCF Data Service metadata using the $metadata query expression, and the results returned will be a CSDL document.

Storage Schema

The Storage Schema is pretty similar to the Conceptual Schema, except that it specifies the attributes and values representing the associated storage provider. The Storage Schema is specified using the *Storage Schema Definition Language (SSDL)* represented by the namespace http://schemas.microsoft.com/ado/2009/02/edm/ssdl.

The following code block represents the Storage Schema associated with the Store database using the SqlClient (System.Data) provider for Microsoft SQL Server databases:

```
<Schema Namespace="StoreModel.Store" Alias="Self" Provider="System.Data.SqlClient"
ProviderManifestToken="2008" xmlns:store="http://schemas.microsoft.com/ado/2007/12/edm/
EntityStoreSchemaGenerator" xmlns="http://schemas.microsoft.com/ado/2009/02/edm/ssdl">
  <EntityContainer Name="StoreModelStoreContainer">
    <EntitySet Name="Contacts" EntityType="StoreModel.Store.Contacts" store:Type="Tables"
Schema="dbo" />
    <EntitySet Name="Orders" EntityType="StoreModel.Store.Orders" store:Type="Tables" Schema="dbo" />
    <AssociationSet Name="FK_Orders_Contacts" Association="StoreModel.Store.FK_Orders_Contacts">
      <End Role="Contacts" EntitySet="Contacts" />
      <End Role="Orders" EntitySet="Orders" />
    </AssociationSet>
  </EntityContainer>
  <EntityType Name="Contacts">
    <Key>
      <PropertyRef Name="ID" />
    </Key>
    <Property Name="ID" Type="int" Nullable="false" StoreGeneratedPattern="Identity" />
    <Property Name="Name" Type="nvarchar" Nullable="false" MaxLength="50" />
    <Property Name="Email" Type="nvarchar" MaxLength="50" />
    <Property Name="State" Type="nvarchar" Nullable="false" MaxLength="2" />
  </EntityType>
  <EntityType Name="Orders">
    <Key>
      <PropertyRef Name="ID" />
    </Key>
    <Property Name="ID" Type="int" Nullable="false" StoreGeneratedPattern="Identity" />
    <Property Name="ContactID" Type="int" Nullable="false" />
    <Property Name="Quantity" Type="int" Nullable="false" />
    <Property Name="Rate" Type="decimal" Nullable="false" />
  </EntityType>
```

```
    <Association Name="FK_Orders_Contacts">
      <End Role="Contacts" Type="StoreModel.Store.Contacts" Multiplicity="1" />
      <End Role="Orders" Type="StoreModel.Store.Orders" Multiplicity="*" />
      <ReferentialConstraint>
        <Principal Role="Contacts">
          <PropertyRef Name="ID" />
        </Principal>
        <Dependent Role="Orders">
          <PropertyRef Name="ContactID" />
        </Dependent>
      </ReferentialConstraint>
    </Association>
  </Schema>
```

▓ **Note** There is an additional attribute `Provider` on the `Schema` element specifying the `SqlClient` provider. The `EntitySet` element also has additional attributes to specify the store type and database schema.

Mapping Schema

The Mapping Schema acts as glue between the Conceptual and Storage Schemas. It is specified using a *Mapping Specification Language (MSL v3)*. The following code block shows the MSL for the Store database Conceptual and Storage Schemas.

```
<Mapping Space="C-S" xmlns="http://schemas.microsoft.com/ado/2008/09/mapping/cs">
  <EntityContainerMapping StorageEntityContainer="StoreModelStoreContainer"
CdmEntityContainer="StoreEntities">
    <EntitySetMapping Name="Contacts">
      <EntityTypeMapping TypeName="StoreModel.Contact">
        <MappingFragment StoreEntitySet="Contacts">
          <ScalarProperty Name="ID" ColumnName="ID" />
          <ScalarProperty Name="Name" ColumnName="Name" />
          <ScalarProperty Name="Email" ColumnName="Email" />
          <ScalarProperty Name="State" ColumnName="State" />
        </MappingFragment>
      </EntityTypeMapping>
    </EntitySetMapping>
    <EntitySetMapping Name="Orders">
      <EntityTypeMapping TypeName="StoreModel.Order">
        <MappingFragment StoreEntitySet="Orders">
          <ScalarProperty Name="ID" ColumnName="ID" />
          <ScalarProperty Name="ContactID" ColumnName="ContactID" />
          <ScalarProperty Name="Quantity" ColumnName="Quantity" />
          <ScalarProperty Name="Rate" ColumnName="Rate" />
        </MappingFragment>
      </EntityTypeMapping>
    </EntitySetMapping>
  </EntityContainerMapping>
</Mapping>
```

■ **Note**   All three schema files are automatically generated by Visual Studio from the Entity Data Model Designer and are stored as embedded resources in the project, as shown in Figure 6-2. You will learn about the Entity Designer in the next chapter.

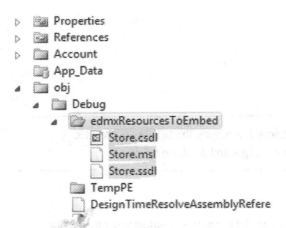

Figure 6-2. Generated EDM resources

Behind the scenes, Visual Studio uses the *EDM Generator Tool* EdmGen.exe to generate the schema files. Let's explore the steps required to use the tool.

EDM Generator Tool

The EdmGen.exe tool is responsible for generating EDM resources, including the EDM schemas and object classes from the conceptual schema, and to pre-generate views for the model. In addition, the tool is used to validate a model.

In order to check the options available with the EdmGen tool, launch the Visual Studio Tools command prompt by searching for the App in the Search charm of your Windows 8 OS, as shown in Figure 6-3.

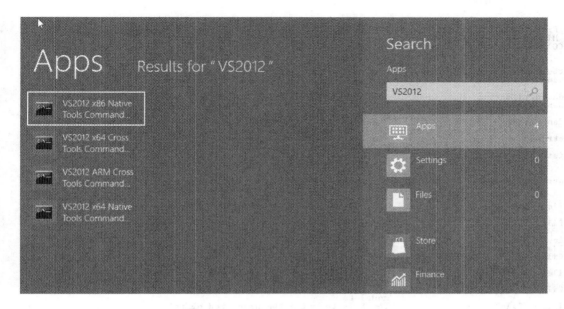

Figure 6-3. *Locating the VS Tools command prompt*

Click *VS2012 x86 Native Tools Command* App and, at the command prompt, enter the edmgen /? command. The options to generate the resources will be displayed, as shown in Figure 6-4.

```
C:\Program Files (x86)\Microsoft Visual Studio 11.0\VC>edmgen /?
EdmGen for Microsoft (R) .NET Framework version 4.5
Copyright (C) Microsoft Corporation. All rights reserved.

                              EdmGen Options
/mode:EntityClassGeneration       Generate objects from a csdl file
/mode:FromSsdlGeneration          Generate msl, csdl, and objects from an
                                  ssdl file
/mode:ValidateArtifacts           Validate the ssdl, msl, and csdl files
/mode:ViewGeneration              Generate mapping views from ssdl, msl,
                                  and csdl files
/mode:FullGeneration              Generate ssdl, msl, csdl, and objects
                                  from the database
/project:<string>                 The base name to be used for all the
                                  artifact files (short form: /p)
/provider:<string>                The name of the ADO.NET data provider to
                                  be used for ssdl generation (short form:
                                  /prov)
/connectionstring:<connection string>  The connection string to the database
                                  that you would like to connect to (short
                                  form: /c)
/incsdl:<file>                    The file to read the conceptual model
                                  from
/refcsdl:<file>                   A csdl file that contains types that the
                                  /incsdl file is dependent upon
/inmsl:<file>                     The file to read the mapping from
/inssdl:<file>                    The file to read the storage model from
/outcsdl:<file>                   The file to write the generated
                                  conceptual model to
/outmsl:<file>                    The file to write the generated mapping
                                  to
/outssdl:<file>                   The file to write the generated storage
                                  model to
/outobjectlayer:<file>            The file to write the generated object
                                  layer to
/outviews:<file>                  The file to write the pre generated view
                                  objects to
/targetversion:<string>           The .NET Framework version that will be
                                  used to compile the generated code. The
                                  supported versions are 4 and 4.5.
                                  Defaults to 4.
/language:CSharp                  Generate code using the C# language
/language:VB                      Generate code using the Visual Basic
                                  language
/namespace:<string>               The namespace name to use for the
                                  conceptual model types
/entitycontainer:<string>         The name to use for the EntityContainer
                                  in the conceptual model
/pluralize                        Automatically pluralize or singularize
                                  entity set name, entity type name, and
                                  navigation property name using English
                                  language rules (short form: /pl)
```

Figure 6-4. *EDM Generator Tool options*

To generate all the resources, you can use the FullGeneration mode with the command, as shown in the following code snippet:

```
edmgen.exe /mode:fullgeneration
/c:"Data Source=%server%; Initial Catalog=Store; Integrated Security=True"
/project:EFWebApplication /entitycontainer:StoreEntities /namespace:StoreModel /language:CSharp
```

Executing the command will generate the CSDL, SSDL, and MSL files for the Store database and the relevant object classes and views in C#. You can then add these files to your project (named EFWebApplication in our case). Note that the /c option is used to specify the connection string information for the Store database.

ADO.NET Metadata

In order to allow tools like Entity Framework to interact with EDM resources, ADO.NET provides metadata services under the `System.Data.Metadata.Edm` namespace. The namespace provides the necessary types and the runtime for describing the Entity Data Model in applications.

The metadata system has a fairly complex hierarchical structure starting with the base abstract class `MetadataItem`. In this section, we will limit our discussion to focus on the most relevant aspects that you must know in order to understand how the system functions. The detail hierarchy of the metadata system is available in the MSDN documentation at `http://msdn.microsoft.com/en-us/library/bb399772.aspx`. You can read it for further guidance.

You have already learned that EDM allows you to define Entities and Relationships. Entities in EDM are represented by the `EntityType` class under the `System.Data.Metadata.Edm` namespace, and Relationships are represented by the `AssociationType` class. Let's now explore the types and relationships in detail.

EDM Types and Relationships

ADO.NET Metadata provides a type system that forms the basis of EDM in Entity Framework. Primarily, there are two abstract types that are exposed by the metadata system:

1. `SimpleType` (derives from `System.Data.Edm.EdmType`) specifies the conceptual primitives. In our Store model CSDL, entity properties like ID represent the primitive types.

```
<Property Name="ID" Type="Int32" Nullable="false" annotation:StoreGeneratedPattern="Identity" />
```

2. `StructuralType` (derives from `System.Data.Edm.EdmType`) specifies the complex types. In our Store model CSDL, Order entity represents a structural type.

```
<EntityType Name="Order">
    <Key>
      <PropertyRef Name="ID" />
    </Key>
    <Property Name="ID" Type="Int32" Nullable="false" annotation:StoreGeneratedPattern="Identity" />
    <Property Name="ContactID" Type="Int32" Nullable="false" />
    <Property Name="Quantity" Type="Int32" Nullable="false" />
    <Property Name="Rate" Type="Decimal" Nullable="false" Precision="18" Scale="0" />
    <NavigationProperty Name="Contact" Relationship="StoreModel.FK_Orders_Contacts"
FromRole="Orders" ToRole="Contacts" />
  </EntityType>
```

Relationships are defined using the AssociationType class that derives from the abstract class RelationshipType.

```
<Association Name="FK_Orders_Contacts">
    <End Role="Contacts" Type="StoreModel.Contact" Multiplicity="1" />
    <End Role="Orders" Type="StoreModel.Order" Multiplicity="*" />
    <ReferentialConstraint>
      <Principal Role="Contacts">
        <PropertyRef Name="ID" />
      </Principal>
      <Dependent Role="Orders">
        <PropertyRef Name="ContactID" />
      </Dependent>
    </ReferentialConstraint>
  </Association>
```

■ **Note**   AssociationType is sealed and cannot be inherited further.

In addition, there is another family of supported base types, which are called the anonymous types, like Collection, Row, and Ref. You will learn about these types when we discuss Entity SQL.

DataSpace Enumerator

The metadata system also provides the DataSpace enumerator to specify if the types are fetched for a conceptual model (CSpace) or a storage model (SSpace). You will see the enumerator in action in the next section.

Metadata Workspace

ADO.NET provides the necessary runtime to allow tools like Entity Framework to operate on EDM metadata and resources. The MetadataWorkspace (System.Data.Metadata.Edm) class is designated for this purpose. The class acts as an aggregator of metadata information from the various EDM resources like conceptual, storage, and mapping schemas. It can then be used in the context of an application to inspect the ADO.NET metadata and perform CRUD operations. In the following exercise, you will review the steps to load the EDM resources and then use the MetadataWorkspace instance to inspect the registered metadata elements.

TRY IT OUT: USE METADATAWORKSPACE TO LOAD EDM RESOURCES AND INSPECT ADO.NET CONCEPTUAL AND STORAGE METADATA

In this exercise, you will learn the steps required to use the MetadataWorkspace class to load the conceptual, storage, and mapping schemas, and then you will inspect the metadata elements present in the context of the Store database. In terms of prerequisites, you will need the Conceptual, Storage, and Mapping Schema files that you generated using the EDM Generator Tool. Follow these steps:

1.   Open your instance of Visual Studio 2012, and create a new ASP.NET Web Application Project named EFWebApplication, as shown in Figure 6-5.

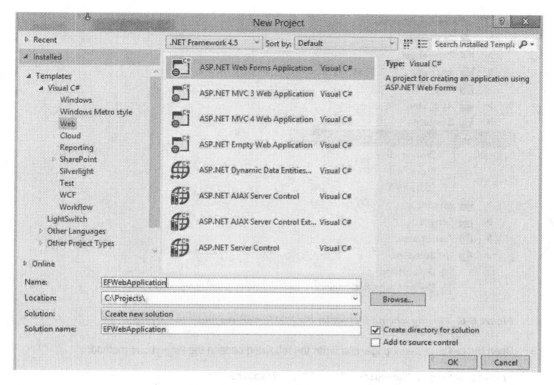

Figure 6-5. *New ASP.NET Web Application Project*

2. Create a folder in the EFWebApplication project named EDMResources. Place the CSDL, SSDL, and MSL files generated for the Store database in the *EDM Generator Tool* section in this folder, as shown in Figure 6-6.

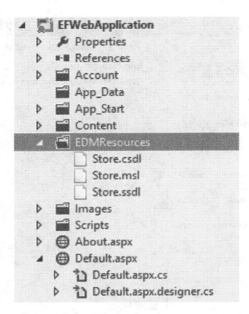

Figure 6-6. *Placing schema files under the EDMResources folder in the project*

3. Open the Default.aspx page, and write the following code in the Page_Load method:

```
private string EDMResourcePath = "~/EDMResources/";
        protected void Page_Load(object sender, EventArgs e)
        {
            try
            {
                MetadataWorkspace context = new MetadataWorkspace();
                EdmItemCollection edmItems = new EdmItemCollection(EDMResourcePath);
                context.RegisterItemCollection(edmItems);
                var conceptualTypes = context.GetItems<EdmType>(DataSpace.CSpace);
                PrintTypes(conceptualTypes);

                StoreItemCollection storeItems = new StoreItemCollection(EDMResourcePath);
                context.RegisterItemCollection(storeItems);
                var storageTypes = context.GetItems<EdmType>(DataSpace.SSpace);
                PrintTypes(storageTypes);
            }
            catch (MetadataException exMetadata)
            {
                Response.Write(exMetadata.Message);
            }
            catch (MappingException exMapping)
            {
                Response.Write(exMapping.Message);
            }

        }
```

The PrintTypes method loops through the read-only collection of EDM types and prints them on the page—nothing fancy there.

```
private void PrintTypes(ReadOnlyCollection<EdmType> edmTypes)
    {
        foreach (var type in edmTypes)
        {
            Response.Write(string.Format(
                "Raw: {0}, Model: {1} ",
                type.GetType().FullName,
                type.FullName));
        }
    }
```

▪ **Note** To build the code successfully, you must resolve the appropriate references while using the code block. You must also add references to the System.Data, System.Data.Entity, and System.Data.DataSetExtensions assemblies, as shown in Figure 6-7.

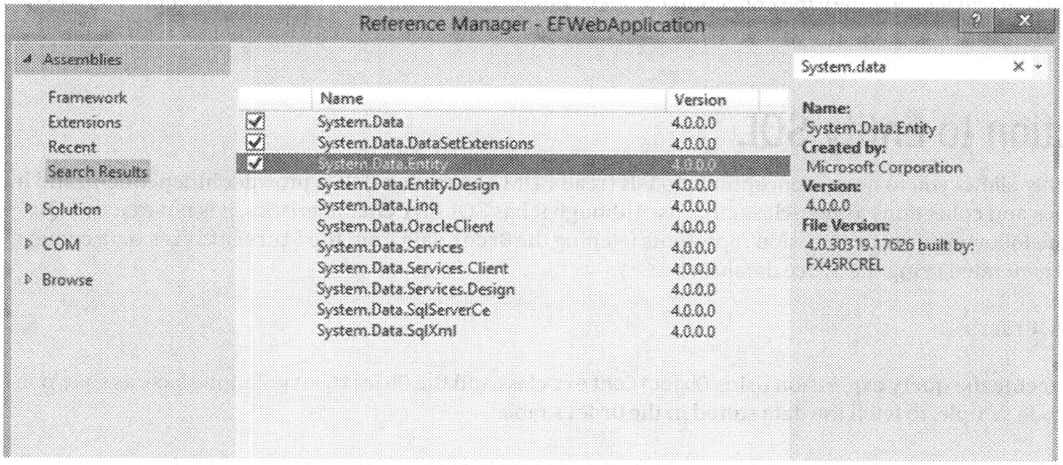

Figure 6-7. *Adding reference to the required assemblies*

When inspecting the code block, you will note that you first created an instance of the MetadataWorkspace class. Then you loaded the conceptual model from the EDM Resources and registered it with the workspace using the EdmItemCollection class. You were able to retrieve the conceptual metadata types by specifying the DataSpace enumerator for conceptual models:

```
EdmItemCollection edmItems = new EdmItemCollection(EDMResourcePath);
            context.RegisterItemCollection(edmItems);
            var conceptualTypes = context.GetItems<EdmType>(DataSpace.CSpace);
```

In a very similar fashion you queried the storage metadata type information using the StoreItemCollection class.

```
StoreItemCollection storeItems = new StoreItemCollection(EDMResourcePath);
            context.RegisterItemCollection(storeItems);
            var storageTypes = context.GetItems<EdmType>(DataSpace.SSpace);
```

■ **Note**   EdmItemCollection and StoreItemCollection inherit from the ItemCollection class responsible for loading metadata information from resource files like CSDL and SSDL.

You have now successfully used the MetadataWorkspace class to load ADO.NET metadata from EDM resources and display the types in context of the application.

Canonical and Store Functions

The ADO.NET Metadata system also provides support for functions. The EdmFunction class can be used to inspect functions in a metadata workspace. *Canonical functions* are the defined part of the conceptual model, and each commonly used canonical function, such as Count, has an equivalent function for the provider-specific storage model.

So far, you have seen that EDM is a powerful mechanism to decouple your data model from the storage provider and how to use EDM to model data in code. The only missing element in Entity Data Modeling is the presence of a query construct that will let you query the conceptual models. *Entity SQL* fills this gap. In the next section, you will be introduced to Entity SQL. You will realize how it is different from native Structured Query Languages, such as T-SQL.

Introduction to Entity SQL

Entity SQL simply allows you to query conceptual models (read EDM abstractions). It is provider independent, and it treats EDM types and collections as first-class citizens. Although it has SQL-like characteristics, it is not exactly SQL. For example, the following query expression represents fetching the Order data from the StoreEntities data context, which you had generated using the Store database:

```
StoreEntities.Orders
```

You can execute the query expression using ObjectContext class and the ObjectQuery<T> interface, as shown in the following code sample, to fetch the data stored in the Orders table:

```
using (ObjectContext context = new ObjectContext(connectionString, "StoreEntities")) {

    context.Connection.Open();

    string queryOrders = "StoreEntities.Orders";

    foreach (Order order in new ObjectQuery<Order>( queryOrders, context)) {

        //TODO: perform operations on the type

    }

}
```

In T-SQL, this would roughly be equivalent to executing the following query:

```
SELECT * FROM Orders
```

Syntactically, you will notice that Entity SQL has first-class support for collections. You could navigate between properties of a collection with the "." operator. In addition, a major difference from T-SQL is that Entity SQL collection expressions are not context driven and are treated uniformly.

The expression will implicitly generate all attributes for the entity. If you need specific attributes to be qualified for the select operation, then you could use the ROW Entity SQL function. A query using the ROW anonymous construct for Orders could look like the following:

```
SELECT VALUE ROW (orders.ID as OrderID, orders.Quantity
    as Quantity, orders.Rate as Rate) FROM StoreEntities.Order AS orders
```

The ROW keyword represents a row instance.

In addition to Object Context services, Entity SQL queries can also be executed using the Entity Client provider. The Entity Client provider is available as part of the System.Data namespace and provides an abstraction to the underlying native database provider. The following code block executes the previous query of fetching orders using the Entity Client provider:

```
using (EntityConnection connection = new EntityConnection("name=StoreEntities"))
        {
            string query = "SELECT VALUE Order FROM StoreEntities.Orders AS Order";
            using (EntityCommand command = new EntityCommand(query))
            {
                using (DbDataReader reader = command.ExecuteReader())
                {
                    while (reader.Read())
                    {
                        //TODO
                    }
                }
            }
        }
```

The Entity Client provider allows querying the conceptual model in a persistence-ignorant fashion. However, it would be a very rare circumstance that you would need to query the conceptual model directly using Entity SQL and Entity Client, since most of it would be handled by Entity Framework while you focus on the presentation and business logic. Nevertheless, it is useful to understand the underlying concepts.

Summary

The concepts discussed in this chapter will be very useful to you going forward as you learn about Entity Framework features in building data-driven applications. In this chapter, you learned about the EDM architecture and gained understanding of how the ADO.NET metadata system is leveraged to load metadata information from EDM resources. You were also briefly introduced to the concept of Entity SQL.

113

CHAPTER 7

■ ■ ■

Designing Data Access Applications Using Entity Framework

In Chapter 1, you were first introduced to the different data access paradigms. You also explored the steps required to create a data access layer easily from an existing database using the Entity Framework *Entity Data Model (EDM) Designer* and the *Database-First* paradigm. In addition, you learned how the EDM and ADO.NET Metadata System together form the core of Entity Framework in the previous chapter.

Up until now, you have merely scratched the surface. In this chapter, you will fully realize the potential of Entity Framework for building data access layers without writing a lot of code.

You will learn about the following in this chapter:

- What constitutes the architecture of Entity Framework.

- How to create and update EDM using Entity Framework Designer.

- How to generate CLR classes automatically from entities that can be programmed in code.

- How to query EDM using LINQ to Entities.

- How to use stored procedures in Entity Framework using complex types.

- How to unit test EDM.

Entity Framework is Microsoft's preferred Object Relation Mapper data access platform for use in data-driven applications built using the .NET Framework. Entity Framework consists of tools, .NET Framework components, language support, and services for Object/Relational Mapping (ORM). In Chapter 6, you explored some of the core .NET Framework components that formed the basis of Entity Framework. In this chapter, we will focus on implementing Entity Framework in building data-driven ASP.NET Web applications. In Chapter 12, you will learn about best practices in doing so.

■ **Note** At the time of this writing, Entity Framework 6.0 Alpha 2 had been released in preview. However, we elected to use the stable Entity Framework version 5 for the exercises in this chapter.

Entity Framework Architecture

Entity Framework is built upon the core principle of ORM; that is, keeping the domain model separate from database design. Figure 7-1 illustrates the various components that together form Entity Framework.

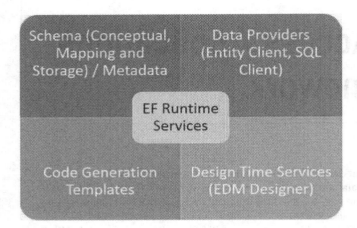

Figure 7-1. *Entity Framework components*

Entity Model Designer is probably the most widely used feature of Entity Framework. It provides a visual experience similar to any *Entity Relationship Diagram (ERD)* tool that you may have used in the past. In addition to this visual experience, it has many features that let you automatically generate the Entity Models from existing database tables and relationships, and it helps you create plain CLR objects (public classes with properties) that can be programmed in code in a persistence-ignorant fashion using languages like LINQ and C#. In the next section, you will explore some of the advanced capabilities of Entity Framework using ADO.NET EDM.

Generating Entity Models

In Chapter 1, you became familiar with the steps required to create an ADO.NET EDM and how it is used to generate a data-driven ASP.NET 4.5 Website. ADO.NET EDM acts as a container for *Entities* and *Associations*. In Entity Framework 5, the entities also generate equivalent *Plain Old CLR* (POCO) classes that can be used in code to create queries and perform data manipulation using .NET Framework-supported languages like LINQ and C#. You will learn more about this in the forthcoming sections of this chapter. Before we do that, however, let's explore the exercise steps from Chapter 1 once again using an ASP.NET MVC 4 Web Application with the addition of testability and then try to understand how the EDM Designer functions. For the purpose of this example, we will use the Store database that you first used in Chapter 5.

▓ **Note**   If you are unfamiliar with ASP.NET MVC 4, you can learn more about it here: www.asp.net/mvc/mvc4.

TRY IT OUT: CREATE TESTABLE DATA ACCESS LAYER FOR AN ASP.NET MVC 4 WEB APPLICATION

The exercise can be executed using Visual Studio 2012 with Entity Framework 5. If you don't have Entity Framework 5, you can get it from *NuGet* services. Launching the NuGet Package Manager or using the Package Manager Console allows you to manage NuGet services for a solution. The interactive NuGet Package Manager can be launched from the solution by right-clicking it and selecting the `Manage NuGet Packages...` command. The relevant program screen is shown in Figure 7-2, and you can search for the Entity Framework 5.0 package.

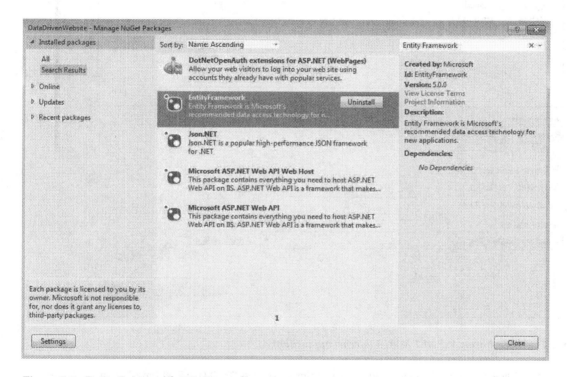

Figure 7-2. *Entity Framework 5 NuGet package*

Follow these steps to complete this exercise:

1. Create a Visual Studio 2012 C# ASP.NET MVC 4 Web Application named DataDrivenWebsite and, from the template selector dialog, select the *Internet Application* template. Make sure to select the *Create a unit test project* checkbox as shown in Figure 7-3.

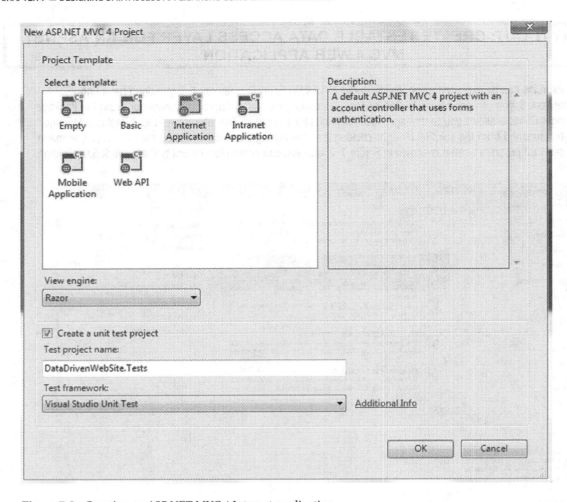

Figure 7-3. *Creating an ASP.NET MVC 4 Internet application*

2. Follow the steps demonstrated in the Chapter 1 exercise "Try It Out: First Data-Driven Page in ASP.NET 4.5" to add a new ADO.NET EDM to the project. However, now use the Store database as the source to generate the model. Once the EDM is generated, it should look like the one shown in Figure 7-4. The entity container context is named StoreEntities.

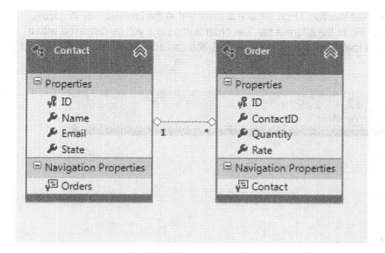

Figure 7-4. EDM generated from Store database

3. Open the *Solution Explorer* and right-click the Controllers folder. Click *Add ➤ Controller...* from the context menu to launch the *Add Controller* dialog. Fill in the details in the *Add Controller* dialog, as shown in Figure 7-5, to create an OrderController class using the Orders entity and StoreEntities entity context. In addition to generating the OrderController, select the *Views* option as *Razor* to generate the views automatically for the controller. You may need to build the solution before adding the controller in order for the model and context classes to be available for selection.

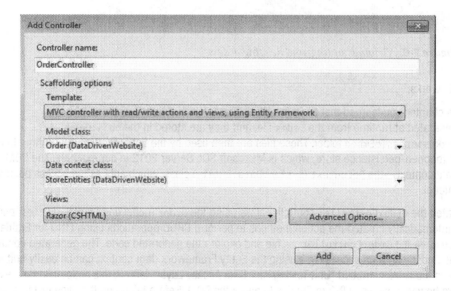

Figure 7-5. Creating OrderController using Order Model and StoreEntities data context

4. Compile and Run the solution. Once the site is launched in the browser, key in /Order at the end of the URL in the address bar. The order items page will be displayed with a default-generated layout, as shown in Figure 7-6. You can add new order items and edit existing ones.

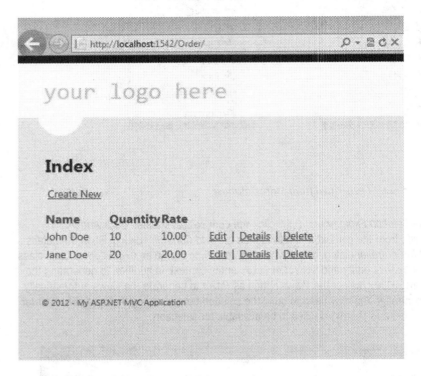

Figure 7-6. *Viewing, adding, and deleting orders*

Here's how this works:

In the previous chapter, you learned that the conceptual, storage, and mapping schema files are dynamically generated at runtime from the .edmx file, and they are stored in the obj\<Debug | Release>\edmxResourcesToEmbed folder. These files are then used by the Entity Framework runtime to execute queries on the mapped-persistence store, which is Microsoft SQL Server 2012 in our example. The EDM Designer generates a data context—the DbContext (System.Data.Entity) class, which acts as the access point for querying the model.

When you created the OrderController controller class using the Order model and StoreEntities DbContext, the template automatically created the action methods to perform CRUD operations using LINQ for Entities. This is evident if you open the OrderController.cs file and explore the generated code. The generated controller actions and the underlying data access logic using the Entity Framework data context can be easily unit tested, as you will see in the section entitled "Unit Testing Your Data Access Layer" later in this chapter. In the next section, you will explore how you can use LINQ to Entities to query the EDM. Before taking on that, you will find out how associations are created when the EDM is generated from an existing database.

Entity Associations

In a Database-First paradigm, Entity Framework creates entity associations for the relationships that exist between tables. The associations allow you to navigate between entities, and Entity Framework loads the associated data only when they are queried. This is known as *Lazy Loading,* and it is Entity Framework's default behavior.

After you open the EDM Designer, right-click the line connecting the Order and Contact entities and click *Properties* to launch the properties pane. You will find the association between the two entities, along with the navigational properties, in this pane, as shown in Figure 7-7.

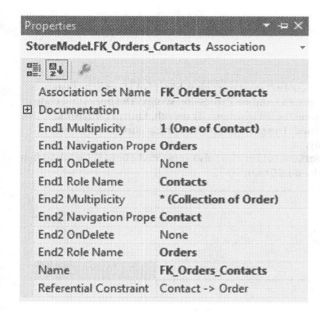

Figure 7-7. *Association between the Order and Contact entities generated from the foreign key relationship in the database*

Query EDM with LINQ to Entities

One of the core ideas behind Entity Framework is to allow developers to query conceptual models in a persistence-ignorant way using CLR-supported languages like C# and LINQ and then somehow magically transform them into database-specific queries. There are several ways that you can query EDM. Entity Framework runtime features Entity SQL, which is an SQL-like language that allows you to construct queries against the EDM. You saw Entity SQL in action in the previous chapter. In this section, you will learn about LINQ to Entities, a feature of Entity Framework that allows you to query EDM using LINQ.

Open the `OrderController.cs` file, and note the code that was generated. The `Index` method, which returns the default view, yields the following code:

```
private StoreEntities db = new StoreEntities();

        //
        // GET: /Order/

        public ActionResult Index()
        {
            var orders = db.Orders.Include(o => o.Contact);
            return View(orders.ToList());
        }
```

The add controller template created an instance of the `DbContext` container class `StoreEntities`. The instance was then used in the `Index` method to return a list of orders using a Lambda Expression syntax. The important code path to remember is to add the `Include` method while returning the list of orders. By default, Entity Framework supports lazing loading, and associated entities are not returned. The preceding code sample illustrates one way of overriding the default behavior to return the associated entity.

In a similar fashion, the steps required to create the `OrderController` class also generated a `Details` method that uses LINQ to Entities to find and display the details of an individual `Order`:

```
//
        // GET: /Order/Details/5

        public ActionResult Details(int id = 0)
        {
            Order order = db.Orders.Find(id);
            if (order == null)
            {
                return HttpNotFound();
            }
            return View(order);
        }
```

The preceding query could also be represented in LINQ syntax as follows:

```
var orderDetails = from order in db.Orders
                                where order.ID == id
                                select order;
        if (orderDetails == null)
        {
            return HttpNotFound();
        }
        return View(orderDetails.FirstOrDefault());
```

■ **Note** The query result returns an `IQueryable<Order>` type. You must use the `FirstOrDefault` method to return a single `Order` to the view.

Code Generation in Entity Framework Using Text Templates

When you create the EDM in Visual Studio 2012, the entity container context (DbContext class) and associated models in the form of Plain Old CLR (POCO) types are automatically generated using a code generation template called *T4*.

▓ **Note**   The T4 (*Text Template Transformation Toolkit*) code generation tool is available out of the box in Visual Studio 2012.

In our example, the StoreEntities class represents the DbContext type. The StoreEntities class also contains a set of DbSet (System.Data.Entity) properties that represent the POCO type collections within the data context.

DbContext and DbSet provide the object services to allow you to create queries against the EDM. The DbContext class provides the runtime context, while the DbSet class allows CRUD operations to be performed on the Entity Models.

▓ **Note**   If you are using Visual Studio 2010, DbContext and POCO types are not generated by default. You need to add the Entity Framework *DbContext Generator* NuGet package to make the DbContext Code Generation Template available. You will then need to add a code generation item to the solution to generate the DbContext and POCO types.

If you explore the StoreEntities class in the Store.Context.cs file organized under Store.edmx in the Solution Explorer, you will see the following code:

```
public partial class StoreEntities : DbContext
    {
        public StoreEntities()
            : base("name=StoreEntities")
        {
        }

        protected override void OnModelCreating(DbModelBuilder modelBuilder)
        {
            throw new UnintentionalCodeFirstException();
        }

        public DbSet<Contact> Contacts { get; set; }
        public DbSet<Order> Orders { get; set; }
    }
```

▓ **Note**   We will discuss the OnModelCreating method in the next chapter.

The constructor provides the named container, which is StoreEntities in our example, and there are two DbSet properties representing a collection of entity sets for Order and Contact entities. LINQ to Entities queries are written against the DbSet properties inside the DbContext class, like the examples shown in the "Query EDM with LINQ to Entities" section earlier in this chapter. DbContext provides methods like SaveChanges to persist data in the persistence tier.

Explore the Create and Delete methods in the OrderController class, and you will notice the SaveChanges method being executed on create and delete operations to persist the state of the DbSet collection in the database. The following code illustrates the Create method:

```
[HttpPost]
        public ActionResult Create(Order order)
        {
            if (ModelState.IsValid)
            {
                db.Orders.Add(order);
                db.SaveChanges();
                return RedirectToAction("Index");
            }

            ViewBag.ContactID = new SelectList(db.Contacts, "ID", "Name", order.ContactID);
            return View(order);
        }
```

■ **Note** DbContext and DbSet are simplified versions of ObjectContext and ObjectSet classes with a limited set of methods. In Entity Framework 5, DbContext and DbSet classes replaced ObjectContext and ObjectSet as alternatives to performing CRUD operations on EDM. Nonetheless, you can revert to the older style of using the ObjectContext by right-clicking an empty area in the EDM Designer and setting the *Code Generation Strategy* property to *Default* in the *Properties* menu, as shown in Figure 7-8.

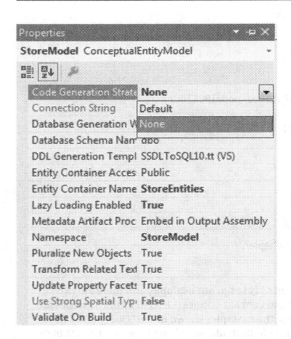

Figure 7-8. *Reverting to old style of code generation using ObjectContext*

DbContext Generator and POCO Classes

Expand the Store.edmx file, and you will see a set of files generated under its hierarchy. This is displayed in Figure 7-9.

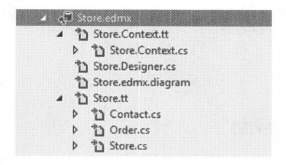

Figure 7-9. *Files generated by T4 templates*

Let's explore the purpose of each of these files and how they function together to allow the creation and manipulation of EDMs in a persistence-ignorant fashion.

1. Store.Context.tt *file*. This is a text template file used for generating the DbContext class. This file is a container that allows data access and manipulation operations with the EDM POCO types in a persistence-ignorant way.

2. Store.Context.cs *file*. This is the generated DbContext class file that enables CRUD operations on the POCO types.

3. Store.edmx.diagram *file*. This is the Designer diagram configuration file.

4. Store.tt *file*. This is a text template file used for generating the persistence-ignorant POCO types.

5. Order.cs *and* Contact.cs *files*. These are files generated for POCO types of the Store EDM.

Creating the Store.edmx file automatically creates code-generated items using the T4 code generation tool.

The tool uses the text template (.tt) files to generate the data context class and the POCO types. If you want a variation of the default code generation process, then you could modify the templates for code generation by creating additional code generation items. To do that, right-click the EDM Designer surface and click *Add Code Generation Item...*, as shown in Figure 7-10.

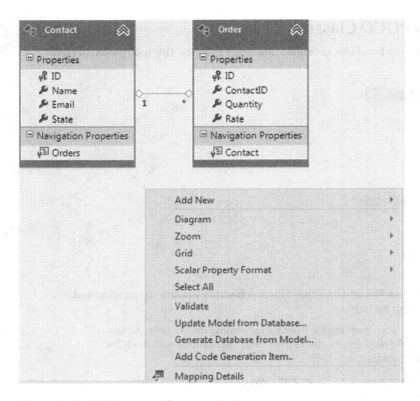

Figure 7-10. *Adding new code generation item*

From the *Add New Item* dialog, select the *Entity Framework 5.x DbContext Generator* under the *Data* tab, as shown in Figure 7-11.

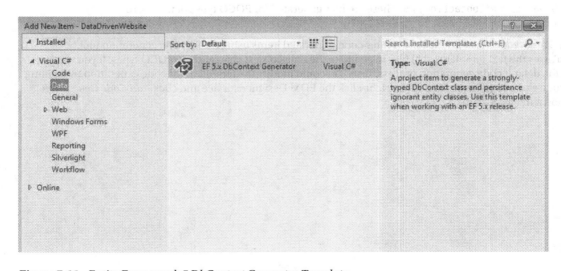

Figure 7-11. *Entity Framework 5 DbContext Generator Template*

Adding a code-generated item will create the POCO types based on the default T4 templates. The T4 infrastructure provides a *Custom Tool* that uses the text templates and generates the context class and POCO types. You will be prompted to run the custom tool every time you make changes in the EDM Designer to update the context and POCO classes appropriately. Alternatively, you can run the custom tool manually by right-clicking the .edmx file and clicking *Run Custom Tool* from the context menu, as shown in Figure 7-12.

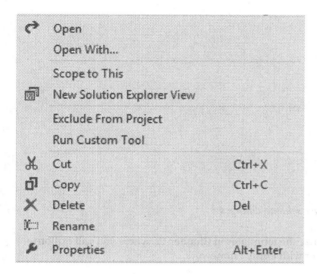

Figure 7-12. *Run code generator custom tool*

■ **Tip**   If there is a change in the Database schema, you can update the model using the *Update Model from Database* option in the EDM Designer, as shown in Figure 7-13. The update model will also run the custom tool to regenerate the POCO types.

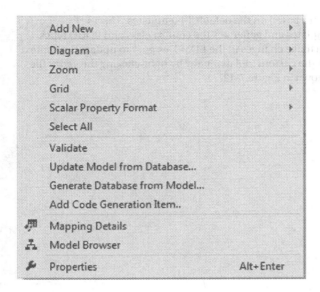

Figure 7-13. *Refreshing model to reflect the updated database schema changes*

You will learn more about the steps required to customize the templates in Chapter 12, where you will explore some of the best practices used in creating a data access layer with Entity Framework.

POCO Proxy

Behind the scenes, Entity Framework does a number of things that are designed to improve performance during a data access operation. One such action is the creation of derived entities from the POCO types when they are instantiated. These derived types act as proxies for the POCO types in order to support features such as lazy loading of associated types. The feature can be disabled, however, by setting the `ProxyCreationEnabled` property of the current `Configuration` instance to false, as shown in the following code snippet.

```
public StoreEntities()
        : base("name=StoreEntities")
    {
        Configuration.ProxyCreationEnabled = false;
    }
```

■ **Caution** POCO derived types are not generated automatically if you are using a new instance of the entity context. You can force their generation, however, using the `Create` method of the `DbSet` properties in the context.

Eager Loading Entities

By default, Entity Framework promotes lazy loading; that is, associated entity data is loaded only when the navigational properties are accessed for the first time. Entity Framework does this by overriding the behavior of navigational properties that are marked virtual. In our example, if you expand the Store.tt file under Solution Explorer and open the Contact.cs file, you will see that Orders collection is marked as a virtual property.

```
public partial class Contact
    {
        public Contact()
        {
            this.Orders = new HashSet<Order>();
        }

        public int ID { get; set; }
        public string Name { get; set; }
        public string Email { get; set; }
        public string State { get; set; }

        public virtual ICollection<Order> Orders { get; set; }
    }
```

■ **Tip**   The generated POCO type classes are all partial. If you need to add other properties that do not participate in mapping, you can create additional partial classes holding these properties. Do not modify the generated POCO type file, as it gets overwritten every time the custom tool runs.

There may be cases where you do not want lazy loading to occur. If you have a scenario where eager loading is preferred, you can do that explicitly by using the Include method while querying the primary property:

```
public ActionResult Index()
    {
        var orders = db.Orders.Include(o => o.Contact);
        return View(orders.ToList());
    }
```

■ **Note**   You can completely disable lazy loading by setting the LazyLoadingEnabled property of the current context configuration to false.

Complex Types

Entity Framework 5 allows you to create complex types to facilitate grouping of several properties under one property. You can refactor existing properties into one complex type from the Entity Framework Designer. Select more than one property under an entity, right-click, and choose the option *Refactor ➤ Move to New Complex Type* to create a complex type, as shown in Figure 7-14.

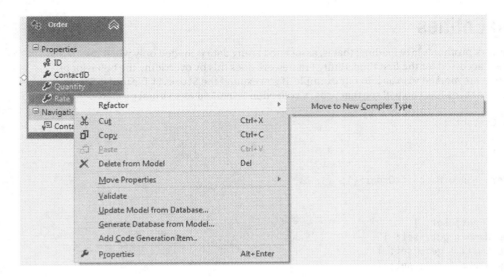

Figure 7-14. *Refactoring to complex type*

You can also create complex types by adding a new complex type from the Designer and then adding properties underneath it. In our example, we created the PriceOptions complex type under the Order entity from the Rate and Quantity properties. The mappings are preserved, as shown in Figure 7-15.

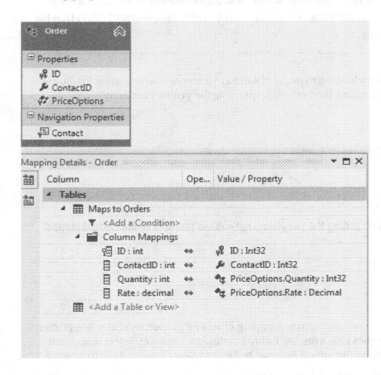

Figure 7-15. *PriceOptions complex type created from Rate and Quantity properties with preserved mappings*

▨ **Note** Complex types do not participate in an association.

Complex Types and Stored Procedures

Entity Framework provides a feature called *Function Imports*, which allows you to call a stored procedure and assign the results to a complex type. You can create a function import from the Entity Framework Designer by right-clicking an empty area and selecting *Add New* ➤ *Function Import....*

Let's create a stored procedure to get the net price for an Order and then use it as a function import in Entity Framework. Run the following script in your SQL Server Store database to create the stored procedure Get_NetPrice:

```
SET ANSI_NULLS ON
GO
SET QUOTED_IDENTIFIER ON
GO

CREATE PROCEDURE Get_NetPrice

@OrderID INT

AS
BEGIN

SELECT (Rate * Quantity) AS Price
FROM Orders
WHERE ID = @OrderID

END
GO
```

Open the Entity Framework Designer and update the model from the database to include the stored procedure in the model, as shown in Figure 7-16.

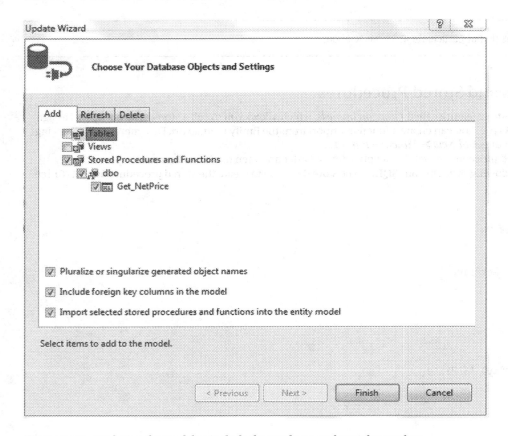

Figure 7-16. *Updating the model to include the newly created stored procedure*

Follow the steps to create a function import:

1. Add a Function Import from the Entity Framework Designer and, in the *Add Function Import* dialog, enter the Name as Get_NetPrice.

2. Select the Get_NetPrice stored procedure from the *Stored Procedure/Function Name* drop-down menu.

3. Click the *Get Column Information* button to get the information about the stored procedure, and then click the *Create New Complex Type* button to generate the complex type.

4. Rename the type to PriceOptions.

Once you have completed the preceding procedure, the dialog should look like the one shown in Figure 7-17.

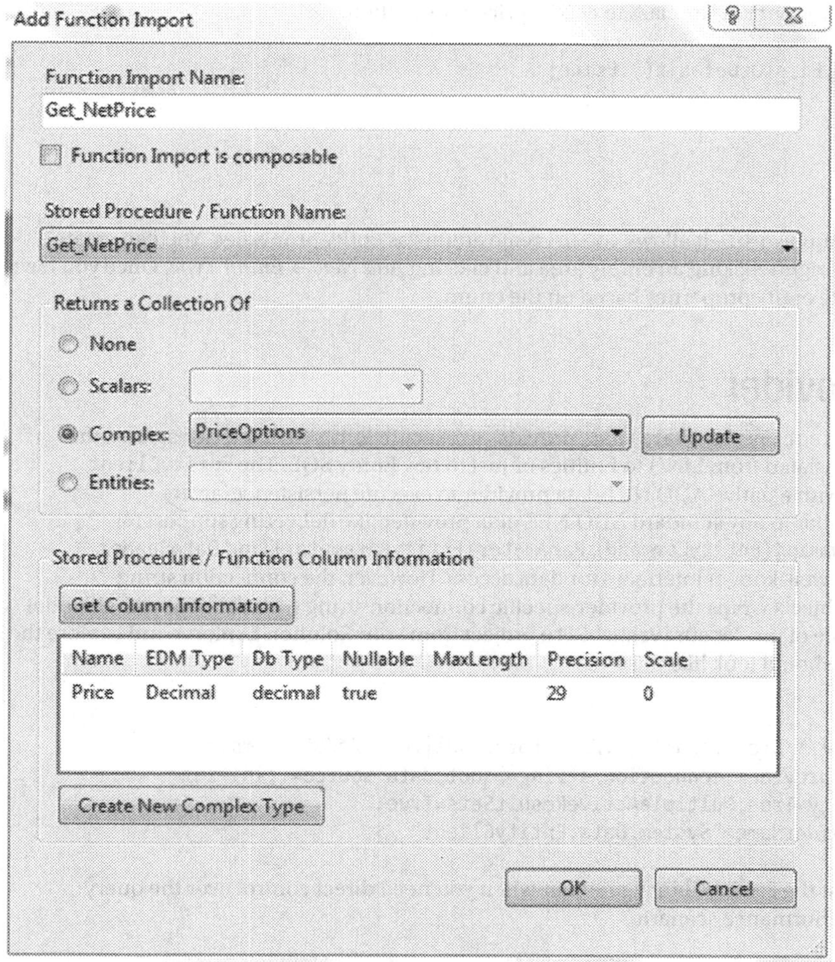

Figure 7-17. Creating a function import using stored procedure

Click *OK* to create the function import. The PriceOptions complex type will be generated as a POCO type, and you will notice that a new method is created in the StoreEntities DbContext class to execute the stored procedure and assign the results to the complex type PriceOptions.

```
public virtual ObjectResult<PriceOptions> Get_NetPrice(Nullable<int> orderID)
    {
        var orderIDParameter = orderID.HasValue ?
            new ObjectParameter("OrderID", orderID) :
            new ObjectParameter("OrderID", typeof(int));

        return
((IObjectContextAdapter)this).ObjectContext.ExecuteFunction<PriceOptions>("Get_NetPrice",
orderIDParameter);
    }
```

You can now use this in your `OrderController` class to access price information.

```
var price = db.Get_NetPrice(id).FirstOrDefault().Price;
```

Enumeration Types

This is also a new feature in Entity Framework 5. It allows you to create enums as entity properties. You can create enum types in the Entity Designer by right-clicking an empty area and clicking *Add New → Enum Type*. Once you have created the enum type, you can create entity properties based on the enum.

Entity Client Data Provider

Entity Framework uses the `EntityClient` (`System.Data`) data provider to execute Entity SQL queries against the conceptual model that are either translated from LINQ to Entities or just to raw Entity SQL. The `EntityClient` data provider works in conjunction with a native ADO.NET data provider to execute persistence-aware queries. Thus, in many ways, it is similar to any standard ADO.NET data provider like delivering support for `Connection` (`EntityConnection`), `Command` (`EntityCommand`), `Parameter` (`EntityParameter`), and `DataReader` (`EntityDataReader`) objects that are well-known interfaces for data access. However, the connection string specified in the `EntityConnection` objects wraps the provider-specific connection string with the conceptual model information. Open the `Web.config` file of the `DataDrivenWebSite` project from your Solution Explorer and explore the `StoreEntities` connection string. It should look like this:

```
    <add name="StoreEntities"
connectionString="metadata=res://*/Store.csdl|res://*/Store.ssdl|res://*/Store.msl;
provider=System.Data.SqlClient;provider connection string=&quot;data source=.;initial
catalog=Store;integrated security=True;MultipleActiveResultSets=True;
App=EntityFramework&quot;" providerName="System.Data.EntityClient" />
```

You can program directly against the `EntityClient` provider when you need direct control over the query execution, as in the case of a high-performance scenario.

Unit Testing Your Data Access Layer

Visual Studio 2012 provides robust unit testing capabilities that can be used to test the accuracy of your code. These capabilities can be extended to testing Entity Framework data context and model behavior in isolation. If you recall, when creating the ASP.NET MVC 4 project, you selected the *Create unit test project* option in the template selection dialog. The ASP.NET MVC 4 project template creates a Visual Studio unit test project and adds a few basic unit tests for the default `HomeController` class. In an enterprise-scale project, you probably would have a separate layer for data access. For simplicity's sake, however, let's assume for a moment that the data access logic is inside the controller actions, and the unit test written against these methods will test data access using Entity Framework.

1. To add a new unit test, right-click the `DataDrivenWebSite.Tests` project and click *Add ➤ New Item*. In the *New Item* dialog, select *Unit Test* from the *Test* tab and name it `OrderControllerTest`, as shown in Figure 7-18.

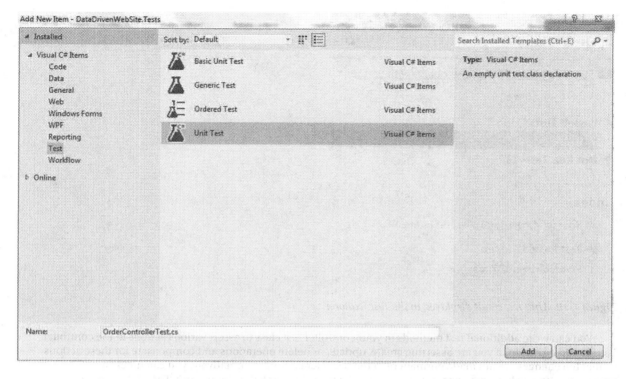

Figure 7-18. *Creating a new unit test*

2. A default unit test template is generated. The TestClassAttribute represents the class containing unit tests. Refer to the following namespaces in the using section:

```
using DataDrivenWebSite;
using DataDrivenWebSite.Controllers;
using System.Web.Mvc;
```

3. If you scroll down, you will see a method decorated with TestMethodAttribute. The TestMethodAttribute represents the unit of code under test. Rename the method to Index and write the following code block inside:

```
[TestMethod]
        public void Index()
        {
            OrderController controller = new OrderController();
            ViewResult result = controller.Index() as ViewResult;
            var model = result.Model;
            Assert.IsNotNull(model);
            Assert.IsInstanceOfType(model, typeof(List<Order>));
        }
```

4. The code block in the preceding step asserts that the model associated with the Order view is of type List<Order>. Right-click the Index method and click *Run Test*. The test is passed, as shown in Figure 7-19.

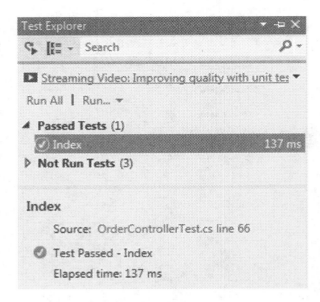

Figure 7-19. *Unit test result displayed in the Test Explorer*

You can write additional test methods in your controller test class to assert various actions in the controller. You should be careful if you are asserting create, update, or delete operations and compensate for these actions so that the changes are not made permanent in the persistence store. Alternatively, you can mock the persistence store using a mocking framework like *MoQ* or *Microsoft Fakes Framework*. The MSDN article http://msdn.microsoft.com/en-us/library/hh549175.aspx provides a good introduction to the Microsoft Fakes Framework.

Summary

This chapter was designed to provide you with an in-depth understanding of the capabilities of Entity Framework. You learned how the EDM Designer is used to create and update an Entity Model from an existing database and how POCO types are generated using T4 templates. You also explored some of the interesting new additions to Entity Framework 5, including complex types and support for enumerations. Finally, you learned how to unit test your data access with Entity Framework using ASP.NET MVC 4 controller templates.

At the time of this writing, Entity Framework 6 Alpha 2 had been released in preview, and Scott Guthrie's blog entry http://weblogs.asp.net/scottgu/archive/2012/12/11/entity-framework-6-alpha2-now-available.aspx elaborates on some of its forthcoming enhancements.

In the next chapter, you will learn more about the advanced capabilities of Entity Framework for supporting different data access paradigms, such as Model First and Code First.

CHAPTER 8

■ ■ ■

Entity Framework Data Access Paradigms

In Chapter 1, you were introduced to modern data access paradigms. To help you remember these, there are three primary strategies for designing a data access layer in your application.

Database First: Start by designing the database (or use a preexisting database as source) and then create an entity container from the database using a conceptual model generator tool. The entity container models will represent the various tables of the relational database and associations representing the relationships. You can then query and manipulate the models and let the tool perform the CRUD operations behind the scenes. This approach is of increasing importance if your application has an existing database with which it can connect and from which it can fetch information.

Model First: You start by designing the conceptual model using the available Designer tools, and then you can either generate the database from the conceptual models or map the data context generated by the tool to a preexisting database.

Code First: This is a developer-friendly approach where you create the conceptual model in code and then uses proprietary APIs to map the model to a physical database.

These paradigms are well supported by the ADO.NET Entity Framework, and this strong support is one of the main reasons behind the growing popularity of Entity Framework in creating robust data access layers in a wide variety of applications.

In the previous chapter, we focused on learning the nuances of Entity Framework, and for the most part you used the Database-First paradigm. This chapter serves as an extension of what you learned previously. Beyond that, you will learn more about the other two paradigms: Model First and Code First.

Specifically, we are going to cover the following in this chapter:

- How to program data access using the Model-First approach.

- How to program data access using the Code-First approach.

- How to perform validations using Data Annotations.

Although you learned about these paradigms in Chapter 1, now you will learn to implement them practically using Entity Framework.

■ **Note**   At the time of this writing, the latest version of Entity Framework was EF 5.0. We have leveraged EF 5.0 for executing the exercises in this chapter.

Model-First Approach

In the previous chapter, you learned how to leverage Entity Framework to build a data access layer in your application quickly and effectively. In the examples in that chapter, you created the *Entity Data Model (EDM)* by generating it from the existing Store database. The tables *Contacts* and *Orders* showed up in the EDM Designer (the edmx file) as entities. The entity associations were also generated automatically using the foreign key relationship between the tables.

This is a reasonable approach if you are working against a database that already exists, and you just need to build an application around it. However, if you are creating a completely new stack from application to database, it is quite likely that you would want to create a visual model and then create the database based on the visual model.

Wouldn't it be great if you could generate the database automatically from the visual model? The Model-First approach lets you do just that. You could model the database in your application and then evolve the model as the application grows. Behind the scenes, Entity Framework will map your model to a physical database based on the EDM conventions. Application developers who are not well versed in relational databases find this approach very useful. They often embrace it for applications that are built from the ground up, along with the storage schema. The benefit of using Entity Framework is that it is capable of translating the model into the database schema using the underlying providers, and it generates the database with one script. Let's try performing the steps designed to create an application data access layer using the Entity Framework Model-First approach.

TRY IT OUT: CREATING A DATA-DRIVEN WEB APPLICATION WITH THE ENTITY FRAMEWORK MODEL-FIRST PARADIGM

You will use the most recent version of the very popular development tool Visual Studio to do this exercise. You will learn to model the Store database that we have been discussing throughout the book using the EDM Designer, and you will then use it to create the database tables and relationships. Follow these steps:

1. Open Visual Studio 2012, and create a Visual C# ASP.NET MVC 4 Web Application project. The project template wizard is displayed. Choose the *Internet Application* template, as shown in Figure 8-1.

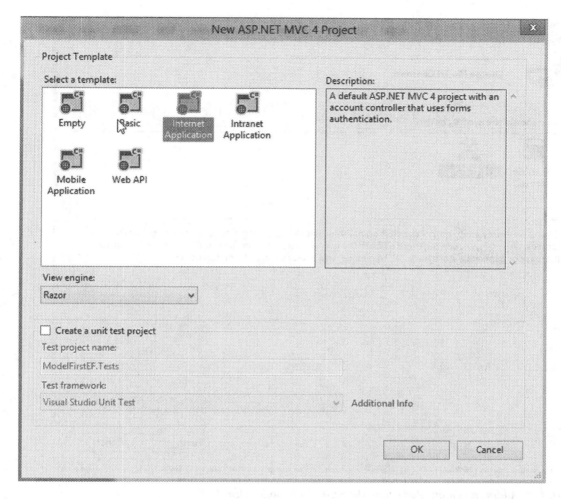

Figure 8-1. *Creating an ASP.NET MVC 4 Web Application*

■ **Note**   You can choose any template for the purpose of this exercise.

---

2.   Add an ADO.NET Entity Data Model as a new item to the project, as shown in Figure 8-2. Select Empty Model in the Choose Model Contents step of the ADO.NET Entity Data Model Wizard.

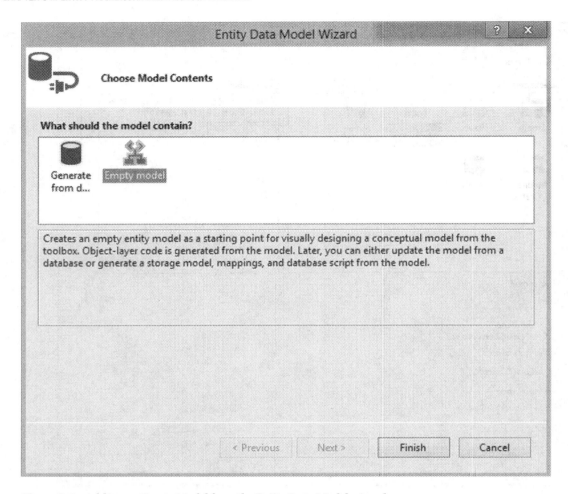

Figure 8-2. Adding an Empty Model from the Entity Data Model wizard

3. Right-click the Designer surface, and click *Add New* ➤ *Entity*, as shown in Figure 8-3.

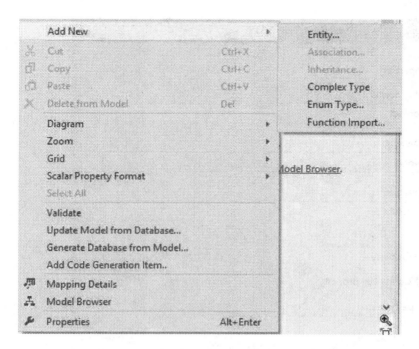

Figure 8-3. *Adding new Entity from the Model Designer surface*

4. In the *Add Entity* dialog, specify the Entity name as Contact. Under the *Key Property* section, select the check box *Create key property* and name the *Property* Id, as shown in Figure 8-4. Click *OK* to close the dialog.

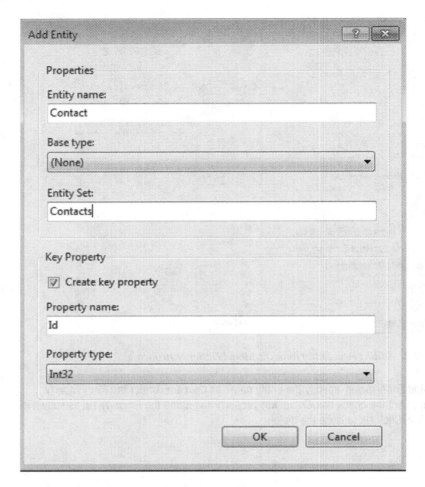

Figure 8-4. *Specifying the Entity name and Key Property*

5. The Contact Entity Model will be created in the Designer surface. Right-click the *Properties* section in the Contact Entity Model, and click *Add New* ➤ *Scalar Property*, as shown in Figure 8-5. Set the property name to Name. In a similar fashion, create the Email and State properties.

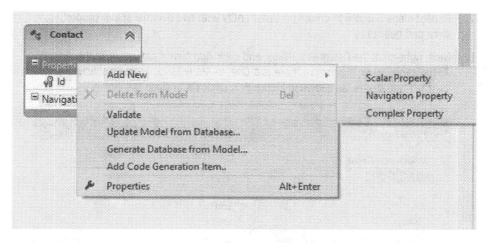

Figure 8-5. *Adding a new Scalar Property to the Contact entity*

6. Select the State property, and press F4 to display the *Properties* pane. In the *Properties* pane, set the *Max Length* property to 2 and *Nullable* to True, as shown in Figure 8-6. This would effectively disallow the State field in the database from storing more than two characters. In a similar fashion, set *Max Length* of the Email property to 100 and *Nullable* to True.

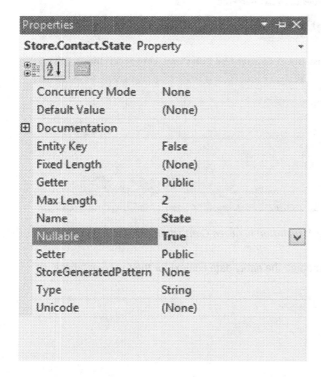

Figure 8-6. *Entity Property constraints*

7. Repeat steps 5 and 6 to create an Order entity with two decimal scalar properties, Rate and Quantity.

8. Next, right-click the Designer surface, and click *Add New Association*. In the *Add Association* dialog, make sure there is a *One-to-Many* association established between Contact and Order, as shown in Figure 8-7. Click *OK* to close the dialog.

Figure 8-7. *Creating Entity Association between Contact and Order*

9. You have now successfully created the entity data context for the Store database, as shown in Figure 8-8.

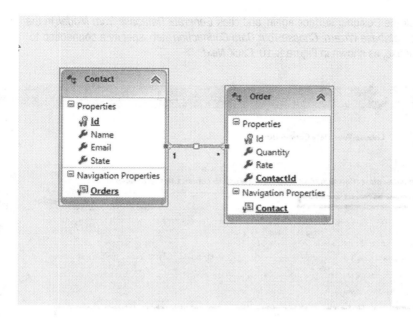

Figure 8-8. *Entity Model created using the Model-First approach using the Designer*

10. Right-click the Designer surface and click *Validate*. You will notice a couple of warnings saying *Entity type < type > is not mapped*, which is displayed under the *Error List* window, as illustrated in Figure 8-9. This is due to the fact that you still haven't mapped the model to a physical database.

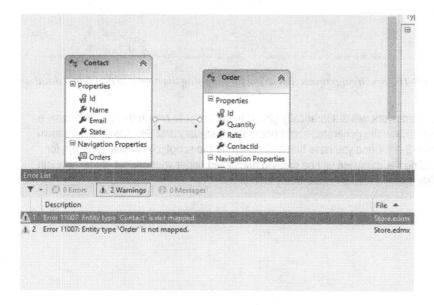

Figure 8-9. *Validation errors in the absence of mapping with a physical store*

11. Right-click the Designer surface again, and click *Generate Database from Model*. In the *Generate Database Wizard: Choose Your Data Connection* step, specify a connection to your database, as shown in Figure 8-10. Click *Next*.

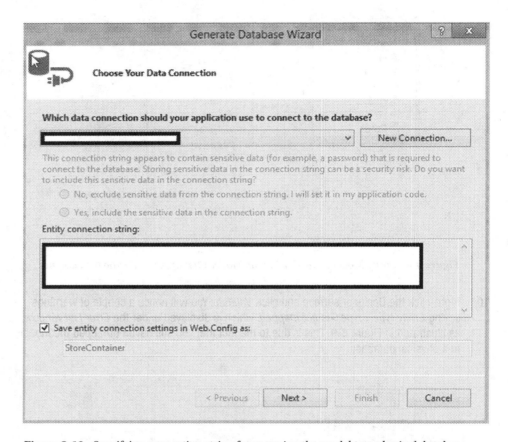

Figure 8-10. *Specifying connection string for mapping the model to a physical database*

12. Entity Framework will automatically generate the script to create the Store database. You can review the generated script under the *Summary and Settings* step, as shown in Figure 8-11. Once you have finished reviewing the script, click *Finish*. A script for generating the database will be created and saved under your project. If you now run *Validate* again, it will run without any errors.

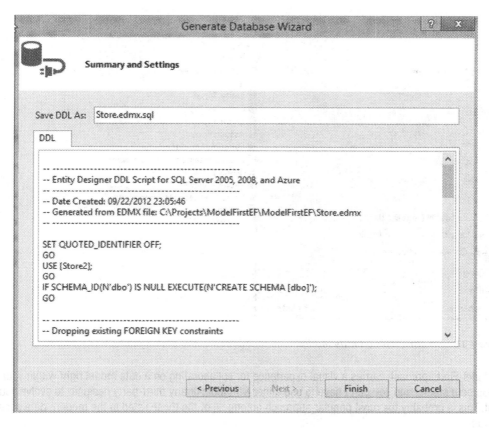

Figure 8-11. *Entity Designer-generated script*

13. Your entity data context is now ready to be built using the Model-First approach.

To use the `Store` data context in your controllers for CRUD operations, create an instance of the `StoreContext` class that is generated by Entity Framework while creating the entities and associations in the Designer.

Visual Studio 2012 provides a *Model Explorer* pane that lists all of the different artifacts related to the conceptual model and the associated physical database. You can create as many conceptual models as you want, which also translates into the possibility that you could potentially create multiple versions of your EDM.

14. Open the *Model Explorer* pane. You can right-click the *Diagrams* folder and click *Add New Diagram* to create different versions of the requisite conceptual model, as shown in Figure 8-12.

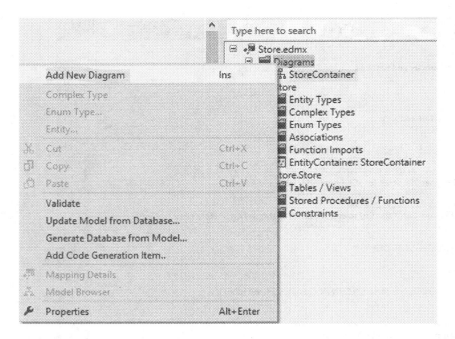

Figure 8-12. *Creating a New Entity Model*

The Model-First approach carries a visual experience for collaborating on a data model right within your development studio, and you don't have to use either SQL tools or any third-party designer to evolve your Entity Model. This is probably the most popular approach among all of the those listed in the modern data access paradigms.

Code-First Approach

Imagine a scenario where multiple teams are working on a program, and they don't yet have the base Entity Model ready to collaborate and improve upon in scoped iterations. Each team probably knows just enough about their own entities to be able to build their own modules. Then consider that a separate team is entrusted to envision the conceptual data model that will be used across all projects in the program. Of course, the stakeholders wouldn't want the teams to be sitting idle just because the data model is not yet ready. Instead, they would like to see progress on the individual modules. In such scenarios, it would be beneficial if developers could use entity classes created in code to act as the data model for their module—just enough to show progress in terms of accessing and manipulating data from the physical store. It would also be great if these classes could seamlessly integrate into the larger conceptual model whenever the data team produces it.

Entity Framework supports this scenario in the form of the Code-First approach. This approach allows each development team to continue to leverage Entity Framework without having to invest time in creating a conceptual model beforehand. Entity Framework allows an entity container to be created around all of the domain classes (POCO) available in code using the Code-First approach. This entity container would behave exactly as it does in a Database- or Model-First approach using Entity Framework, and it can be used to perform CRUD operations on a relational database.

▒ **Note** .NET Framework domain classes are often referred to as *POCO* classes. POCO stands for <u>P</u>lain <u>O</u>ld <u>C</u>LR <u>O</u>bjects.

Let's look at the steps needed to create an entity data context using the Code-First approach.

TRY IT OUT: CREATING A DATA-DRIVEN ASP.NET MVC 4 APPLICATION WITH THE ENTITY FRAMEWORK CODE-FIRST PARADIGM

In this exercise, you will create the familiar `Order` and `Contact` POCO classes. Then you will build the `Store` entity data context using the POCO classes to leverage Entity Framework features in mapping the entities to physical database tables and perform CRUD operations on them. Follow these steps:

1. Create an ASP.NET MVC 4 Web Application project using the steps you have learned previously. Although you could use any template for the purpose of this exercise, for simplicity's sake, we will continue to use the Internet template in our example.

2. Create a Contact class with the properties listed in the following code snippet:

```
namespace CodeFirstEF.Models
{
    public class Contact
    {
        public int ContactId { get; set; }
        public string Name { get; set; }
        public string Email { get; set; }
        public string State { get; set; }
        public List<Order>Orders { get; set; }
    }
}
```

Notice that `Orders` is a navigation property, and you have to add it to the `Contact` entity after you have created the `Order` entity.

▒ **Note** For automatic mapping of primary keys for the repository, you must have an `Id` property for the `Contact` class named `ContactId`. Alternatively, you can also use the data annotation attribute `KeyAttribute`. We will discuss this further in the "Validation with Data Annotations" section.

---

3. In a similar fashion, create the `Order` class.

```
public class Order
    {
        public int OrderId { get; set; }
        public int ContactId { get; set; }
        public decimal Rate { get; set; }
        public decimal Quantity { get; set; }
        public Contact Contact { get; set; }
    }
```

> **Note** The ContactId property in the Order class will allow Entity Framework to form the foreign key relationship in the database. You will learn how to specify a foreign key relationship using Data Annotations explicitly in a forthcoming section.

4. Create a StoreContext class inheriting DbContext (System.Data.Entity), and specify the Contact and Order classes as DbSet instances as follows:

```
public class StoreContext : DbContext
{
    public StoreContext() : base("name=StoreContext")
    {
    }

    public DbSet<Contact>Contacts { get; set; }
    public DbSet<Order>Orders { get; set; }
}
```

5. Finally, update the Web.config to specify a connection string for the repository, and you are ready to perform CRUD operations on your entity classes using Entity Framework.

```
<connectionStrings>
    <add name="StoreContext" connectionString="Data Source=
(localdb)\v11.0; Initial Catalog=StoreContext-20120926224002;
Integrated Security=True; MultipleActiveResultSets=True;
AttachDbFilename=|DataDirectory|StoreContext-20120926224002.mdf"
        providerName="System.Data.SqlClient" />
</connectionStrings>
```

> **Note** The connection string name has to be the same as the name of the data context class, unless you have specifically mentioned the instance name in the data context class constructor.

You have successfully mapped your entities to a SQL Server LocaDB database. Create an instance of the StoreContext class in your controller classes and use it to perform data access and manipulation operations. Next, you will learn how to configure the physical database programmatically from within your application using Entity Framework.

Database Initializer

Entity Framework provides the IDatabaseInitializer<TContext> (where TContext is constrained to be of type DbContext) interface, which can be used to customize the steps for initializing a database from your application code. This is very useful for the Code-First approach specifically, as it provides you with a way to update the database programmatically as the model evolves. There are a few default implementations already provided, such as DropCreateDatabaseIfModelChanges (System.Data.Entity), which will re-create the database in the store if model changes are detected (Data Context file is update) by Entity Framework. The System.Data.Entity.Database. SetInitializer method is used to specify the database initialization rules.

In order to setup the database when the application starts, you can execute the following code to get the database created with one-time or sample data added for reference:

```
protected void Application_Start()
    {
        AreaRegistration.RegisterAllAreas();

        FilterConfig.RegisterGlobalFilters(GlobalFilters.Filters);
        RouteConfig.RegisterRoutes(RouteTable.Routes);
        BundleConfig.RegisterBundles(BundleTable.Bundles);

        Database.SetInitializer(new DropCreateDatabaseIfModelChanges<StoreContext>());
    }
```

In this case, the code is inside the Application_Start method under the Global.asax file. Entity Framework will check for model changes whenever the application starts, and it will recreate the database based on the new model.

▓ **Caution**   You must be careful when using the database initializer. The DropCreateDatabaseIfModelChanges class will drop the database and any existing data that was previously stored. It would be most ideal to create your own initializer using the IDatabaseInitializer<TContext> interface, which is suitable for your scenario.

Next, we will explore a different method for creating the entity container based on the Code-First paradigm and using native ASP.NET MVC 4 features.

TRY IT OUT: CREATING A DATA CONTEXT CLASS USING ADD CONTROLLER

In ASP.NET MVC 4, there is also a way of using the Visual Studio templates to generate the entity container quickly from existing domain entities.

1. Open the ASP.NET MVC 4 project that you created in the previous section.

2. Right-click the *Controllers* folder in the *Solution Explorer*, and click *Add ➤ Controller....*

3. In the *New Controller* dialog, specify the *Controller name* as Contact and select the template *MVC controller with read/write actions and views, using Entity Framework*.

4. Under the *Model class* drop-down, select the Contact class.

5. Under *Data context class*, choose the first option *<New data context>*. The *New Data Context* dialog will be displayed with the data context class name specified as StoreContext.

6. Click *OK* to return to the *Add Controller* dialog. The *Add Controller* dialog should appear as illustrated in Figure 8-13.

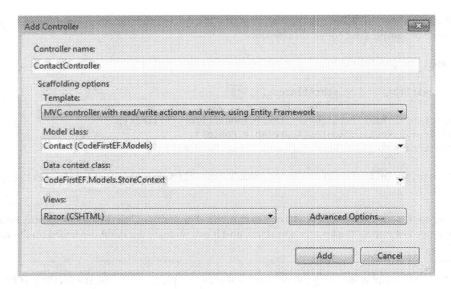

Figure 8-13. *Creating a Data Context class using the Add Controller wizard*

7. Click *Add* to generate the `ContactController` class, associated views, and the `StoreContext` data context class.

8. Create the `OrderController` controller class in a similar fashion, only this time pick the `StoreContext` class as the data context option, which is now available under the *Data context class* drop-down.

Now you are all set to perform data access operations with the template generating the code for you all the way from the views to the data access layer using ASP.NET MVC 4 and Entity Framework.

The preceding approach uses the default conventions in Entity Framework. Next, we will discuss how the Code-First default conventions can be overridden using the Data Annotations and Fluent API features in Entity Framework.

Custom Mapping with Fluent API

In a real, data-driven application development scenario using Entity Framework, it is quite possible that you will deal with complex entities and relationships. It may be nearly impossible for the default conventions to map such relationships with the physical database.

Entity Framework allows you to override the default mappings in code using the `ModelBuilder` class and a number of methods that it exposes, collectively known as *Fluent API*. As such, the `ModelBuilder` class enables several powerful capabilities for manipulating the default Entity Framework data context behaviors in mapping to a physical database. However, we will limit our discussion in this section to the relationship mapping overrides.

The `DbContext` (`System.Data.Entity`) class, which you use to create your entity container, has an `OnModelCreating` method that can be overridden in the implementation of your data context class (`StoreContext` in our example). The `OnModelCreating` method receives a derived version of the `ModelBuilder` class, called `DbModelBuilder`, as a parameter that exposes the methods to specify the relationship mappings with the physical database.

Continuing with the `Store` data context, imagine that you want to name the `ContactId` property in the `Order` class differently and still maintain the foreign key relationship in the database with this renamed property.

The default convention cannot figure this out, and you will need to specify the foreign key relationship between the Orders and Contacts table explicitly in the Store database using Fluent API syntax as follows. (Assume that you want to name the property PersonId.)

```
protected override void OnModelCreating(DbModelBuilder modelBuilder)
{
    modelBuilder.Entity<Order>()
        .HasRequired<Contact>(order => order.Contact)
        .WithMany(order => order.Orders)
        .HasForeignKey(contact => contact.PersonId);
}
```

As the code illustrates, you need to use three Fluent API methods in combination to override the foreign key relationship in the database. The HasRequired method specifies a navigation reference followed by WithMany that represents the type of relationship, and then HasForeignKey subsequently specifies the property in the related entity to be used as foreign key reference. When you run the application again, the DropCreateDatabaseIfModelChanges will fire and you will notice that the foreign key constraint is now set on the PersonId column. This is an overly simplified example designed to provide you with a glimpse of the capabilities of Fluent API. You can explore it further in the following MSDN article: http://msdn.microsoft.com/en-US/data/jj591620.

■ **Note** Data Annotations are an alternative to Fluent API and follow the attribute-driven model to override the default mapping behavior. The previous example would have been much easier to implement if you had just decorated the PersonId property with the ForeignKey (System.ComponentModel.DataAnnotations.Schema) data annotation attribute. However, the example demonstrated how Fluent API can be used to your advantage. It may not be possible to use Data Annotations in certain complex mapping scenarios, and you may need to use Fluent API. Both of these approaches provide you with a choice of the programming paradigm that you prefer. As far as Data Annotations are concerned, we will explore them further under the section "Validation with Data Annotations."

Code-First Migrations

The Code-First approach with Entity Framework comes with a very important feature called *Migrations*. Migrations allow you to maintain a history of changes as the model evolves and it allows them to be applied to your database. It also allows adding *Seed Data* for initialization.

To enable migrations, you can run the command Enable-Migrations on the *Package Manager Console* under *Tools* ➤ *Library Package Manager* in your Visual Studio 2012 instance. Once you have enabled migrations, a folder named Migrations will be created in your project containing a couple of files: a Configurations class file to define the settings for migration and <timestamp>_InitialCreate class file representing the changes made. You can use the Add-Migration command to let the Entity Framework Code-First Migrations scaffold the migration best on the default conventions whenever a change occurs in the model. You can modify the generated scaffolding template to make appropriate changes.

This topic requires further investigation, and we will discuss this in detail when exploring strategies and best practices for building data-driven web sites in Chapter 12.

Reverse Engineering Code First from Database

If you are brought into the Code-First approach (which is very likely given its flexibility), and you want to use it against an existing database, it is possible to autogenerate the POCO classes and the data context from the physical database using the *Entity Framework Power Tools*. Currently in its Beta 2 avatar, the Entity Framework Power Tools includes a reverse engineering feature, as shown in Figure 8-14, which can be used to generate your Code-First classes from the physical database.

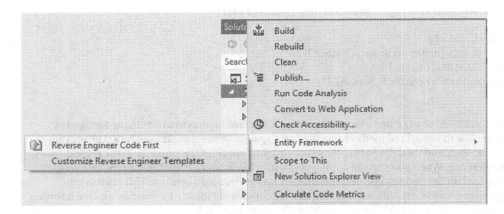

Figure 8-14. *Reverse engineering Code First*

You can download and install the Power Tools from this site: `http://visualstudiogallery.msdn.microsoft.com/72a60b14-1581-4b9b-89f2-846072eff19d`.

▓ **Note**   The Power Tools also allow you to customize the reverse engineering template using T4, which lets you to control the way you generate the POCO classes and follows your naming conventions.

Validation with Data Annotations

If you favor attribute-driven programming, you will love what *Data Annotations* can do with Entity Framework POCO classes. Data Annotations are a feature of Entity Framework, which allow you to define validation rules and several other rules cleanly to override the default Entity Framework Code-First conventions.

Data Annotations are an alternative to using Fluent API conventions. Fluent API provides better control in overriding Code-First conventions; however, Data Annotations are more readable and reduce the code footprint in overridding a convention. In the preceding section, you saw how you can override the default Code-First conventions in creating a Foreign Key Relationship using Fluent API. In Data Annotation style, this can simply be achieved using the ForeignKey Attribute as [ForeignKey("PersonID")]. Data Annotations, however, cannot be used in scenarios that require complex relationships to be established between entities and you must use Fluent API.

A natural extension to using Data Annotations is for validation. In this section, we will focus on the data validation rules.

Entity Framework Data Annotation attributes are available in Entity Framework 5 under the namespace `System.ComponentModel.DataAnnotations`. There are a number of validation attributes available under this namespace, which can be used to implement constraints in your model POCO class properties in order to maintain data integrity and consistency in the database. For example, the following code uses the `EmailAddress` Attribute to specify that the `Email` property must receive data that conforms to the norms of an e-mail address format.

```
public class Contact
    {
        public int ContactId { get; set; }
        public string Name { get; set; }
        [EmailAddress]
        public string Email { get; set; }
        [MaxLength(2, ErrorMessage="Max allowed length is 2 characters")]
        public string State { get; set; }
        public List<Order>Orders { get; set; }
    }
```

Notice that there is also a MaxLength data annotation attribute set on the State property, which displays the specified error message if more than two characters are entered. If you now run the Code-First application and try to enter a value for an e-mail address in the *Create Contact* form which doesn't follow the e-mail address format, a validation error will be displayed and you will be prevented from submitting the form, as shown in Figure 8-15.

Figure 8-15. *Data Annotations e-mail address validation*

▓ **Note**   There is also a set of special attributes available under the System.ComponentModel.DataAnnotations.Schema namespace. Thus, if you previously worked in Entity Framework 4, then you should be looking under that namespace for attributes such as ForeignKey, Table, and so on.

Although the validation errors are triggered when the `DbContext SaveChanges` method is executed, you can get the validation errors by explicitly invoking the `GetValidationErrors` method exposed by your data context class.

Summary

This chapter primarily served as an extension of the previous chapter, in which you learned to use Entity Framework effectively. In this chapter, the focus was on exploring two of the most important data access paradigms made popular by Entity Framework, namely, Model First and Code First. You learned about the steps required to create data-driven ASP.NET MVC 4 Web Applications using Entity Framework and the Model-First and Code-First paradigms. You also learned how you could easily implement validations in your model using the Entity Framework Data Annotations framework.

In the next chapter, you will learn how to use the Open Data Protocol (OData) specifications to expose your data for access and manipulation using RESTful HTTP services.

CHAPTER 9

■ ■ ■

Consuming Data Using WCF Data Services

Technologists invested their time trying to expose data as service over nearly the entire past decade. In doing so, the focus was inadvertently shifted from "data" to application logic. There are numerous reasons for this. While the need was for enterprises to distribute data to their partners and to consumers, there were concerns centering on security and transactions that led the shift in focus to *Remote Procedure Calls (RPC)*–style operations. The RPC style provided the much-needed abstraction for accessing and manipulating data, but it wasn't intuitive for consumers. As a result, metadata had to be provided to consumers to help them understand the operations they could perform.

Simple Object Access Protocol (SOAP) was at the forefront of this effort, and everyone acknowledged its dominance in the world of web services (RPC-style operations exposed over the Web). However "web services" sounded a little confusing, since SOAP lacked true characteristics of accessing resources using Web *URIs (Uniform Resource Identifiers)* that HTTP possessed. Nevertheless, it provided full support for transactions, security, and everything else needed to build an enterprise-class service in the form of WS-* specifications.

The realization of being able to move away from the basic ability to expose data came sooner. As web services started getting more complex, technologists felt the need for something simpler to support heterogeneous application-to-application communication. HTTP appeared to be most promising to tackle this job. It was almost as if HTTP was reborn. Built-in HTTP commands like GET, POST, PUT, and DELETE seemed to fit best for Create, Read, Update, and Delete (CRUD) operations on Data. This style of access to data, known as *REST (REpresentational State Transfer)*, also supported a variety of formats like *JSON (JavaScript Object Notation)*, apart from XML. This is a huge advantage over traditional web services given that consumers now have a choice of the way in which they want to consume the data. The current decade will be the one where RESTful services gain prominence, as the performance and usability benefits are realized and its simplicity is appreciated.

Microsoft has made significant investments in REST-style data access and manipulation. *WCF Data Services* provides the necessary runtime features to allow you to expose *Entity Data Models (EDM)* as *Open Data (OData)* feeds. In addition, it also provides the necessary client libraries to support consumption of OData feeds in client applications built using the .NET Framework. The runtime will be core to building data-driven web applications in the future.

In this chapter, we are going to cover the following:

- What are RESTful services?
- What is OData, and how can it let you access data from heterogeneous platforms?
- How can you expose your data as OData feeds using WCF Data Services?
- How can you consume OData feeds in your client applications using WCF Data Services Client Library?

The concepts you will learn in this chapter will go a long way in building modern responsive web applications that consume data from multiple sources, building interconnected applications sharing data and growing an ecosystem that breaks the storage silos in which data exists today.

Overview of REST Semantics

REST architecture was first proposed to simplify distributed operations over the World Wide Web in conjunction with the semantics of the HTTP protocol. It allowed interactions between clients and servers generally in a loosely coupled way, and it also allowed systems to be deployed as independently accessible resources. REST specifies that all resources can be accessed using an addressable URI. *RESTful HTTP* is designed to be simpler than SOAP, and it provides for better performance. The fact that the REST architecture is well suited for the HTTP protocol encouraged programmers to build services that are interoperable across firewall boundaries and leverage the caching benefits of the protocol to boost performance.

▨ **Note**   Although REST is well suited for HTTP, the architectural concepts are not limited to HTTP alone.

The architecture has several proposed constraints within which the applications that use it should operate. One of the major constraints is to leverage the architecture style of the Web as the core engine for application state. The architecture also proposed that a common set of interfaces should be used by all resources to provide uniformity in the way that they can be accessed. This works well for the HTTP protocol, with verbs like GET, PUT, POST, and DELETE being used to perform actions on the resources. You can read further about the architecture in Chapter 5 of Roy Fielding's thesis: `www.ics.uci.edu/~fielding/pubs/dissertation/rest_arch_style.htm`.

In the next section, we will look at how Microsoft invested in this architecture and how they built the OData protocol, aimed at creating a global paradigm for data access and manipulation.

Introduction to WCF Data Services

Microsoft's enthusiasm and commitment for creating a simple and easy-to-use data access platform are nothing new. It has been investing heavily in ADO and subsequently ADO.NET over the years, and it has continuously evolved the framework to allow developers build data-driven applications with ease, unlocking the potential of data living in silos. Microsoft was quick to realize the effectiveness of the REST architecture in building data services that are simple and scalable, and it created the OData protocol for this purpose. Microsoft, along with companies like SAP AG, IBM, and Citrix, has proposed the OData protocol to OASIS, an open standards consortium. How does the OData protocol help you build RESTful data services? You will find this out shortly. Read on.

The Open Data Protocol

OData lets you perform CRUD operations on data using open web technologies like HTTP, JSON, and *ATOM (Atom Publishing)*. The protocol resonates with the REST style, allowing resources to be identified using URIs and performing operations using a set of common interfaces. Figure 9-1 represents the OData ecosystem consisting of Producers, Consumers, and Applications.

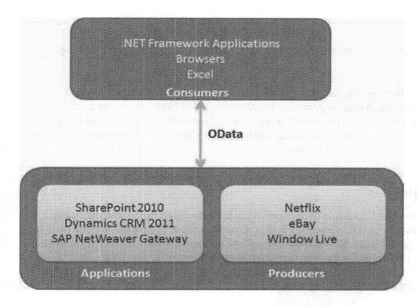

Figure 9-1. *The Open Data protocol ecosystem*

Notice that there are several OData producers, which are available online today, such as the Netflix movie catalog. Servers in the Microsoft stack, like SharePoint 2010 and Dynamics CRM 2011, are also capable of exposing data stored in their object models as OData feeds.

Using OData for Data Access and Manipulation

OData uses an EDM to describe the data exposed as service. The data abstraction using EDM is something with which you are already familiar, since we discussed it in detail in Chapter 6. OData allows resources such as entity, entity sets, relationships, properties, and operations to be accessed using addressable URI. The resource URI consists of three parts:

- **The Root URL:** Representing the OData service root end point.
- **Resource Path:** Identifies the resource.
- **Query Options:** Perform parameterized operations.

Netflix. the popular movie rental service, has exposed its catalog as an OData feed. To understand how the protocol operates, enter the following URI in your browser address bar:

```
http://odata.netflix.com/Catalog/Genres('20th%20Century%20Period%20Pieces')/Titles.
```

The part `http://odata.netflix.com/Catalog` represents the root URL. `Genres('20th Century Period Pieces')/Titles` represents the resource path. To filter the list of titles displayed, you can provide a System Query Option $top. The following query returns the top five titles.

```
http://odata.netflix.com/Catalog/Genres('20th%20Century%20Period%20Pieces')/Titles?$top=5
```

■ **Note** All System Query Options start with the $ symbol.

You could also create a filter condition, such as the following one, where you get the list of titles that are not rated:

```
http://odata.netflix.com/Catalog/Genres('20th%20Century%20Period%20Pieces')/Titles?$filter=Rating
eq 'NR'.
```

There is a host of OData conventions that you can use to structure your URI for accessing and manipulating a data feed. You can learn more about it here: www.odata.org/media/30002/OData%20URL%20Conventions.html.

To make it easier for .NET developers who want to use the OData protocol, Microsoft also introduced the WCF Data Services runtime to let you expose your data as an OData feed, and it also developed Client Libraries to consume OData services in client applications built on the .NET Framework.

WCF Data Services Architecture

The WCF Data Services runtime can be used with a variety of data providers including, but not limited to, Entity Framework and LINQ to SQL to expose data in the OData format. It also provides a client library that can be used to consume OData services in .NET-based applications, allowing developers use some of the framework features like LINQ to query OData sources. Figure 9-2 illustrates the architecture of WCF Data Services.

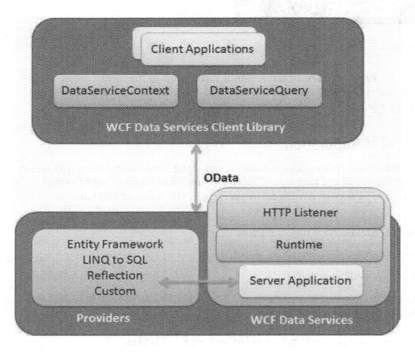

Figure 9-2. *WCF Data Services architecture*

Next, you will learn how to use WCF Data Services in exposing data as a service and consuming OData feeds.

Exposing Data as Service

With WCF Data Services, the runtime allows you to create an OData service using a variety of providers. ADO.NET Entity Framework is a popular choice among all the supported providers, given the ease with which it allows you to build data layers in .NET Framework applications. In addition to the supported providers listed in Figure 9-2, it is also possible for you to leverage your own provider as long as it supports IQueryable. In the following exercise, you will learn the steps required to make a WCF Data Service feed on the entity container created using Entity Framework.

TRY IT OUT: EXPOSE ADO.NET ENTITITY FRAMEWORK ENTITIES AS ODATA FEEDS

In this exercise, you will create a Visual Studio 2012 C# Web Application Project to expose an Entity Data Model as a data feed using WCF Data Services. Following are the prerequisites:

- Visual Studio 2012 (Express and above).

- The example will use the Store database created in Chapter 5. You will also need the Entity Model created using ADO.NET Entity Framework on the Store database.

▓ **Note** WCF Data Services come integrated with versions of Visual Studio or stand-alone. At the time of this writing, WCF Data Services 5.0 was released as an add-on version for Visual Studio 2010 and .NET Framework 4.0. If you are still using Visual Studio 2010, then you can download WCF Data Services 5.0 for OData V3 from www.microsoft.com/en-in/download/details.aspx?id=29306.

Follow these steps to complete the exercise:

1. Create a Visual Studio 2012 C# Web Application Project and name it DataAsService, as shown in Figure 9-3.

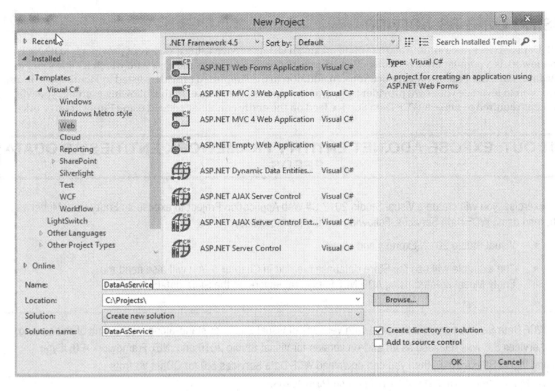

Figure 9-3. *Visual Studio 2012 C# Web Application Project*

2. Create an ADO.NET Entity Data Model using the Store database and the steps illustrated in Chapter 7.

3. Right-click the project and click *Add New Item....* in the *Add New Item* dialog. Then, select *WCF Data Service* under the *Web* tab and name it StoreService.svc, as shown in Figure 9-4.

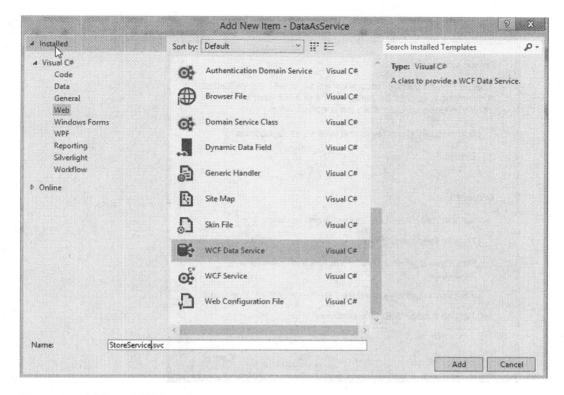

Figure 9-4. *Adding a WCF Data Service*

4. In the generate template, specify the `StoreService` class to be inheriting `DataService` of type `StoreEntities`. `StoreEntities` is the generated Entity Model container containing the entities `Orders` and `Contacts` from the `Store` database tables.

```
public class StoreService : DataService< StoreEntities >
```

5. Inside the `InitializeService` method, specify the read permissions on the `Orders` and `Contacts` entities.

```
public static void InitializeService(DataServiceConfiguration config)
        {
                config.SetEntitySetAccessRule("Orders", EntitySetRights.
AllRead);
                config.SetEntitySetAccessRule("Contacts", EntitySetRights.
AllRead);
                config.DataServiceBehavior.MaxProtocolVersion =
DataServiceProtocolVersion.V2;
        }
```

6. Build the solution. Before you can browse the service, turn off the feed reading view in Internet Explorer by unchecking the *Feed Reading View* check box under *Tools* ➤ *Internet Options* ➤ *Content* ➤ *Feed Settings,* as shown in Figure 9-5.

Figure 9-5. *Turning off the feed reading view*

7. Right-click the StoreService.svc file and click *View in Browser (Internet Explorer)*.
    You will see the results being displayed as XML. You can now run OData commands in
    the URI to filter the results further. To display the list of Contacts, run
    http://localhost:<generated port>/StoreService.svc/Contacts. You will see
    all of the contacts being displayed, as shown in Figure 9-6.

```
<?xml version="1.0" encoding="utf-8" ?>
- <feed xml:base="http://localhost:1103/StoreService.svc/" xmlns="http://www.w3.org/2005/Atom" xmlns:d="http://schemas.microsoft.com/ado/2007/08/dataservices"
    xmlns:m="http://schemas.microsoft.com/ado/2007/08/dataservices/metadata">
    <id>http://localhost:1103/StoreService.svc/Contacts</id>
    <title type="text">Contacts</title>
    <updated>2012-09-09T09:56:50Z</updated>
    <link rel="self" title="Contacts" href="Contacts" />
  - <entry>
      <id>http://localhost:1103/StoreService.svc/Contacts(1)</id>
      <category term="StoreModel.Contact" scheme="http://schemas.microsoft.com/ado/2007/08/dataservices/scheme" />
      <link rel="edit" title="Contact" href="Contacts(1)" />
      <link rel="http://schemas.microsoft.com/ado/2007/08/dataservices/related/Orders" type="application/atom+xml;type=feed" title="Orders" href="Contacts
        (1)/Orders" />
      <title />
      <updated>2012-09-09T09:56:50Z</updated>
    - <author>
        <name />
      </author>
    - <content type="application/xml">
      - <m:properties>
          <d:ID m:type="Edm.Int32">1</d:ID>
          <d:Name>John Doe</d:Name>
          <d:Email />
          <d:State>CA</d:State>
        </m:properties>
      </content>
    </entry>
  - <entry>
      <id>http://localhost:1103/StoreService.svc/Contacts(2)</id>
      <category term="StoreModel.Contact" scheme="http://schemas.microsoft.com/ado/2007/08/dataservices/scheme" />
      <link rel="edit" title="Contact" href="Contacts(2)" />
      <link rel="http://schemas.microsoft.com/ado/2007/08/dataservices/related/Orders" type="application/atom+xml;type=feed" title="Orders" href="Contacts
        (2)/Orders" />
      <title />
      <updated>2012-09-09T09:56:50Z</updated>
    - <author>
        <name />
      </author>
    - <content type="application/xml">
      - <m:properties>
          <d:ID m:type="Edm.Int32">2</d:ID>
          <d:Name>Jane Doe</d:Name>
          <d:Email />
          <d:State>AZ</d:State>
        </m:properties>
      </content>
    </entry>
  </feed>
```

Figure 9-6. *List of contacts from the Store DB Contacts table*

You can now run all sorts of OData commands in your browser address bar. For example, to sort the Contacts by State, you can run http://localhost:<generated port>/StoreService.svc/Contacts?$orderby=State. Another example is to display the name of the first contact: http://localhost:<generated port>/StoreService.svc/Contacts(1)/Name. Figure 9-7 shows the result of this action.

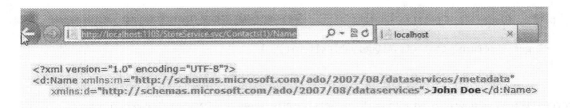

```
<?xml version="1.0" encoding="UTF-8"?>
<d:Name xmlns:m="http://schemas.microsoft.com/ado/2007/08/dataservices/metadata"
    xmlns:d="http://schemas.microsoft.com/ado/2007/08/dataservices">John Doe</d:Name>
```

Figure 9-7. *Name of the first Contact entity*

Behind the scenes, the WCF Data Services runtime parses the OData commands executed in the browser and performs the necessary operations on the EDM. Addtionally, access to data is controlled using the entity access rules as mentioned in step 5. The entity access rules allow you to set read/write permissions on the entity accessed over the service.

■ **Note** The `DataServiceConfiguration` class provides a host of configuration options that you can specify to constrain access to the entities. Other than the entity access rules, you can also set behaviors such as the supported protocol version.

If you are not using Entity Framework, then it is also possible to expose your data as service through different providers that are supported by the runtime. We discuss this next.

WCF Data Service Providers

In the previous section, you learned that Entity Framework–generated EDMs can be very easily exposed as a data feed. Of course, there are different supported providers if you don't have the option of using Entity Framework. You could use *LINQ to SQL* or a *Reflection Provider*. The Reflection Provider allows you to expose your existing classes as feeds. This is useful if you already have a set of *DTOs (Data Transfer Objects)* which the application stack is using. You can now expose them as feeds to your consumers. You need to create an entity container (database context) class that exposes your custom entities as queryable types. The following code illustrates this with the `StoreService` example:

```
public partial class StoreEntities
    {
        static IList<Order> _orders;
        static IList<Contact> _contacts;
        static StoreEntities()
        {
            //TODO: Fetch and populate orders and contacts
        }

        public IQueryable<Order> Orders
        {
            get { return _orders.AsQueryable<Order>(); }
        }
        public IQueryable<Contact> Contacts
        {
            get { return _contacts.AsQueryable<Item>(); }
        }
    }
```

`StoreEntities` can now be used with the `StoreService` class inheriting `DataService` generic type.

```
public class StoreService : DataService< StoreEntities >
    {
        public static void InitializeService(IDataServiceConfiguration
                                    config)
        {
            config.SetEntitySetAccessRule("Orders", EntitySetRights.All);
            config.SetEntitySetAccessRule("Contacts", EntitySetRights.All);
        }
    }
```

Also the entity classes should specify a DataServiceKeyAttribute to uniquely identify an instance of the entity.

```
[DataServiceKeyAttribute("ID")]
    public class Order
    {
            //Order Properties
    }
```

▓ **Caution**   Relational data cannot be exposed using the Reflection Provider. You must use providers like EF.

In order to allow updates, the StoreEntities class must also implement IUpdatable, which exposes the necessary methods for insert and update operations. The Reflection Provider uses reflection to infer the data model. It can derive entity containers, sets, types, and keys. In addition to the Reflection Provider, you could also write your own custom provider using the data services runtime contracts.

Although exposing your Entity Model as feeds is easy, you don't always have to go this route to expose your services as OData feeds. If you have made investments in creating an abstraction around your data (like repository-style data access) and you have been using services like *ASP.NET MVC WebAPI* to expose controller-style web operations, then you can easily convert them to be accessed as OData feeds. You will learn more about the steps for doing this in the next section.

Exposing ASP.NET MVC WebAPI Services as OData Feeds

If you are working on an *ASP.NET MVC 4* web application and leveraging WebAPI services, you can easily convert your WebAPI Controller methods to be queried using OData commands.

▓ **Note**   If you are not familiar with ASP.NET WebAPI, you can find out more about it at www.asp.net/web-api.

TRY IT OUT: EXPOSE WEBAPI SERVICES AS ODATA FEEDS

Follow these steps:

1. Create a C# ASP.NET MVC 4 Web Application Project in Visual Studio and name it ApiAsDataFeeds, as shown in Figure 9-8.

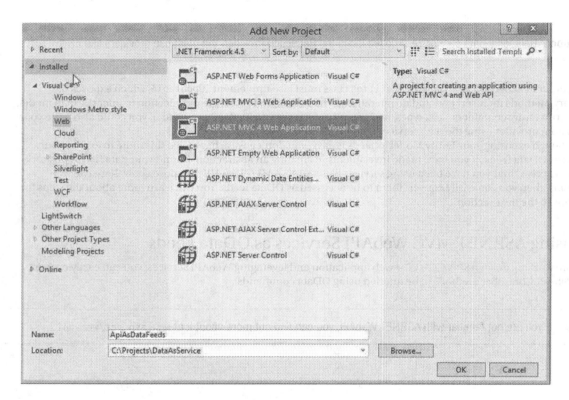

Figure 9-8. *Creating an ASP.NET MVC 4 web application*

2. In the *New ASP.NET MVC 4 Project* dialog, select *Web API* as the template. Figure 9-9 illustrates how to do this.

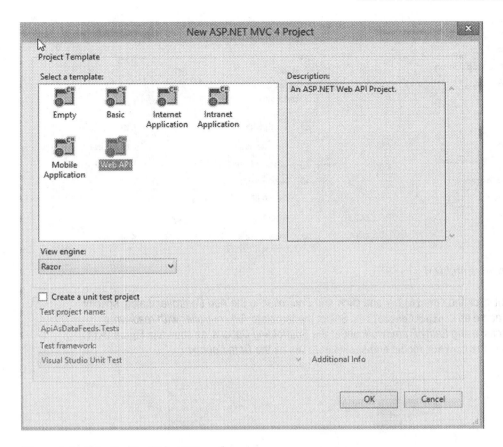

Figure 9-9. Selecting the Web API template

3. Create the Store database EDM. You have done this several times by now, so the steps to do this need no further elaboration. Figure 9-10 illustrates a quick action in the context menu to do this.

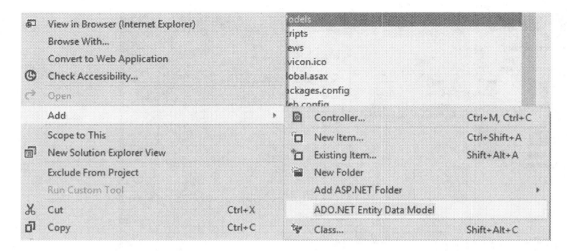

Figure 9-10. *Creating an EDM*

4. Right-click the Controller and click *Add Controller*. In the *Add Controller* dialog, specify the name as ContactController. Select the template *API controller with read/write actions, using Entity Framework* under the *Scaffolding Options,* as shown in Figure 9-11. Select the Contact model and StoreEntities as the *Data Context*.

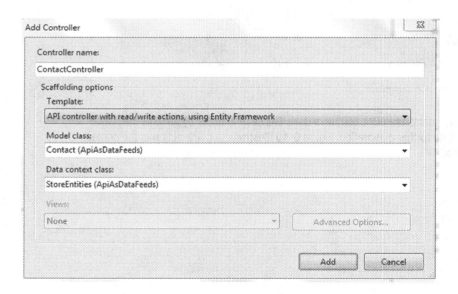

Figure 9-11. *Creating a Controller class using the EDM*

■ **Note** Make sure to build the solution to get the EDMs while adding the Controller.

---

5. The scaffolding template generates the necessary methods for CRUD operations using the `StoreEntities` entity container instance. Modify the `Get` method to return the type as `IQueryable` and specify the `QueryAttribute` as follows:

```
private StoreEntities db = new StoreEntities();

        // GET api/Contact
        [Queryable]
        public IQueryable<Contact> GetContacts()
        {
            return db.Contacts;
        }
```

6. Build the solution. Run the application. In the browser address bar, enter the URI `http://localhost:<generated port>/api/contact`. You will see results similar to the one displayed in the previous section (Internet Explorer sends `application/json` by default, so it would prompt for a download of the result. This will also work fine in Chrome, where you can see the result in the browser window). You can now run OData queries like `http://localhost:<generated port>/api/contact?$orderby=state`.

The `QueryableAttribute` allows access to the controller action in the form of OData feeds, and all the commands are supported.

■ **Note**   The `QueryableAttribute` can be equally applied to `IEnumerable` and `IQueryable` types.

The OData support in WebAPI is built on the same foundations as WCF Data Services. The example demonstrated only a `GET` operation. Additionally, you can create implementations for `POST`, `PUT`, and `DELETE` operations.

Now that you have a couple of ways to expose your data as feeds, which one is generally preferred? WebAPI style is the preferred mechanism if you need a little bit of abstraction over the way you want to expose data and reuse existing infrastructure for additional clients requesting OData feeds. You can create additional HTTP Verbs–mapped actions to allow a constrained access to data.

Consuming Data Services in a Client Application

Now let's discuss the ways in which you can consume OData feeds in different client applications. In Chapter 5, you learned how the LINQPad client can query WCF Data Services and perform LINQ operations on the result. This is made possible with the help of the WCF Data Services Client Libraries, which transform the LINQ queries into equivalent OData commands on the resource URI. We will soon discuss how the WCF Data Service Client Libraries function, but first let's learn about the steps used to consume OData feeds in JavaScript-based rich Internet applications.

Consuming OData Feeds using jQuery Ajax

Today, with the advent of HTML 5, you have the capability to build rich data-driven web applications that are responsive and provide the kind of experience that could only be imagined previously in desktop-based applications. OData feeds can be consumed asynchronously using jQuery Ajax and bound to HTML controls in a Razor or

ASPX View in your ASP.NET MVC 4 application. The following code snippet illustrates how you can consume the StoreService.svc WCF Data Service, which you previously created in your ASP.NET MVC 4 views using jQuery:

```
function DisplayContacts() {
    var storeServiceUrl = "/StoreService.svc/Contacts?$orderby=State";

    $.ajax({
      type: "GET",
      url: storeServiceUrl,
      contentType: "application/json; charset=utf-8",
      dataType: "json",
      success: function (result) {
        loadContacts(result.d);
      }
    });
}
```

The storeServiceUrl variable specifies the OData URL, and you can pass commands to this URI based on the operations that you want to perform. In this case, it will return the list of contacts.

■ **Note**　Notice that for WCF Data Service query, the results translated to JSON are actually stored under the "d" property.

The loadContacts method receives the response asynchronously, and you can use it to parse the result as shown here:

```
function loadContacts(results) {
    var contactsTable = '<table><thead><tr><th>Name</th><th>Email</th><th>State</th>
    </thead><tbody>';

    for (var contact in results) {
      var row = '<tr>';

      row += '<td>' + results[contact].Name + '</td>';
      row += '<td>' + results[contact].Email + '</td>';
      row += '<td>' + results[contact].State + '</td>';
      row += '</tr>';

      contactsTable += row;
    }

    contactsTable += '</tbody></table>';

    $('#contactsTable).html(contactsTable);
```

Here the #contactsTable is the HTML DIV control, which acts as a container to display the results. Notice that the results displayed are ordered by State.

▦ **Tip** It is also possible to query OData feeds asynchronously using the $.getJSON() method in jQuery if you need the results to be processed as JSON only. With the Ajax method, you can specify the format in which you want the results.

Consuming OData Feeds Using WCF Data Services Client Library

The WCF Data Services runtime also provides a client library, which supports consuming OData feeds in .NET Framework–based applications. In the previous section, you learned that consuming OData feeds is fairly straightforward if your application can send an HTTP request to the feed and process the response. However, the client libraries provide a better programming experience, and they do most of the heavy lifting in transforming the actions to appropriate resource URI. For example, with the client libraries, you could run LINQ queries against an OData source, and the client library runtime will do the job of translating your query into appropriate OData URI.

DataServiceContext and DataServiceQuery Classes

The DataServiceContext and the DataServiceQuery are the core classes of the WCF Data Services Client Library, allowing you to do the following:

1. Create an entity container using the feed reference.

2. Perform queries on the entities.

To consume a WCF Data Service like StoreService.svc, which we built previously, you need to right-click your client project (ASP.NET MVC 4 application) and click *Add Service Reference*.... The framework is capable of identifying that you are trying to add a reference to a WCF Data Service, and it will create an entity container based on the DataServiceContext class. Figure 9-12 illustrates how to add a service reference.

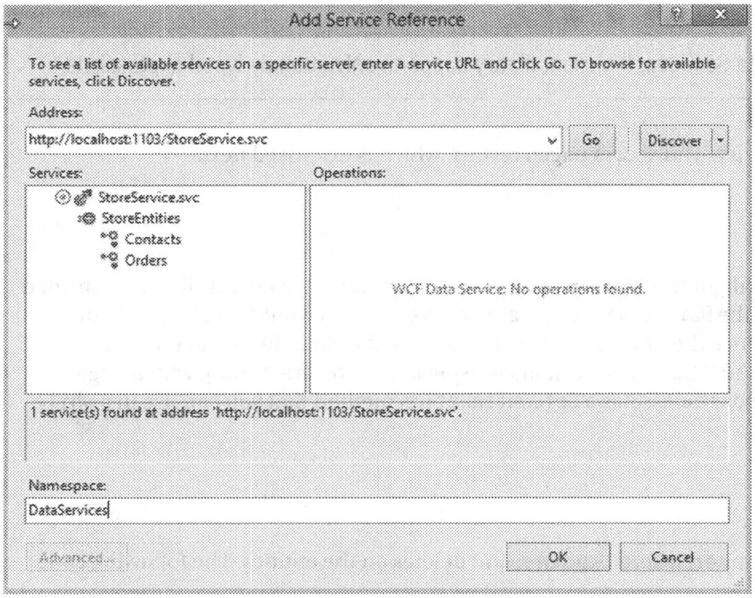

Figure 9-12. Adding WCF Data Service reference

The following code demonstrates how you can query the data feed and pass the results to an MVC 4 View:

```
public ActionResult Index()
    {
        var serviceUri = new Uri("http://localhost:1103/StoreService.svc");
        DataServices.StoreEntities dbContext = new DataServices.StoreEntities(serviceUri);
        var results = from order in dbContext.Orders
                        where order.Quantity > 5
                        select order;
        return View(results.ToList());
    }
```

The preceding code sample showcases the ability to run LINQ queries on the entity container created from the WCF Data Service feed. This is possible because the DataServiceQuery class under the System.Data. Services.Client namespace inherits IQueryable. In addition, you can also run direct OData commands using the DataServiceQuery class as shown in the following code sample:

```
DataServices.StoreEntities dbContext = new DataServices.StoreEntities(serviceUri);
DataServiceQuery<Contact> contacts = dbContext.Contacts;
        contacts.AddQueryOption("$orderby", "State");
```

There are a couple of ways that the query gets executed. One is if you loop through the results in a foreach loop. The second approach is to use the QueryOperationResponse class. The benefit of using QueryOperationResponse is that you can get additional information about the query result like Error, StatusCode, and TotalCount.

```
DataServices.StoreEntities dbContext = new DataServices.StoreEntities(serviceUri);
DataServiceQuery<Contact> contacts = dbContext.Contacts;
QueryOperationResponse<Contact> response = contacts.Execute() as QueryOperationResponse<Contact>;
```

■ **Note**   While executing queries on WCF Data Services, the client library supports only strongly typed expressions.

The QueryOperationResponse class also lets you access paged results, which is discussed next.

Pagination

In the WCF Data Service, you can provide configuration instructions to limit the number of records that are returned using the SetEntitySetPageSize method of the DataServiceConfiguration class. You would set this inside the InitializeService method of the service. Once the page size is set, you can use the client library to retrieve paginated results. This is a good technique, and it boosts performance, especially if you are dealing with a large number of records. The QueryOperationResponse class has a GetContinuation method that you can use in a while loop to get paged results from the data feed.

Inserts, Updates, and Deletes

In addition to read, the client libraries also support inserts, updates, and deletes on the entities. The following code shows how to create a new Contact.

```
DataServices.StoreEntities dbContext = new DataServices.StoreEntities(serviceUri);
```

```
Contact newContact = Contact.CreateContact(3, "Henry Doe", "MA");
            dbContext.AddToContacts(newContact);
```

Delete and Update can be performed using the DeleteObject and UpdateObject methods exposed by the entity container dbContext.

Eager Loading Entities

By default, WCF Data Services do not load entities that are related to the one being queried. However, the $expand command is available with OData, which the WCF Data Services client library can leverage.

```
DataServices.StoreEntities dbContext = new DataServices.StoreEntities(serviceUri);
DataServiceQuery<Order> result =
    dbContext.Orders.Expand("Contact");
```

▪ **Tip** You can specify multiple related entities by separating them with a comma delimiter.

Summary

In this chapter, you learned how the REST architecture is used to build data services, which can be accessed and manipulated over the World Wide Web using the OData protocol. You also learned how the WCF Data Services runtime and client libraries make it really easy to leverage the OData protocol in building scalable data services.

In the next chapter, we will focus on some of the core capabilities of ASP.NET 4.5 and consider how we can build data-driven web sites using the framework.

CHAPTER 10

■ ■ ■

Data Binding in ASP.NET 4.5

The chapters you have explored so far in this book have been focused on data access. You learned how easily you can create a data access layer using Entity Framework. You also learned about the different data access paradigms and how data access technologies are becoming standardized by means of protocols like OData for universal distribution.

In this chapter, we will shift gears and focus on data presentation. Although it is not unfamiliar territory, there has been continuous improvement in this area since ASP.NET 2.0. While ASP.NET 2.0 brought with it the addition of powerful data presentation capabilities in the form of *Data Source Controls* and an array of Web controls, ASP.NET 4.5 has taken it further by introducing features like *Strongly Typed Data Controls* and the all-new *Model Binding* capability—straight out of the ASP.NET MVC Framework—that you will learn about shortly.

A significant and visible improvement has also occurred in the area of ASP.NET MVC and, with increasing popularity, ASP.NET MVC 4 is aiming to take its fair share of the new Web application development market that supports modern Web platforms like HTML 5. ASP.NET MVC also introduced a new view engine called *Razor*. Although not strictly tied to ASP.NET MVC, Razor brings to the table a host of data presentation capabilities. Coupled with Ajax, you will learn how easy it is to fetch data asynchronously and bind it to HTML controls for display.

In this chapter, we will cover the following:

- How to perform CRUD operations using LinqDataSource and EntityDataSource Controls.

- How the new data presentation controls work with the data source controls.

- What the new data-binding features in ASP.NET 4.5 are.

- How to do data binding in ASP.NET MVC 4.

Furthermore, in this chapter, you will apply your knowledge of data access and learn how to create useful visualizations using presentation tier components.

Data Source Controls

Data source controls are not new. They have provided easy access to data from a variety of sources, including databases like Microsoft SQL Server and CLR objects, since ASP.NET 2.0. They can be used either declaratively or in code, providing lots of flexibility and ease when performing CRUD operations in conjunction with presentation Web controls like GridView. There has been continuous improvement in ASP.NET Web controls—stack and newer controls are added with each new version of .NET. You explored the SqlDataSource control in ASP.NET 2.0 that allowed you to perform data access and manipulation operations on a Microsoft SQL Server database. In this section, you will explore two new data source controls, LinqDataSource and EntityDataSource, which have been introduced to support ORM-style data access using LINQ to SQL and Entity Framework.

■ **Note**   Data source controls like SqlDataSource have been discussed in detail in the previous version of this book, *Beginning ASP.NET 2.0 Databases: From Novice to Professional.* You are strongly encouraged to pick up a copy of it if you are not familiar with the concept.

LinqDataSource

The LinqDataSource (System.Web.UI.WebControls) control allows you to use a LINQ to SQL data context class as a source of data and then perform CRUD operations. A LinqDataSource control can be associated with data presentation controls like GridView and ListView. The following code demonstrates a simple example of LinqDataSource control used declaratively in an ASPX file:

```
<asp:LinqDataSource ID="StoreDataSource" runat="server"
            ContextTypeName="DataSourceControls.StoreDataContext"
            TableName="Contacts"
            Select="new (Name, Email, State, ID)">
        </asp:LinqDataSource>
```

The preceding code uses a LINQ to SQL data context class generated from the Store database, and it fetches information from the Contacts table. Associated with a GridView control, it will display the records present in the Contacts table.

```
<asp:GridView ID="StoreContactsView" runat="server" DataSourceID="StoreDataSource"
AutoGenerateColumns="False">
        <Columns>
            <asp:BoundField DataField="Name" HeaderText="Name" ReadOnly="True"
            SortExpression="Name" />
            <asp:BoundField DataField="Email" HeaderText="Email" ReadOnly="True"
            SortExpression="Email" />
            <asp:BoundField DataField="State" HeaderText="State" ReadOnly="True"
            SortExpression="State" />
            <asp:BoundField DataField="ID" HeaderText="ID" ReadOnly="True"
            SortExpression="ID" />
        </Columns>
    </asp:GridView>
```

The control opens up lot of possibilities in querying data. For example, you could filter the results using the Where clause. To select Contacts in the State of CA, you could provide the following Where clause:

```
<asp:LinqDataSource ID="StoreDataSource" runat="server"
            ContextTypeName=" DataSourceControls.StoreDataContext"
            TableName="Contacts"
            Where='State = "CA"'
            Select="new (Name, Email, State, ID)">
        </asp:LinqDataSource>
```

A more useful and practical possibility will be to let users choose the State from a drop-down, and the results will automatically be filtered based on the selected State. To implement this feature, first create a DropDownList control holding the filter condition values (AZ and CA in our case).

```
<asp:DropDownList AutoPostBack="true" ID="StateDropDown" runat="server">
          <asp:ListItem Value="CA"></asp:ListItem>
          <asp:ListItem Value="AZ"></asp:ListItem>
      </asp:DropDownList>
```

░ **Note**   The AutoPostBack attribute of the DropDownList control is set to true. This will enable the display to be refreshed when you select an option in the drop-down.

Create a ControlParameter as part of the WhereParameters parameter collection of the StoreDataSource control. The data source control should look like this:

```
<asp:LinqDataSource ID="StoreDataSource" runat="server" ContextTypeName=" DataSourceControls.
StoreDataContext"
          TableName="Contacts" Where='State = @State' Select="new (Name, Email, State, ID)">
          <WhereParameters>
              <asp:ControlParameter Name="State" DefaultValue="CA" ControlID="StateDropDown"
                  Type="String" />
          </WhereParameters>
      </asp:LinqDataSource>
```

When you run the application, the record with State CA will be displayed. If you select AZ from the drop-down, the data will get refreshed in the grid and you will see the record associated with State AZ.

In addition to the Where and Select clauses, the LinqDataSource control also supports OrderBy, GroupBy, and Insert clauses and parameters. Potentially, you could display complex aggregated results using the GroupBy clause along with Select. Aggregate functions are equally supported in the Select clause.

While the declarative format is pretty straightforward and readable, you may find yourself in a situation where a complex operation needs to be performed involving the LinqDataSource control, and it may not be accomplished easily in declarative mode. There are several events associated with the LinqDataSource control. You could write an event handler in code to perform a complex operation while the event is being triggered. For example, the earlier Where clause could be made part of an event handler for the Selecting event of the control.

```
protected void StoreDataSource_Selecting(object sender, LinqDataSourceSelectEventArgs e)
    {

        var result = from contact in context.Contacts
                     where contact.State == "CA"
                     select contact;
        e.Result = result;
    }
```

This will display the same behavior as the previous example and it will display records for the State of CA. The handler must be specified in the StoreDataSource control's onselecting event:

```
<asp:LinqDataSource ID="StoreDataSource" runat="server" ContextTypeName=" DataSourceControls.
StoreDataContext"
          TableName="Contacts"
          Select="new (Name, Email, State, ID)" onselecting="StoreDataSource_Selecting">
      </asp:LinqDataSource>
```

▦ **Note**   In the examples showcased here, the result is same whether you favor a declarative style or programmatic control. However, the programmatic control provides greater flexibility in performing the data access and manipulation operations.

Next, you will learn about another data source control named `EntityDataSource`. It is in many ways is very similar to `LinqDataSource`, but it works with Entity Framework data context classes as opposed to LINQ to SQL. In case you were wondering why data manipulation was not discussed previously, this is exactly what you will be learning to do with the `EntityDataSource` control.

EntityDataSource

The `EntityDataSource` control lets you use an EDM as a source of data for presentation controls like the `GridView` and `DetailsView`. Similar to the `LinqDataSource` control, you can specify a data context class from where the entity details will be fetched. Let's explore the steps required to configure an `EntityDataSource` control.

TRY IT OUT: CREATE AN ENTITYDATASOURCE CONTROL AND CONFIGURE IT TO PERFORM CRUD OPERATIONS ON THE STORE DATABASE

You could run this exercise equally well with Visual Studio 2010 or Visual Studio 2012. Other than that, there are no prerequisites. So, here are the steps to follow:

1.   Create a new *Visual C# ASP.NET Web Forms Application* project from your instance of Visual Studio and name it `DataSourceControls`, as shown in Figure 10-1.

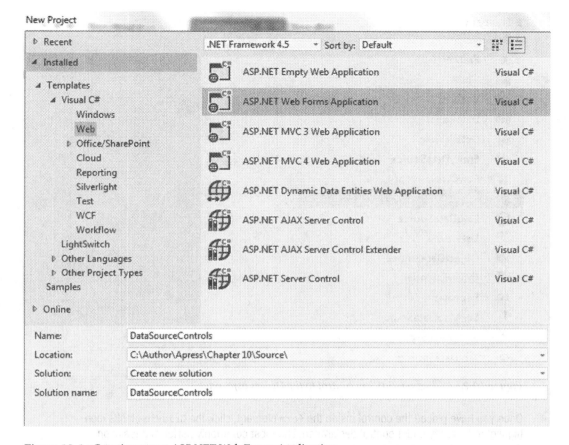

Figure 10-1. Creating a new ASP.NET Web Forms Application

2. Create an EDM named StoreEntities generated using the Store database from your instance of SQL Server. While generating the EDM, make sure to save the named *Entity Connection String* (StoreEntities by default for the Store database) in the Web.config file as prompted.

3. Add a new *Web Form* to the project and name it Orders.aspx. In the Orders.aspx page, drag and drop a GridView control from the toolbox. It is available under the *Data* tab, as shown in Figure 10-2.

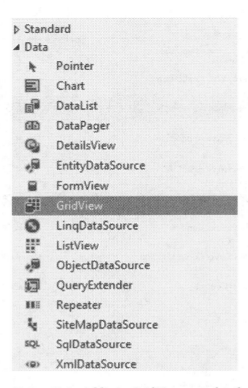

Figure 10-2. Adding a GridView control to the Orders.aspx page

4. Once you have placed the control inside the form element, click the GridView tasks icon highlighted directly under control declaration. The most commonly performed tasks on the GridView appear as a menu, as shown in Figure 10-3. As you can see, *Choose Data Source* is listed as an option.

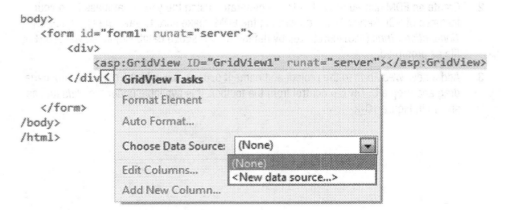

Figure 10-3. Choosing Data Source from the GridView Smart Task pane

▧ **Note** If you are using Visual Studio 2012, you will notice that the ability to launch the most commonly performed tasks menu is also available in the *Source* view. This is known as *Smart Tasks*. Earlier, this was possible only in the *Design* view.

5. Under the *Choose Data Source* option in the GridView tasks menu, select *<New data source>*. The *Choose a Data Source Type* dialog is displayed. Choose the *Entity* option from the list of available types, type the name as StoreDataSource, and click *OK*. This is illustrated in Figure 10-4.

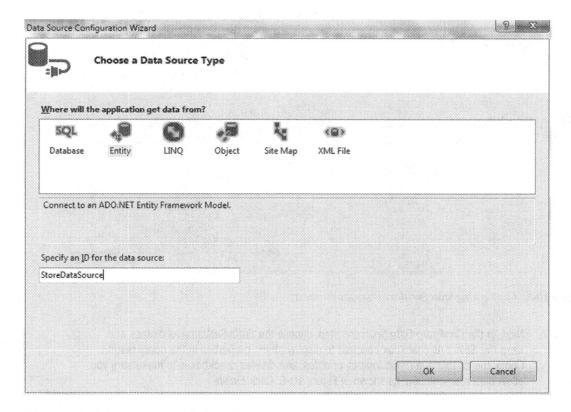

Figure 10-4. *Selecting Entity as the Data Source Type*

6. In the *Configure ObjectContext* dialog, select the StoreEntities connection string under *Named Connection* and the *DefaultContainerName* as StoreEntities, as shown in Figure 10-5. Click *Next*.

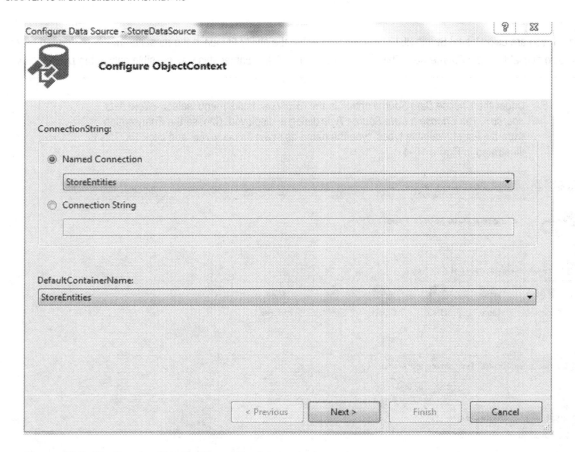

Figure 10-5. *Configuring StoreEntities as the data context*

7. Next, in the *Configure Data Selection* step, choose the *EntitySetName* as Orders and keep the *Select All* checkbox checked to display all the properties in the query result. Check the *Enable automatic inserts*, *updates*, and *deletes* checkboxes to make sure you allow data manipulation, as shown in Figure 10-6. Click *Finish*.

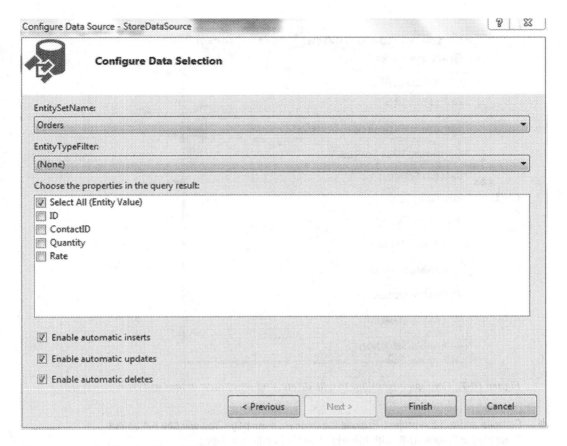

Figure 10-6. *Configuring Data Selection*

8. You will return to the *GridView* tasks menu. Select the *Enable Editing*, *Deleting*, and *Selection* options, as shown in Figure 10-7.

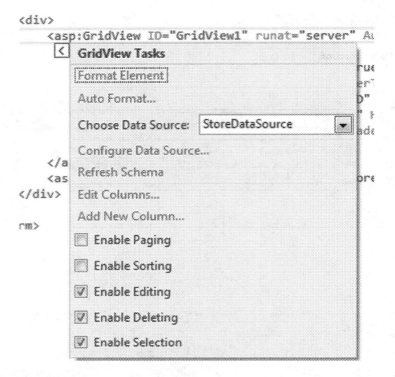

Figure 10-7. *Configuring options to edit, delete, and select data in the GridView*

9. Compile and run the project. Browse the Orders.aspx page. You will see the output illustrated in Figure 10-8, with the added ability to edit and delete.

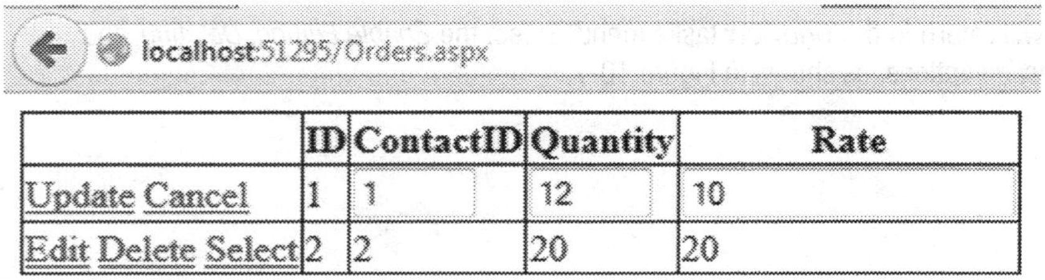

localhost:51295/Orders.aspx

	ID	ContactID	Quantity	Rate
Update Cancel	1	1	12	10
Edit Delete Select	2	2	20	20

Figure 10-8. *Results displayed in GridView*

How It Works

If you inspect the source closely, you will find out that it is similar to one that you wrote in the earlier `LinqDataSource` example, with the addition of few attributes to support data manipulation. This time, however, all of the code was generated automatically with the help of wizards and dialogs. The following code illustrates the generated source:

```
<div>
        <asp:GridView
            ID="GridView1"
            runat="server"
            AutoGenerateColumns="False"
            DataKeyNames="ID"
            DataSourceID="StoreDataSource">
            <Columns>
                <asp:CommandField ShowEditButton="True" ShowDeleteButton="True"
                ShowSelectButton="True"></asp:CommandField>
                <asp:BoundField DataField="ID" HeaderText="ID" ReadOnly="True"
                SortExpression="ID"></asp:BoundField>
                <asp:BoundField DataField="ContactID" HeaderText="ContactID"
                SortExpression="ContactID"></asp:BoundField>
                <asp:BoundField DataField="Quantity" HeaderText="Quantity"
                SortExpression="Quantity"></asp:BoundField>
                <asp:BoundField DataField="Rate" HeaderText="Rate"
                SortExpression="Rate"></asp:BoundField>
            </Columns>
        </asp:GridView>
        <asp:EntityDataSource
            runat="server"
            ID="StoreDataSource"
            DefaultContainerName="StoreEntities"
            ConnectionString="name=StoreEntities"
            EnableFlattening="False"
            EnableDelete="True"
            EnableInsert="True"
            EnableUpdate="True"
            EntitySetName="Orders">
        </asp:EntityDataSource>
    </div>
```

If you are wondering what happened to Insert, then know that `GridView` doesn't natively support inserts. You will now learn about the `DetailsView` control that could be used to allow inserts. That and more presentation controls are next.

Data-Bound Controls

Now that you have seen data source controls in action, let us explore some of the data presentation controls. You have already learned some of them with the `GridView` control in the previous section.

DataList

Like any other presentation control, the DataList control is capable of being associated with a data source like EntityDataSource. The DataList control requires an ItemTemplate element to be specified in order to determine the display format. The ItemTemplate element provides the look and feel to the data fields from the data source control. It provides great flexibility, and you can customize the look and feel of individual data elements. In addition, the control also provides some default templates. To generate an ItemTemplate quickly, you can click *Refresh Schema* from the Smart Task pane once you have associated the DataList control with the EntityDataSource. In addition, there is a *Property Builder* option available in the Smart Task pane that can be used to customize the template for display. This is illustrated in Figure 10-9.

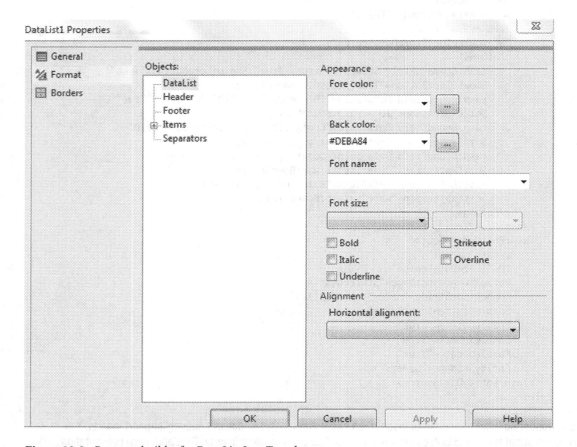

Figure 10-9. *Property builder for DataList ItemTemplate*

The following code illustrates an automatically generated DataList ItemTemplate for the StoreDataSource:

```
<asp:DataList ID="DataList1" runat="server" DataSourceID="StoreDataSource" BackColor="#DEBA84"
BorderColor="#DEBA84" BorderStyle="None" BorderWidth="1px" CellPadding="3" GridLines="Both"
CellSpacing="2" DataKeyField="ID" RepeatLayout="Flow">

        <FooterStyle BackColor="#F7DFB5" ForeColor="#8C4510"></FooterStyle>
```

```
        <HeaderStyle BackColor="#A55129" Font-Bold="True" ForeColor="White"></HeaderStyle>

        <ItemStyle BackColor="#FFF7E7" ForeColor="#8C4510"></ItemStyle>

        <ItemTemplate>
            ID:
            <asp:Label ID="IDLabel" runat="server" Text='<%# Eval("ID") %>' />
            <br />
            ContactID:
            <asp:Label ID="ContactIDLabel" runat="server" Text='<%# Eval("ContactID") %>' />
            <br />
            Quantity:
            <asp:Label ID="QuantityLabel" runat="server" Text='<%# Eval("Quantity") %>' />
            <br />
            Rate:
            <asp:Label ID="RateLabel" runat="server" Text='<%# Eval("Rate") %>' />
            <br />
            Contact:
            <asp:Label ID="ContactLabel" runat="server" Text='<%# Eval("Contact") %>' />
            <br />
            <br />
        </ItemTemplate>

        <SelectedItemStyle BackColor="#738A9C" Font-Bold="True" ForeColor="White">
        </SelectedItemStyle>
    </asp:DataList>
```

DetailsView

DetailsView is an interesting addition, and it can be used in conjunction with GridView to create a master detail format for display, editing, and creation of new records. Replacing the earlier example from the EntityDataSource control scenario to use now a DetailsView instead of the GridView, the following code will be generated:

```
<asp:DetailsView
            ID="DetailsView1"
            runat="server"
            Height="50px"
            Width="125px"
            AutoGenerateRows="False"
            DataKeyNames="ID"
            DataSourceID="StoreDataSource"
            AllowPaging="True">
    <Fields>
        <asp:BoundField DataField="ID" HeaderText="ID" ReadOnly="True"
        SortExpression="ID"></asp:BoundField>
        <asp:BoundField DataField="ContactID" HeaderText="ContactID"
        SortExpression="ContactID"></asp:BoundField>
        <asp:BoundField DataField="Quantity" HeaderText="Quantity"
        SortExpression="Quantity"></asp:BoundField>
        <asp:BoundField DataField="Rate" HeaderText="Rate"
        SortExpression="Rate"></asp:BoundField>
```

```
                    <asp:CommandField ShowInsertButton="True" ShowEditButton="True"
                    ShowDeleteButton="True"></asp:CommandField>
                </Fields>
            </asp:DetailsView>
            <asp:EntityDataSource
                runat="server"
                ID="StoreDataSource"
                DefaultContainerName="StoreEntities"
                ConnectionString="name=StoreEntities"
                EnableFlattening="False"
                EnableDelete="True"
                EnableInsert="True"
                EnableUpdate="True"
                EntitySetName="Orders">
            </asp:EntityDataSource>
```

In the DetailsView Smart Tasks, the following options are enabled, as shown in Figure 10-10.

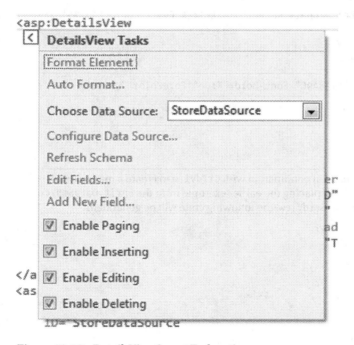

Figure 10-10. *DetailsView Smart Task options*

When you run the application, you will see a paged list of records that you can edit, update, and delete. In addition, you can click the *New* link to create a new record.

QueryExtender

While the filtering options in a data source control are quite robust, the filters can be a very complex combination of conditions that may not be easily constructed. The QueryExtender control augments a data source control to enable complex filters on data. You could specify different expressions within the QueryExtender to support searching in order to narrow the scope of results returned by the data source. The following code illustrates the usage of QueryExtender with a RangeExpression to search for a range of quantities in the Orders entity set:

```
<asp:QueryExtender
                ID="QueryExtender1"
                runat="server"
                TargetControlID="StoreDataSource">
                <asp:RangeExpression
                    DataField="Quantity"
                    MinType="Inclusive"
                    MaxType="Inclusive">
                    <asp:ControlParameter ControlID="From" />
                    <asp:ControlParameter ControlID="To" />
                </asp:RangeExpression>
            </asp:QueryExtender>
```

Now, all you need to do is to place two TextBox controls, named *From* and *To*, respectively, and a Button control, which allows the page to submit the entered filter conditions.

Like RangeExpression, there are additional expression elements that are provided by default. If the existing ones are not helpful to you, and you prefer writing your expressions in code, then you could also use a CustomExpression element inside the QueryExtender control to provide your own expression logic. CustomExpression lets you use a LINQ expression to filter data.

There are other presentation controls that are commonly used, such as the Chart control, which is used to display useful data visualizations. Although each presentation control provides you with the opportunity to connect to a data source and display data differently, you must evaluate the abilities based on the solution you are seeking to implement in your application.

In the forthcoming sections, you will learn about some of the interesting new additions to Web Forms provided by ASP.NET 4.5.

Strongly Typed Data Controls

You can truly appreciate this feature if you are a front-end developer and have been spending a lot of time working on data presentation controls. Often, you are frustrated by the lack of any IntelliSense and compile time check while wiring up the data-bound fields. You had to use the Eval and Bind functions along with the data-binding expression, none of which was very friendly. This is no longer the case with this new feature. Let's explore the enhancements with Strongly Typed Data Controls.

ItemType Attribute

ASP.NET 4.5 introduces the concept of Strongly Typed Data Controls, where a data presentation control provides support for declaring an associated entity type using the ItemType attribute. Once set, you will see the type properties available in IntelliSense while binding them to individual fields. Figure 10-11 illustrates a Repeater control showcasing IntelliSense while creating an ItemTemplate for the Order entity.

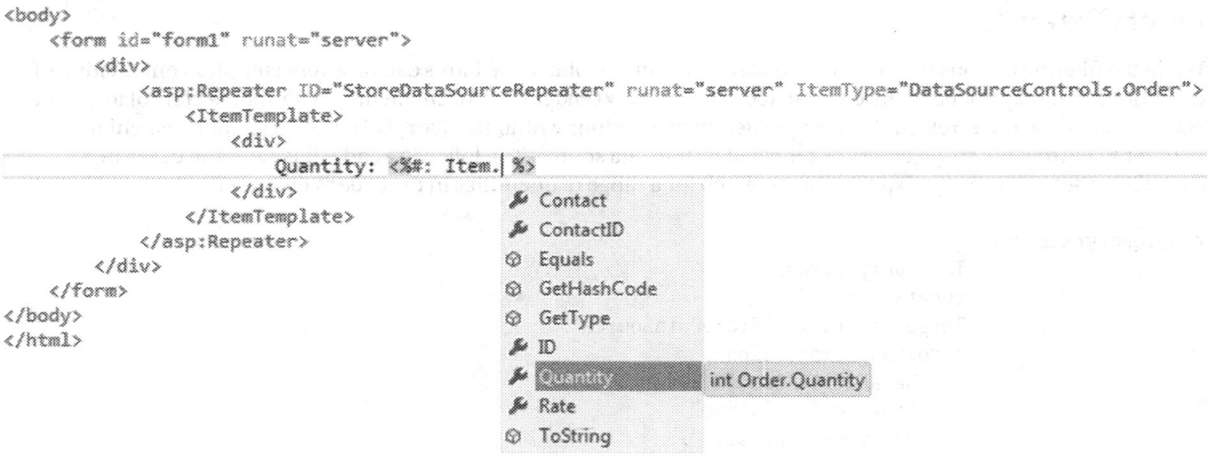

```
<body>
    <form id="form1" runat="server">
        <div>
            <asp:Repeater ID="StoreDataSourceRepeater" runat="server" ItemType="DataSourceControls.Order">
                <ItemTemplate>
                    <div>
                        Quantity: <%#: Item.| %>
```

```
                    </div>
                </ItemTemplate>
            </asp:Repeater>
        </div>
    </form>
</body>
</html>
```

🔧 Contact
🔧 ContactID
◉ Equals
◉ GetHashCode
◉ GetType
🔧 ID
🔧 Quantity   int Order.Quantity
🔧 Rate
◉ ToString

Figure 10-11. *ItemType attribute for Strongly Typed Data Presentation Controls*

HTML-Encoded Expression

It is important to HTML encode the data-binding expression to prevent usage of unsafe characters. Earlier, you had to encode a binding expression programmatically. In ASP.NET 4.5, you can simply use a colon (:) character before the expression to declare it as HTML encoded. Notice the use of this new feature in Figure 10-11.

Model Binding

Model binding is a feature introduced in ASP.NET MVC and extended to ASP.NET Web Forms due to its popularity. In model binding, a model acts as an intermediary to allow data to be posted from client to the data repository via the server. This allows data to be validated and processed before being retrieved or saved. It is the natural way in which ASP.NET MVC applications do data binding. This style of data binding is now available in ASP.NET Web Forms. In conjunction with Strongly Typed Controls, this feature brings easy-to-implement data-binding capabilities to ASP.NET 4.5 Web Forms.

In the earlier section, you learned how Strongly Typed Data Controls work. If you execute the code as presented in the example, however, you won't see any output. What is the reason for this? There is no associated data source. This is where model binding comes in and completes the implementation.

■ **Note** Data presentation controls along with data source controls were the most widely used mechanism for data binding since the advent of ASP.NET 2.0. Strongly Typed Controls and model-binding capabilities are new to ASP.NET 4.5 and provide an alternative, giving you an implementation choice in building data-driven websites. Strongly Typed Controls are easier to implement, and you should use these newer capabilities wherever there is an opportunity.

Extending the earlier example, if you add a SelectMethod attribute to the Repeater control, the implementation should look like this:

```
<div>
        <asp:Repeater
            ID="StoreDataSourceRepeater"
            SelectMethod="StoreDataSourceRepeater_GetData"
            runat="server"
            ItemType="DataSourceControls.Order">
            <ItemTemplate>
                <div>
                    Quantity: <%#: Item.Quantity %>
                </div>
            </ItemTemplate>
        </asp:Repeater>
</div>
```

When you type the *equal to* (=) symbol after adding the SelectMethod attribute, you will be prompted to generate a method. If you open the code behind the file, you will notice that a method with the name StoreDataSourceRepeater_GetData is already created with the return type specified as an enumerable collection of the Order type. Update the method to return all Orders from the StoreEntities data context.

```
public IEnumerable<DataSourceControls.Order> StoreDataSourceRepeater_GetData()
    {
        return context.Orders.AsEnumerable();
    }
```

Now, if you compile and run the project, you will see a list of Order Quantity properties being displayed without having to do any explicit data binding. All you did was to use a Strongly Typed Data Control and specify the SelectMethod attribute.

Value Providers

The earlier SelectMethod was simple, and there were no filter conditions. You could use *Value Providers* to filter your queries or provide data for inserts and updates. Value Providers act as a source of data for model binding. For example, you could modify the preceding SelectMethod with the following code:

```
public IEnumerable<DataSourceControls.Order> StoreDataSourceRepeater_GetData([QueryString("qty")]
int? quantity)
    {
        if(quantity.HasValue)
            return context.Orders.Where(order => order.Quantity > quantity).AsEnumerable();
        return context.Orders.AsEnumerable();
    }
```

With this additional condition, if there is a QueryString parameter "*qty*" in the URL, it will be used to filter the results further. The QueryStringAttribute is an example of a value provider. Additional providers could be FormAttribute, ControlAttribute, CookieAttribute, SessionAttribute, RouteDataAttribute, and ProfileAttribute. When you run the application, if you append your URL with the qty query string parameter (for example, http://.../Orders.aspx?qty=10), then all records with a quantity greater than the value specified in the parameter will be displayed. Pretty cool, isn't it? There are many more interesting additions to ASP.NET 4.5, but they would be outside the scope of this book. You can learn more about them, however, in the book *Beginning ASP.NET 4.5 in C#* by Matthew MacDonald (Apress, 2012).

This is all you need to know to start building data-driven websites in ASP.NET 4.5. Next, you will explore some of the data-binding concepts in ASP.NET MVC 4.

Data-Binding in ASP.NET MVC 4

You have seen ASP.NET MVC 4 in action in several chapters in this book. You know how controllers function and how, along with Entity Framework, ASP.NET MVC 4 helps you to build modern data-driven Web applications. Nevertheless, you can always learn more from the ASP.NET MVC home page at http://asp.net/mvc.

In this section, you will explore some of the data-binding concepts using the *Razor view engine*. Although it is independent of ASP.NET MVC, it was introduced concurrently with it and it is steadily becoming the preferred choice when it comes to building a data-driven user interface in the framework.

Razor View Engine

Razor is a compact view engine with a very easy-to-learn syntax. You can quickly build a UI with data elements from a Model class. It can be built in isolation, making it suitable for unit testing. These unique features makes it a very good tool to use in ASP.NET MVC. First introduced in ASP.NET MVC 3, it continues to gain popularity among developers. If you recall the DataDrivenWebSite project you created in Chapter 7, you know that ASP.NET MVC 4 is capable of automatically generating the View based on the Model. You created the Order model based on the Orders table in the Store database, and the associated views were generated in the Order folder under Views, as shown in Figure 10-12.

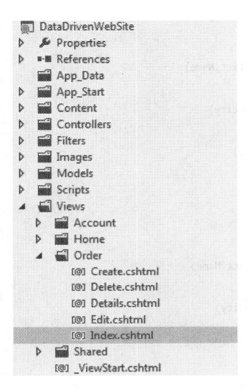

Figure 10-12. *Automatically generated Order View using the controller builder feature in ASP.NET MVC 4*

Razor views are created as .cshtml files for a Visual C# ASP.NET MVC 4 project. If you open the Index.cshtml file under the Order folder, you will notice the following code structure:

```
@model IEnumerable<DataDrivenWebSite.Order>
```

1. First, the associated model is declared on the top of the page.

2. In Razor, a code block starts with an @ character. Razor is aware of C#/VB semantics, so the code blocks need not be explicitly closed.

3. This is followed by the Create action link that will redirect you to the Create View.

   ```
   <p>
       @Html.ActionLink("Create New", "Create")
   </p>
   ```

4. The action link is followed by a table that displays all of the order records in the store.

   a. The ActionLink method will render a hyperlink on the page to allow users to be redirected to the page for creating new orders.

```
<table>
    <tr>
        <th>
            @Html.DisplayNameFor(model => model.Contact.Name)
        </th>
        <th>
            @Html.DisplayNameFor(model => model.Quantity)
        </th>
        <th>
            @Html.DisplayNameFor(model => model.Rate)
        </th>
        <th></th>
    </tr>

@foreach (var item in Model) {
    <tr>
        <td>
            @Html.DisplayFor(modelItem => item.Contact.Name)
        </td>
        <td>
            @Html.DisplayFor(modelItem => item.Quantity)
        </td>
        <td>
            @Html.DisplayFor(modelItem => item.Rate)
        </td>
        <td>
            @Html.ActionLink("Edit", "Edit", new { id=item.ID }) |
            @Html.ActionLink("Details", "Details", new { id=item.ID }) |
            @Html.ActionLink("Delete", "Delete", new { id=item.ID })
        </td>
    </tr>
}

</table>
```

b. A couple of methods are worth noting here: the DisplayNameFor and the DisplayFor. The DisplayNameFor displays the column header, and the DisplayFor is inside the loop displaying data in each cell.

5. The data is returned from the Controller Index action:

```
public ActionResult Index()
        {
            var orders = db.Orders.Include(o => o.Contact);
            return View(orders.ToList());
        }
```

When you run the project and browse the Order route (http://..<server>/Order), the details will be displayed, as shown in Figure 10-13.

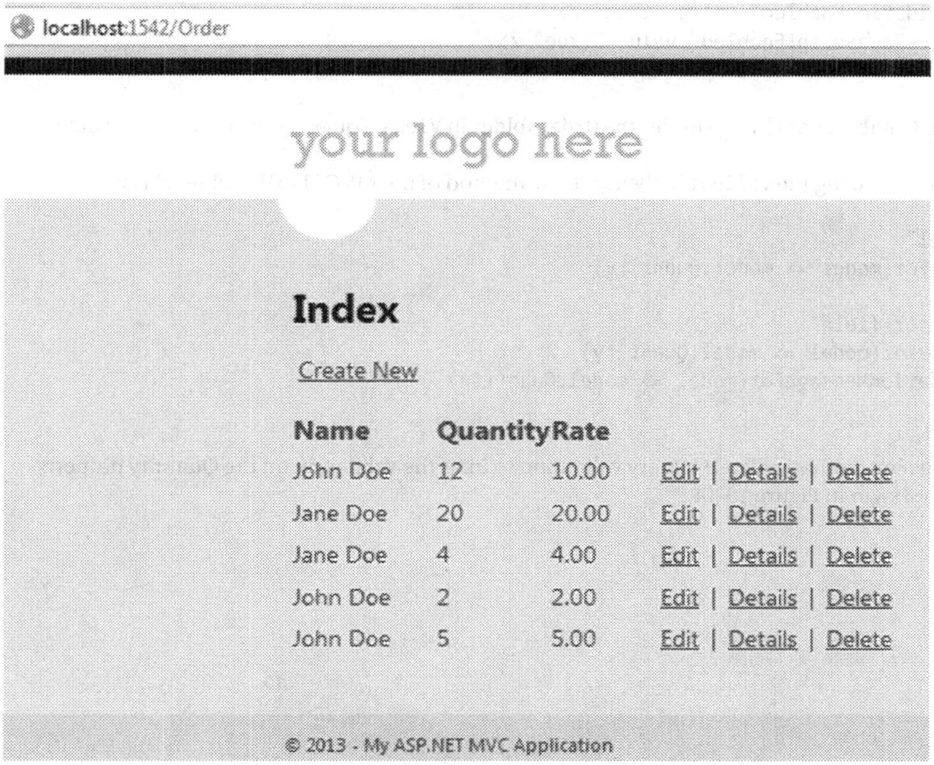

Figure 10-13. *Display Order data using an ASP.NET MVC 4 application*

Unobtrusive JavaScript

In a typical Web application, if you intend to use client-side validation, you will end up generating a clumsy-looking page with lot of JavaScript rendered to support it. There is an *Unobtrusive* feature in ASP.NET MVC 4, which allows JavaScript code to remain clean and in isolation without cluttering the actual page where it is referenced. For validations, it supports external validator plug-ins, like *Jquery*, with well-known attributes in HTML 5 scripts.

■ **Note** If you are interested in learning more about Unobtrusive JavaScript, then we would recommend reading the original article on the subject by Stuart Langridge at www.kryogenix.org/code/browser/aqlists/.

To enable Unobtrusive JavaScript, you first need to set an AppSettings key in your Web.config file called UnobtrusiveJavaScriptEnabled.

```
<appSettings>
    <add key="webpages:Version" value="2.0.0.0" />
    <add key="webpages:Enabled" value="false" />
    <add key="PreserveLoginUrl" value="true" />
```

```
      <add key="ClientValidationEnabled" value="true" />
      <add key="UnobtrusiveJavaScriptEnabled" value="true" />
  </appSettings>
```

Now, if you explore the Create.cshtml page under the Order folder in Views, you will see methods for validating input controls.

Input controls are validated using the ValidationMessageFor method of the MVC HTML Helper class:

```
<div class="editor-label">
        @Html.LabelFor(model => model.Quantity)
      </div>
      <div class="editor-field">
          @Html.EditorFor(model => model.Quantity)
          @Html.ValidationMessageFor(model => model.Quantity)
      </div>
```

The ValidationMessageFor method will use JQuery validation to infer the validation on the Quantity property and display the message, as shown in Figure 10-14.

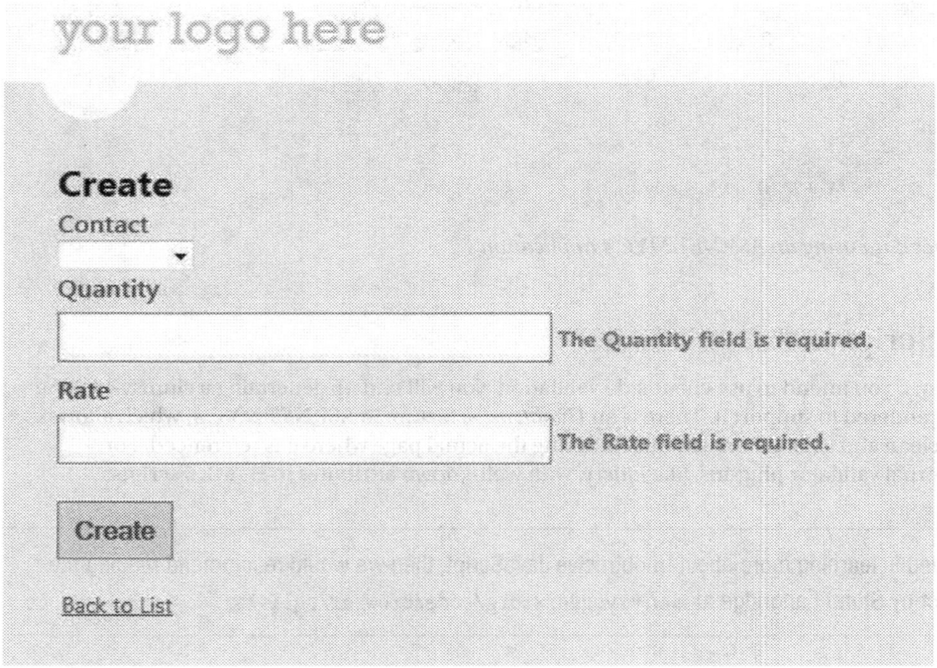

Figure 10-14. *Unobtrusive JavaScript validation*

You will notice that the bundled JQuery validation script is added to the `Scripts` section at the bottom of the page:

```
@section Scripts {
    @Scripts.Render("~/bundles/jqueryval")
}
```

▓ **Note** *Bundling* and *minification* are relatively new concepts that have been added to ASP.NET 4.5. Bundling allows you to bundle multiple script files into one. Minification shrinks the script file sizes by removing whitespace and irrelevant characters. The preceding Scripts section renders a bundled script.

If you look at the source of the rendered `Create` view in a browser, you will see that there isn't any cluttered JavaScript that has been rendered on the page, and it looks clean and crisp.

```
<div class="editor-label">
        <label for="Quantity">Quantity</label>
    </div>
    <div class="editor-field">
        <input class="text-box single-line" data-val="true" data-val-number="The field Quantity
        must be a number." data-val-required="The Quantity field is required." id="Quantity"
        name="Quantity" type="number" value="" />
        <span class="field-validation-valid" data-valmsg-for="Quantity" data-valmsg-
        replace="true"></span>
    </div>

    <div class="editor-label">
        <label for="Rate">Rate</label>
    </div>
    <div class="editor-field">
        <input class="text-box single-line" data-val="true" data-val-number="The field Rate must
        be a number." data-val-required="The Rate field is required." id="Rate" name="Rate"
        type="text" value="" />
        <span class="field-validation-valid" data-valmsg-for="Rate" data-valmsg-
        replace="true"></span>
    </div>
```

The data validation attributes are recognized by Jquery, and the inputs are accordingly validated.

Asynchronous Display with Ajax

There are scenarios where you may be dealing with a large data set or a complex processing operation that takes a long time to return results. In such scenarios, it's advantageous not to keep users waiting for the data to be fetched before proceeding to the next operation. This is made possible by fetching the data asynchronously from a Web service or a controller using Ajax. The following code snippet illustrates the use of JQuery Ajax to retrieve data asynchronously from a controller action.

```
<script>
    $.ajax({
        type: 'GET',
        url: '/Order/Details/2',
        success: function (result) {
            //TODO: Process result
        },
        error: function (xhr, status, error) {
            alert('error', error);
        }
    });
</script>
```

On successful processing, the result variable holds the data returned by the controller action. In this example, you would see the Order model properties being returned, and you can place the values returned in an HTML control like literal or label.

The preceding code is probably not an ideal representation of a time-consuming operation. Nevertheless, it illustrates how you can run a GET operation using the controller action. In the Order controller, your method would appear as follows:

```
public ActionResult Details(int id = 0)
    {
        Order order = db.Orders.Find(id);
        return Json(order, JsonRequestBehavior.AllowGet);
    }
```

Notice the use of the JsonRequestBehavior enum. It allows GET requests from the client. The controller action returns a JSON (JavaScript Object Notation) result that is parsed by the client asynchronously and displayed in the page once processing is complete. Users can continue to work on other areas of the page, and they don't have to wait on the results to be returned.

Summary

This chapter completes the cycle of learning to build data-driven websites. While the earlier chapters were focused on fetching data from repositories, this chapter concentrated on data presentation. You learned about the new data source controls and how they work with the data presentation controls to allow you to display data in a highly customized fashion and also perform data manipulations. You also learned about some of the new data-binding features in ASP.NET 4.5, including Strongly Typed Controls and model binding. In addition, you explored how data binding is performed in ASP.NET MVC 4.

In the next chapter, you will learn about the concept of Dynamic Data in ASP.NET 4.5.

CHAPTER 11

■ ■ ■

Building Extensible Data-Driven Web Applications Using Dynamic Data

To be honest, many front-end developers in the world of .NET hate it when it comes to writing queries against a database and figuring out if the data is consistent with the state of the application. They are more content working within the limits of Visual Studio and would line up to get their hands on a tool that would let them access relational data without having to write SQL queries. They are also pretty happy operating on data in memory using their language of choice, be it C#, VB, or LINQ, but not SQL. This is primarily due to the fact that each native relational database has its own flavor of SQL, and it is simply overwhelming to try and learn each one of them.

The fact that ORM tools have become so popular is a testament to the fact that developers worldwide are looking for tools and frameworks that can create a data layer nearly automatically by mapping the relational database tables with a conceptual model. It then would become fairly easy for them to program against the model classes, as the rest of the heavy work on the database would be dealt with by the tool.

In ASP.NET, apart from the support for Entity Framework and other ORM tools like LINQ to SQL, there is another fascinating feature that allows you to create data-driven websites automatically by deriving the *User Interface (UI)* from the data context generated by Entity Framework. This feature is called *ASP.NET Dynamic Data*, and it has been around since version 3.5 of .NET Framework. With Dynamic Data, you can easily create views for your database tables (with minimal code) and start performing CRUD operations on them. Sound exciting? In this chapter, you will learn about the different ways of leveraging ASP.NET Dynamic Data.

We will cover the following in this chapter:

- How ASP.NET Dynamic Data works.

- How to use Dynamic Data in data-bound controls.

- How to use Dynamic Data scaffolding.

ASP.NET Dynamic Data is a concept that is not discussed very often, as there are no major changes from .NET Framework 4 to 4.5. However, it is extremely useful if you are seeking to create a quick view of your database tables and provide an interface with which administrators can add and update data.

Dynamic Data Layers

ASP.NET Dynamic Data leverages Entity Framework features, and it allows you to create Dynamic views for data elements like rows, fields, and tables. The Dynamic views let you display and edit data stored in these data elements. Now let's find out how Dynamic Data actually works with different layers within your application.

Figure 11-1 illustrates the different templates available in ASP.NET Dynamic Data Entity websites, which are used to create a view for your data elements and let you perform CRUD operations using the ADO.NET *EDM (Entity Data Model)* and ASP.NET routing features.

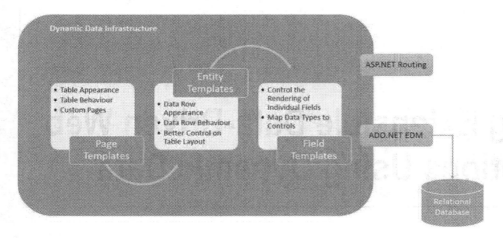

Figure 11-1. *Dynamic Data layers*

As you can see in the figure, the *Field Templates* provide a set of controls that map the Entity Model types with ASP.NET controls. Field Templates are the most basic unit of Dynamic Data websites, and they are used internally by Entity Templates for creating row-level UI elements.

Entity Templates provide the UI for data row elements, and they provide better control for manipulating the default table layout.

Page Templates contain pages for high-level table views and appearance. You can customize the appearance of all tables by modifying the Default pages or do this for specific tables by using *Custom Pages*. Custom Pages are discussed later in this chapter.

Visual Studio 2012 provides a Scaffolding Template for building ASP.NET Dynamic Data websites. First, we'll see Dynamic Data in action using this Scaffolding Template, and then we will explore the internals to learn how Dynamic Data really works.

■ **Note**   ASP.NET Dynamic Data capabilities are available with the System.Web.DynamicData assembly.

Dynamic Data Scaffolding

Scaffolding is a quick and dirty way of demonstrating the capabilities of the feature in question. Microsoft has truly implemented this to the developer's advantage by providing basic skeletons for various capabilities of .NET Framework 4.5, which allows them to build functional prototypes that can evolve through customizations as needed.

Dynamic Data is no exception. There is a Scaffolding Template that lets you create Dynamic Data-driven websites with minimal coding. It is extensible, so once you learn how it works, you can master it by customizing the artifacts based on your needs.

TRY IT OUT: CREATE AN EXTENSIBLE DATA-DRIVEN WEBSITE USING ASP.NET DYNAMIC DATA

Let's quickly explore the steps required to create an ASP.NET 4.5 Dynamic Data Web Application; after that, you will learn just how it works. Regarding prerequisites, the steps listed in this exercise will work with the Visual Studio 2012 Express Web through Ultimate editions, so you should be able to use whichever one is available to you.

■ **Note** We will use the Store database that we have been using for all of the exercises in this book.

---

1. Launch your instance of Visual Studio 2012 and create a new project. In the *New Project* dialog, Select *ASP.NET Dynamic Data Web Application* on the *Web* tab under Visual C# root, as shown in Figure 11-2.

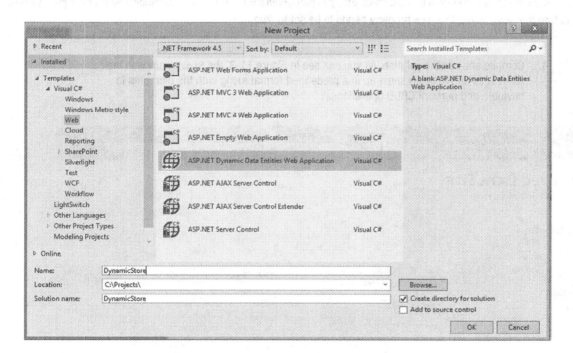

Figure 11-2. *New ASP.NET Dynamic Data Entities Web Application Project*

2. Use the Store database to create an EDM in the project using Entity Framework. The steps need no illustration. If necessary, you may revisit the exercises in Chapter 8.

3. Open the `Global.asax.cs` file. You will see a bunch of generated code with commented instructions. The file hosts the most important instructions to connect to the data context and specify routing commands. Locate the `RegisterRoutes` method and place the following code inside it:

```
DefaultModel.RegisterContext(typeof(StoreEntities), new ContextConfiguration() {
ScaffoldAllTables = true });

                routes.Add(new DynamicDataRoute("{table}/{action}.aspx")
                {
                        Constraints = new RouteValueDictionary(new { action =
"List|Details|Edit|Insert" }),
                        Model = DefaultModel
                });
```

■ **Note** `StoreEntities` is the data context class that you just generated in the `Store` database using Entity Framework. Also note that the `ScaffoldAllTables` property needs to be set to *true*.

---

4. Compile and run the solution. As you can see in Figure 11-3, the `Store` database tables (`Contacts` and `Orders`) show up in a predefined format along with the elements to navigate and perform CRUD operations.

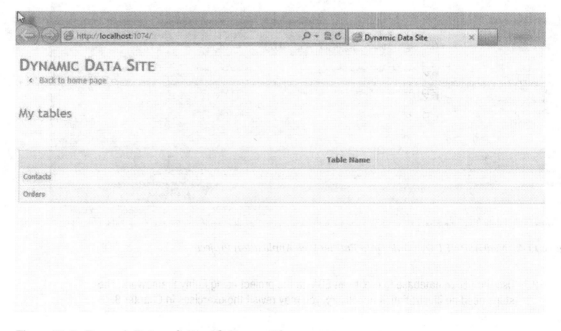

Figure 11-3. *Dynamic Data website with Store entities*

5. Click the Contacts table link, and it will show the records that you have entered in the table (see Figure 11-4).

DYNAMIC DATA SITE
‹ Back to home page

Contacts

	Name	Email	State	Orders
Edit Delete Details	John Doe		CA	View Orders
Edit Delete Details	Jane Doe		AZ	View Orders

✦ Insert new item

Figure 11-4. *Contacts table entries*

6. To create a new item, click the *Insert new item* link and it will take you to a dynamically generated form that shows all of the field values for creating a new Contact, as shown in Figure 11-5.

Figure 11-5. *Creating new Contact*

7. Create a new Contact with the *Name* "Eric Doe" and *State* "AZ" and click *Insert*. You will be returned to the *Contacts* page, and you will see the new contact added and displayed in the *Contacts* grid. Click the *View Orders* link of the newly created Contact Eric Doe. It will display a message indicating that no associated orders are available for the contact, since it is newly created, as illustrated in Figure 11-6.

205

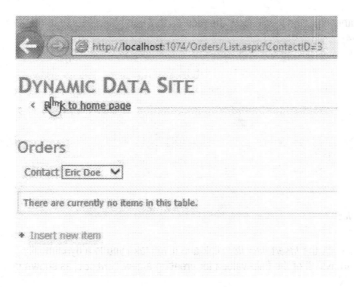

Figure 11-6. Contact Orders

■ **Note** The URL uses action verbs as commands that leverage the ASP.NET routing module.

---

8. Click *Insert new item* in the Orders page. Enter values for *Quantity* and *Rate*. Notice that the *Contact* field is already selected as Eric (see Figure 11-7). Click *Insert*.

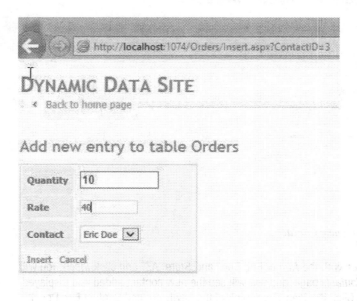

Figure 11-7. Creating a new Order

9. You will now get redirected to the *Orders* page and see the Order created for the Contact Eric Doe. There is a *Contact* drop-down at the top of the page that you can use that to filter the results in the *Orders* grid. You can also perform *Edit* and *Delete* operations by clicking the respective links in the grid (See Figure 11-8).

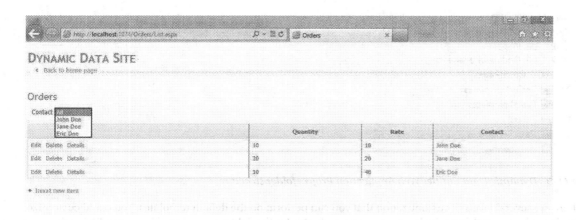

Figure 11-8. *Filtering Orders by Contact*

■ **Note** In addition to Page, Field, and Entity Templates, the Dynamic Data Scaffolding Template also contains Filter Templates that allow you to filter records based on a specific criterion, as shown in Figure 11-8. The Filter Templates allow filters in Boolean, Enumeration, and Foreign Key Field relationships.

Setting aside for a moment the default naming conventions for pages and tables, the template is extremely useful for navigating and manipulating data structures from a relational database. You have successfully entered data and performed modifications without actually writing any code for the views.

Your next question is probably how to manipulate the default Scaffolding Template to create views that actually give it the behavior and appearance of your choice. In the next section, we explore how to do just that.

Customizing the Scaffolding Templates

If you expand your solution structure, you will notice that there is a Dynamic Data folder, as illustrated in Figure 11-9. The folder again contains multiple subfolders representing the presentation- and entity-tier elements of ASP.NET Dynamic Data.

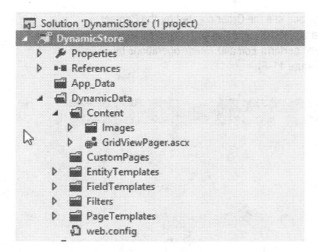

Figure 11-9. Dynamic Data Entities Web Application Project folder structure

There are several levels of customization that you can perform on the default templates. You could customize the table behavior by modifying the Page Templates or do this for the field-specific behavior by modifying the Field Templates. You could also choose to customize the behavior of specific tables or the template as a whole, in which case the changes are applied to all the tables in the database.

The page-level templates are available under the *Page Templates* folder in the ASP.NET Dynamic Data Entities Web Application Project. If you want to customize the appearance of all of the entities, then edit the files under this folder to change the behavior. For example, if you want to change the way the heading is displayed on all of the table pages, modify the List.aspx page in the folder to change the heading, as shown in Figure 11-10.

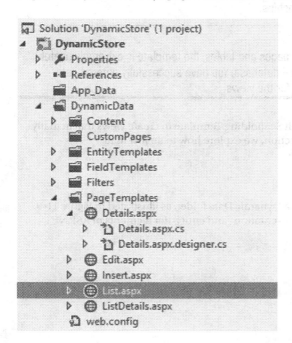

Figure 11-10. Modifyinsg the List.aspx page to customize the appearance of the header in all table pages

In a similar fashion, if you want to change the behavior of a text box in edit mode, then you could do that in the Text_Edit.ascx file under the FieldTemplates folder. However, these changes are applied globally.

There is also the possibility that you might want to change the behavior and appearance of individual entities mapped to the database tables based on a particular condition. Read the following note carefully to understand the rules of customizing the behavior of individual tables.

■ **Note** Identify the Entity Set name of the mapped entity in the dmx file for the table whose behavior you want to customize; then, create a folder with the Entity Set name in the Custom Pages folder in your Dynamic Data project. This is generally a pluralized name for the Entity unless specified otherwise.

Now let's explore the steps required to customize table-specific behavior.

TRY IT OUT: CUSTOMIZE THE APPEARANCE OF THE ORDERS TABLE USING DYNAMIC DATA SCAFFOLDING CUSTOMIZATION

Follow these steps to customize the behavior or appearance of the Orders table:

1. Create a folder called Orders under the CustomPages folder in your Dynamic Data Entities Web Application Project. You can now create your customized template pages inside this folder, as shown in Figure 11-11.

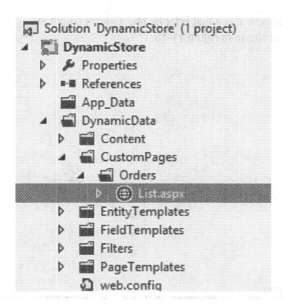

Figure 11-11. Dynamic Data Custom Pages

2. To customize the appearance of the Orders list page, create a page named List.aspx under the newly created Orders folder. Make sure to set the Site.Master as the master page.

3. Copy the contents of the List.aspx page from under PageTemplates/List.aspx. Copy the markup and the code behind contents without changing the namespace of the newly created page.

4. The Orders page has a Contact filter. To make it more descriptive, add the text *Filter By* in the QueryFilterRepeater control's Label ItemTemplate, as shown in Figure 11-12.

```
<asp:UpdatePanel ID="UpdatePanel1" runat="server">
    <ContentTemplate>
        <div class="DD">
            <asp:ValidationSummary ID="ValidationSummary1" runat="server" EnableClientScript="true"
                HeaderText="List of validation errors" CssClass="DDValidator" />
            <asp:DynamicValidator runat="server" ID="GridViewValidator" ControlToValidate="GridView1" Display="None" CssCla

            <asp:QueryableFilterRepeater runat="server" ID="FilterRepeater">
                <ItemTemplate>
                    <asp:Label ID="Label1" runat="server" Text='<%# string.Format("Filter By {0}",Eval("DisplayName")) %>'
                    <asp:DynamicFilter runat="server" ID="DynamicFilter" OnFilterChanged="DynamicFilter_FilterChanged" /><b
                </ItemTemplate>
            </asp:QueryableFilterRepeater>
            <br />
        </div>
```

Figure 11-12. *Modifying the appearance of the Orders table only*

5. Compile and run the project. You will now notice that Filter By text appears before the Contact filter in the Orders page, as shown in Figure 11-13.

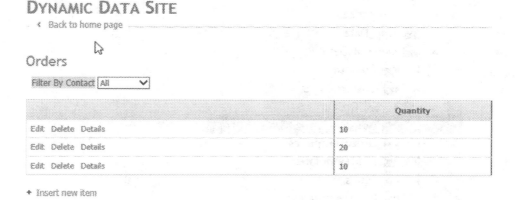

Figure 11-13. *Updated filter by label*

You have now successfully customized table-specific appearance using the Dynamic Data scaffolding customization features. If you look at your Dynamic Data project, you will notice that there is also an `EntityTemplates` folder. This folder contains the files for displaying rows in the page grids. You can customize the row-level behavior by modifying the pages in this folder.

▓ **Note** `EntityTemplates` can also be used in your Custom Pages.

Template Behaviors

The templates provide three modes in which you can run your customizations:

1. **Display:** Appearance when content is displayed in the Dynamic website.

2. **Edit:** Appearance and behavior when the content is edited.

3. **Insert:** Appearance and behavior when new records are inserted.

You can customize the specific display, edit, and insert behavior of tables and rows using Page and Entity Templates. Field Templates provide default mappings for display and edit (which also doubles as insert).

So far, you have learned how the Scaffolding Templates can be customized to modify default and table-specific behavior. In the next section, you will explore how this works and also how routing works with Dynamic Data.

How Dynamic Data Works

Now that you know how to use Dynamic Data, we will look at the internals of the ASP.NET Dynamic Data infrastructure.

MetaModel

The `System.Web.DynamicData` namespace contains a class called `MetaModel`, which is responsible for associating one or more databases used by your ASP.NET Dynamic Data Application. It is the conduit between the Entity Model created using Entity Framework or LINQ to SQL and Dynamic views generated by ASP.NET Dynamic Data. Let's go back and explore the code generated by the Scaffolding Template inside the `Global.asax` file. The file contains a static default instance of the `MetaModel` class, and it also has a property representing the default `MetaModel` instance.

```
private static MetaModel s_defaultModel = new MetaModel();
        public static MetaModel DefaultModel
        {
            get
            {
                return s_defaultModel;
            }
        }
```

You register one or more data context classes with this instance of the `MetaModel` representing the databases on which you will operate using the Dynamic Data infrastructure. You do this inside the `RegisterRoutes` method, which is called once the application is loaded for the first time. The `MetaModel` class provides a `RegisterContext` method for the purpose shown in the following code snippet:

```
DefaultModel.RegisterContext(typeof(StoreEntities), new ContextConfiguration()
{ ScaffoldAllTables = true });
```

In our example, we associated the StoreEntities data context class that was generated on the Store database using the Entity Designer with the Dynamic Data MetaModel. One important thing to note here is the ScaffoldAllTables property. You may choose to let the template create Dynamic views for all tables or for specific tables only.

If the ScaffoldAllTables is set to *true*, then Dynamic Data will take all of the entities into consideration. If you want to scaffold a selected few tables only, then set this property to *false*. Create a partial class for the entity you want to scaffold, and use the ScaffoldTableAttribute on it. It will be picked up by the Dynamic Data infrastructure, and Dynamic views will be generated only for the tables on which the ScaffoldTableAttribute is set. In our example, you can put the ScaffoldTables attribute on the generated entities in the Store.Designer.cs file.

▩ **Note**   In addition to ScaffoldTables, there is also a ScaffoldColumns attribute that can be used to specify whether a Data Column participates in scaffolding.

Routing

ASP.NET Dynamic Data uses the built-in routing infrastructure to route commands for CRUD operations on tables. There are two ways to use the routing infrastructure:

1. Default mode, where different actions are handled by different pages of the Scaffolding Template. The following code block illustrates the default mode in the RegisterRoutes method:

```
routes.Add(new DynamicDataRoute("{table}/{action}.aspx")
          {
                  Constraints = new RouteValueDictionary(new { action =
"List|Details|Edit|Insert" }),
                  Model = DefaultModel
          });
```

2. Combined-page mode, where all of the actions are handled by a single page. The following code illustrates this mode:

```
routes.Add(new DynamicDataRoute("{table}/ListDetails.aspx")
          {
              Action = PageAction.List,
              ViewName = "ListDetails",
              Model = DefaultModel
          });

routes.Add(new DynamicDataRoute("{table}/ListDetails.aspx")
          {
              Action = PageAction.Details,
              ViewName = "ListDetails",
              Model = DefaultModel
          });
```

■ **Note**   Although either of the modes could be used for routing, the default mode is preferred for its ability to separate the handling of the commands cleanly. The combined-page mode could potentially require you to do a lot of customization.

Dynamic Data in Existing Controls

The System.Web.DynamicData assembly provides several artifacts, including the requisite controls (like DynamicControl to generate Dynamic views), and extension methods that allow leveraging Dynamic Data functionality in existing ASP.NET controls.

For example, if you add a reference to the System.Web.DynamicData assembly in your project, controls like GridView and FormView will have an extension method, SetMetaTable, available to them, allowing Dynamic table data to be displayed automatically in these controls.

The following code inside the Details.aspx page in the PageTemplates folder illustrates the use of Dynamic controls:

```
protected void Page_Init(object sender, EventArgs e)
    {
        table = DynamicDataRouteHandler.GetRequestMetaTable(Context);
        FormView1.SetMetaTable(table);
        DetailsDataSource.EntityTypeFilter = table.EntityType.Name;
    }
```

FormView1 is a FormView control that displays the details of the selected data row.

Summary

ASP.NET Dynamic Data is an interesting concept that allows you to write minimal code in order to build data-driven applications relatively quickly. In this chapter, you learned how the Dynamic Data Scaffolding Template gives you quick access to your database tables and lets you perform CRUD operations with just a few lines of code. You also learned about the internals of the Dynamic Data infrastructure and how you can choose to create views for tables selectively in the Scaffolding Template. Then, you learned how Dynamic Data capabilities can be extended to existing ASP.NET controls.

In the next chapter, you will learn about some real-world issues that you will encounter while building data-driven websites and the best practices you can use to overcome these issues.

CHAPTER 12

■ ■ ■

Best Practices and Techniques in Building Data-Driven Websites

In reaching this point, you have gained a firm understanding of building modern data-driven Web applications using some of the key new features in .NET Framework. Since its 2.0 avatar, continuous enhancements in .NET Framework have been driven by extracting many of the heavy lifting operations you perform fetching and manipulating data through Web applications. The idea behind these enhancements was to help you focus on core business functionalities. In parallel, the developer community has invested significant time trying to create best practices from what they learned by using these new features in real-world scenarios.

In this chapter, you will learn some of these best practices and useful techniques to deal with the issues involved in building data-driven applications.

Specifically, we are going to cover the following:

- What are the best practices in using Entity Framework as a data access layer?

- How can you ensure data consistency using the Unit of Work pattern?

- How do you handle concurrency issues?

- How can you perform historical debugging using the IntelliTrace tool?

The best practices are largely driven by experiences from the developer community in implementing Entity Framework. The previous book in the series, *Beginning ASP.NET 2.0 Databases, 2nd Edition*, by Damien Foggon (Apress, 2006), covers some useful techniques that are generally applicable to building data-driven websites. The ones discussed in this chapter are in the context of Entity Framework. However, they can also be utilized with other object-relational mapping (ORM) tools that can be used to build a data layer.

Data Access Layer Patterns

Entity Framework abstracts most of the mundane work of transforming conceptual queries into database-specific CRUD operations, saving you hours of hard work. If not designed and implemented correctly, however, it can lead to severe performance bottlenecks. Over the years, technologists have learned a lot from enterprise-scale Entity Framework implementations, and their knowledge has resulted in the formulation of patterns to guide teams in following best practices while implementing Entity Framework as a data access layer.

In this section, you will learn about the *Repository Pattern*, which allows you to abstract your ORM implementation out from the rest of your application code. Before you do that, however, let's review the steps necessary to isolate the Entity Models in a separate project for you to be able to share them across different layers in your application.

Isolating the Data Layer and Entity Models

In Chapter 7, you learned that creating a new ADO.NET Entity Data Model from an existing database automatically generates the POCO classes along with the DbContext class. It is a good practice, however, to keep the POCO classes isolated so that they can be shared across layers and easily extended. This can be achieved by customizing the T4 template files responsible for generating the POCO classes. Recall that in the DataDrivenWebSite ASP.NET MVC 4 project from Chapter 7, there are two T4 template files added to the project once the Store ADO.NET EDM file is added. They are the Store.Context.tt and Store.tt files, which represent the templates for generating the DbContext and POCO classes, respectively. Let's re-create this project now a bit differently so that the data access layer and models are isolated in their self-contained projects, and the website can refer to them in the Controller classes. Follow these steps:

1. Create a Visual C# ASP.NET MVC 4 Web application project using your instance of Visual Studio 2012. This requires no illustration, since you had been creating MVC projects throughout this book.

2. Create two Visual C# Class Library projects named DataAccess and Entities in the solution.

3. Add a new ADO.NET Entity Data Model named Store.edmx in the DataAccess project, and generate the EDM from the Store database, again using the familiar steps.

4. Now comes the tricky part: Open the location of the EDMX file in File Explorer and move the Store.tt and generated POCO class files (Order.cs and Contact.cs in this case) to the Entities project folder.

5. Right-click the Entities project in *Solution Explorer* and select *Add Existing Item* from the context menu. Add the Model.tt and POCO class files. Remove reference to the Store.tt file from the DataAccess project. Save your solution.

6. Open the Store.tt file in the Entities project and update the inputFile parameter to set the following path:

   ```
   const string inputFile = @"..\DataAccess\Store.edmx";
   ```

This is the path of the EDMX file, which is under the DataAccess project.

7. Run the *Custom Tool* and build the Entities project. *Add reference* of Entities assembly in DataAccess. Resolve references of the POCO classes in the Store DbContext file.

8. Build the solution. Add the DataAccess and Entities assembly references to the DataDrivenWebSite project. The solution structure will look like the one shown in Figure 12-1.

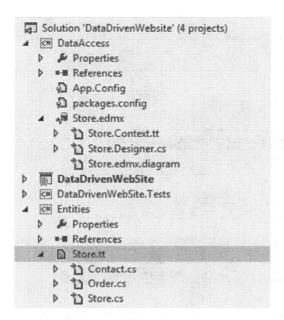

Figure 12-1. *Solution structure after creating the DataAccess and Entities projects*

9. Now you can create the OrderController by right-clicking the Controller folder in the DataDrivenWebSite project and clicking *Add Controller*. In the *Add Controller* dialog, you can get the Order model from Entities and the DbContext references from the DataAccess project, as shown in Figure 12-2. This is the only change from what you did in Chapter 7.

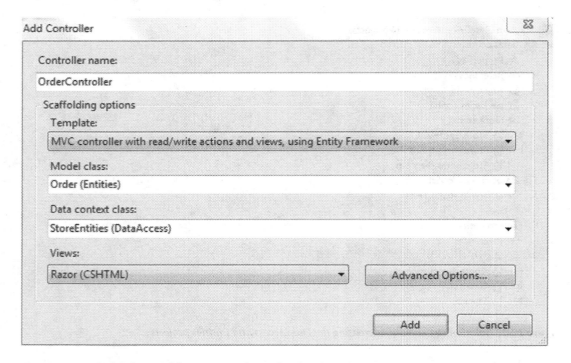

Figure 12-2. *Model class and data context class references from the Entities and DataAccess projects, respectively*

Compile and run the Web application. Navigate to Order, and you will see the expected result of all orders displayed.

The steps you performed above are significant in isolating the data layer and POCO classes. This paves the way for implementing the repository pattern that you will learn next. You now have successfully taken the first step towards creating a truly decoupled data access layer!

Repository Pattern

Not only is a truly robust data access layer decoupled, but it is also abstracted from the business logic of the application. This abstraction provides you with the ability to focus on the core functionalities of the application without having to worry too much about the persistence mechanism. This is also important from the testability perspective of the data access layer. You may want to write unit tests against the data access layer but don't want the tests to hit the Entity Framework DbContext and the associated persistence store. Your tests could point to a mocked persistence store if a repository pattern is implemented.

A basic repository pattern is not hard to implement. You need some additional artifacts created in the DataAccess project. The first item you will need to build is the repository contracts. Ideally, each entity should be represented by a repository to allow CRUD operations to be performed on it in isolation. For example, the following interface defines the operations for the OrderRepository:

```
public interface IOrderRepository : IDisposable
    {
        public IEnumerable<Order> GetAllOrders();
        public Order GetByOrderId(int orderId);
```

```
    public void Create(Order order);
    public void Update(Order order);
    public void Delete(int orderId);
}
```

▓ **Note**   You must create a separate project named `Repository` to host all of the common repository interfaces, and the concrete implementation could be in the `DataAccess` project.

In the implementation, you create a `Repository` folder in the `DataAccess` project and add an `OrderRepository` class under it. Make sure to reference the `Repository` project in `DataAccess`. The `OrderRepository` should provide an implementation for `IOrderRepository` and, in addition, should support disposing the context once the usage is over:

```
public class OrderRepository : IOrderRepository, IDisposable
```

Inside the class, first create a constructor to allow passing a `DbContext` instance to the repository:

```
private StoreEntities context;
    private bool disposed = false;

    public OrderRepository(StoreEntities context)
    {
        this.context = context;
    }
```

Ignore the `disposed` variable for now. It will be used to implement Dispose. The CRUD operations are implemented as follows:

```
public IEnumerable<Order> GetAllOrders()
    {
        return context.Orders.AsEnumerable();
    }

    public Order GetByOrderId(int orderId)
    {
        return context.Orders.Find(orderId);
    }

    public void Create(Order order)
    {
        context.Orders.Add(order);
    }

    public void Update(Order order)
    {
        context.Entry(order).State = System.Data.EntityState.Modified;
    }
```

```
public void Delete(int orderId)
{
    var order = context.Orders.Find(orderId);
    context.Orders.Remove(order);
}
```

In addition, there is a Save method to allow persisting the changes to database after one or more Create/Update/Delete operations from the controller.

```
public void Save()
{
    context.SaveChanges();
}
```

This is followed by the standard Dispose implementation to dispose the DbContext instance after the repository usage is over:

```
protected virtual void Dispose(bool disposing)
{
    if (!this.disposed)
    {
        if (disposing)
        {
            context.Dispose();
        }
    }
    this.disposed = true;
}

public void Dispose()
{
    Dispose(true);
    GC.SuppressFinalize(this);
}
```

■ **Note**   If you are not very familiar with the Dispose pattern, then we would strongly recommend reading about it in this MSDN article: http://msdn.microsoft.com/en-us/library/fs2xkftw.aspx.

With this completed, the Order repository implementation is ready. In a similar fashion, create the Contact repository. This is required at this point since the OrderController uses both the Order and Contact entities.

Now you need to implement the created repositories in the OrderController class, replacing the direct DbContext instance reference.

10.   First, add a reference to the Repository assembly in the DataDrivenWebSite project.

11. Open the OrderController class and create an instance of the Order and Contact repository as shown:

```
private IOrderRepository orderRepository;
        private IContactRepository contactRepository;
        public OrderController()
        {
            orderRepository = new OrderRepository(new StoreEntities());
            contactRepository = new ContactRepository(new StoreEntities());
        }
```

■ **Note**   Don't forget to remove the StoreEntities instance.

---

12. Now that the repository instances are created, you can start replacing the StoreEntities context reference with it inside the action methods. The following code illustrates the Index and Details method:

```
public ActionResult Index()
        {
            var orders = orderRepository.GetAllOrders();
            return View(orders.ToList());
        }


        //
        // GET: /Order/Details/5

        public ActionResult Details(int id = 0)
        {
            Order order = orderRepository.GetByOrderId(id);
            if (order == null)
            {
                return HttpNotFound();
            }
            return View(order);
        }
```

13. The Create method requires you to have a list of Contacts that can be associated with the Order. The Contact information is fetched using the ContactRepository instance.

```
public ActionResult Create()
        {
            ViewBag.ContactID = new SelectList(contactRepository.GetAllContacts(), "ID", "Name");
            return View();
        }

        //
        // POST: /Order/Create
```

```
        [HttpPost]
        public ActionResult Create(Order order)
        {
            if (ModelState.IsValid)
            {
                orderRepository.Create(order);
                orderRepository.Save();
                return RedirectToAction("Index");
            }

            ViewBag.ContactID = new SelectList(contactRepository.GetAllContacts(), "ID",
            "Name", order.ContactID);
            return View(order);
        }
```

14. Replace the StoreEntities DbContext instance in a similar fashion for the Update and Delete methods:

```
[HttpPost]
        public ActionResult Edit(Order order)
        {
            if (ModelState.IsValid)
            {
                orderRepository.Update(order);
                orderRepository.Save();
                return RedirectToAction("Index");
            }
            ViewBag.ContactID = new SelectList(contactRepository.GetAllContacts(), "ID",
            "Name", order.ContactID);
            return View(order);
        }

[HttpPost, ActionName("Delete")]
        public ActionResult DeleteConfirmed(int id)
        {
            orderRepository.Delete(id);
            orderRepository.Save();
            return RedirectToAction("Index");
        }
```

15. In Dispose, replace the DbContext Dispose call with the Dispose functions of the repositories.

```
protected override void Dispose(bool disposing)
        {
            orderRepository.Dispose();
            contactRepository.Dispose();
            base.Dispose(disposing);
        }
```

This is a fairly simple representation of a repository. This repository implementation is incapable of managing changes across multiple repositories, and there is a possibility that not all of them refer the same data context in the implementation. A *Unit of Work* pattern is more appropriately used in conjunction with the repository pattern to make the repositories function under a defined constraint.

Unit of Work

To implement the Unit of Work pattern, the first thing you need to do is to create a common interface for persisting the changes back to the store. A generic or base repository will use this to make the persistence tier consistent for all the repositories. The following code illustrates the interface:

```
public interface IUnitOfWork
{
    void SaveChanges();
}
```

Next, provide an implementation for IUnitOfWork on an extended context class that represents the type of repository. In our example, this is precisely represented by an Entity Framework repository in the DataAccess project:

```
public class EfStoreDataContext : StoreEntities, IUnitOfWork
    {
        public new void SaveChanges()
        {
            base.SaveChanges();
        }
    }
```

This is all you need to create a Unit of Work implementation. Now, let's explore the steps required to create a base repository that utilizes the Unit of Work pattern.

Create a class named BaseRepository in the DataAccess project and add the following code within it:

```
protected IUnitOfWork UnitOfWork { get; set; }

        protected StoreEntities Context
        {
            get { return (EfStoreDataContext)this.UnitOfWork; }
        }

        /// <summary>
        /// .ctor
        /// </summary>
        /// <param name="unitOfWork"></param>
        public BaseRepository(IUnitOfWork unitOfWork)
        {
            if (unitOfWork == null) throw new ArgumentNullException("unitOfWork");
            this.UnitOfWork = unitOfWork;
        }
```

```
public void Save()
    {
        this.Context.SaveChanges();
    }

    protected virtual DbSet<TEntity> GetDbSet<TEntity>() where TEntity : class
    {
        return this.Context.Set<TEntity>();
    }

    protected virtual void SetEntityState(object entity, EntityState entityState)
    {
        this.Context.Entry(entity).State = entityState;
    }
```

Notice that the implementation allows an IUnitOfWork type to be dependency injected via the constructor.

■ **Tip** *Unity* is a popular tool for implementing dependency injection. In general, if you are not familiar with concepts such as *Inversion of Control, Dependency Injection,* and *Unity,* then this project is a good start: http://unity.codeplex.com/. These patterns and tools are extremely useful in creating decoupled systems.

The base repository provides a generic implementation for fetching the DbSet instance, and it uses the Unit of Work interface to derive the DbContext.

■ **Tip** You can also move the Dispose implementation from each individual repository implementation to the BaseRepository class.

Now you are ready to create the individual repositories from the BaseRepository. Here is an example of the OrderRepository:

```
public class OrderRepository : BaseRepository, IOrderRepository
    {

        public OrderRepository(IUnitOfWork unitOfWork)
            : base(unitOfWork)
        {

        }

        public IEnumerable<Order> GetAllOrders()
        {
            return this.GetDbSet<Order>();
        }
```

```
public Order GetByOrderId(int orderId)
{
    return this.GetDbSet<Order>().Find(orderId);
}

public void Create(Order order)
{
    this.GetDbSet<Order>().Add(order);
}

public void Update(Order order)
{
    this.SetEntityState(order, System.Data.EntityState.Modified);
}

public void Delete(int orderId)
{
    var order = this.GetDbSet<Order>().Find(orderId);
    this.GetDbSet<Order>().Remove(order);
}
```

With this completed, your data access layer is ready with the base repository and Unit of Work implementation. The most challenging part you now face is in using the repository in your controllers and ensuring that the data context is consistent across Create/Update/Delete operations. This constraint can be enforced by dependency-injecting the data context along with using a command pattern. Although not absolutely necessary, the command pattern provides a much cleaner implementation.

■ **Note**   To enable Unity support, you can install the *Unity NuGet* package on the DataDrivenWebSite project. In addition, you need to add the Unity configuration to your Web.config file to store the mapping information.

The first artifact you would create in your Controller folder is a BaseController class, as follows:

```
public class BaseController : Controller
    {
        private readonly IServiceLocator serviceLocator;

        public BaseController(IServiceLocator serviceLocator)
        {
            this.serviceLocator = serviceLocator;
        }

        protected T Using<T>() where T : class
        {
            var handler = serviceLocator.GetInstance<T>();
```

```
        if (handler == null)
        {
            throw new NullReferenceException("Unable to resolve type with service locator;
            type " + typeof(T).Name);
        }
        return handler;
    }
}
```

The Using method will resolve the type of command you are trying to execute, and it will perform the operation using the repositories that are needed. The following code illustrates an example of a CreateOrder command:

```
public class CreateOrder
    {
        private readonly IOrderRepository orderRepository;

        public CreateOrder(IOrderRepository orderRepository)
        {
            this.orderRepository = orderRepository;
        }

        public virtual void Execute(Order order)
        {
            if (order == null) throw new ArgumentNullException("invalid order");

            try
            {
                orderRepository.Create(order);
                orderRepository.Save();
            }
            catch (Exception)
            {
                //LOG
                throw;
            }
        }
    }
```

In a similar fashion, create commands necessary for the operations in the OrderController.

■ **Note** While this is a simple command implementation, you have the potential to execute complex commands involving multiple repositories.

Next, open the `OrderController` class and modify the implementation to make it inherit the `BaseController` as shown here:

```
public class OrderController : BaseController
    {
        public OrderController(IServiceLocator serviceLocator)
            :base (serviceLocator)
        {

        }
    }
```

You can now use the commands to implement the action methods in the controller. Here is an example of Create:

```
[HttpPost]
        public ActionResult Create(Order order)
        {
            if (ModelState.IsValid)
            {
                Using<CreateOrder>().Execute(order);
                return RedirectToAction("Index");
            }

            ViewBag.ContactID = new SelectList(Using<GetAllContacts>().Execute(), "ID", "Name",
            order.ContactID);
            return View(order);
        }
```

The mapping configuration must be set in the `Unity` section of your `Web.config` file or in a separate Unity configuration file.

```
<unity>
        <typeAliases>
                    <typeAlias alias="string" type="System.String, mscorlib" />
                    <typeAlias alias="singleton" type="Microsoft.Practices.Unity.
                    ContainerControlledLifetimeManager, Microsoft.Practices.Unity" />
        </typeAliases>
        <containers>
                    <container name="container">
                                <types>
        <type type="Repository.IOrderRepository, Repository, Version=1.0.0.0, Culture= neutral, PublicKeyToken= null"
mapTo="DataAccess.Repositories.OrderRepository, DataAccess">
        </type>
        <type type="Repository.IContactRepository, Repository, Version=1.0.0.0, Culture= neutral,
        PublicKeyToken= null"
mapTo="DataAccess.Repositories.ContactRepository, DataAccess">
        </type>
```

```
      <type type="Repository.IUnitOfWork, Repository, Version=1.0.0.0, Culture= neutral, PublicKeyToken= null"
mapTo="DataAccess.EfStoreDataContext, DataAccess">
      </type>

   </type>
                                                    </types>
                       </container>
            </containers>
</unity>
```

■ **Note**   You must add the Unity container instantiation logic in the `Global.asax` file's `Application_Start()` method for enabling support for dependency injection.

This completes the implementation of the Unit of Work. There is some additional refactoring you could do to your code depending on the similarity of your repositories. You could potentially make a generic repository that lists the CRUD operations and totally do away with individual repositories if your operations are consistent across entities. This can be an exercise for you to try out on your own.

Next, you will explore some of the techniques used to deal with most common issues you will encounter when building data-driven websites.

Techniques to Deal with Issues

The earlier book in this series, *Beginning ASP.NET 2.0 Databases, 2nd Edition*, by Damien Foggon (Apress, 2006), explored some of the issues you will encounter while building data-driven websites, presenting techniques to deal with them. While the issues are roughly the same today, the techniques have evolved in the context of enhancements in the .NET Framework, most visibly in ADO.NET with the addition of Entity Framework.

Concurrency

It is a common possibility in data-driven websites that while one user is editing a record, someone else has already deleted it. During update, this will cause a concurrency exception in Entity Framework. By default, Entity Framework supports *optimistic concurrency*, meaning that it will assume the best-case scenario (in this case, referring to the fact that the data hasn't changed while being updated). The DbContext SaveChanges method call will throw a DbUpdateConcurrencyException (System.Data.Entity.Infrastructure) exception in such a case. There are a few suitable approaches that you could choose based on your implementation requirements. Primarily, the approaches revolve around the deciding factor of who wins the state war. If you choose to do a *Database-Win*, then you could handle the exception to notify the client about the changes in the database using the following code:

```
try
      {
            this.Context.SaveChanges();
      }
      catch (DbUpdateConcurrencyException concurrencyException)
      {

            concurrencyException.Entries.Single().Reload();
      }
```

The Reload method refreshes the entity values from the store.

Another option is to make the client win. In this case, you could set the original values of the entry to be the values fetched from database:

```
var concurrencyEntry = concurrencyException.Entries.Single();
concurrencyEntry. OriginalValues.SetValues(concurrencyEntry.GetDatabaseValues());
```

In addition, you could also provide the ability to the end user to choose a suitable option in a conflicting update.

Transactions

While Entity Framework internally handles transactions, and you could safeguard your implementation from partial updates by implementing Unit of Work, however, there could be scenarios where you would need to run updates across multiple data context instances and you may want them in a transaction. In such scenarios, you could wrap your SaveChanges operation in a TransactionScope (System.Transactions). The following code illustrates this action:

```
using(var scope = new TransactionScope(TransactionScopeOption.RequiresNew))
                {
                        //save changes to multiple db context operations
                }
```

Debugging Issues

While new techniques have evolved to deal with issues in building data-driven websites, the debugging capabilities of Visual Studio have also been progressively enhanced over the multiple releases of this most popular development tool. First introduced in Visual Studio 2010, *IntelliTrace* offers some interesting new updates in Visual Studio 2012, such as tracing and debugging issues in production using the *Standalone Collector*. Most importantly, it works behind the scenes in collecting trace information as you use the application, and it can pinpoint exceptions in code while debugging the application using the trace log collected by the tool. This generally reduces the time and effort spent in debugging issues within websites and applications that are built using .NET Framework. Let's try out an exercise to explore the steps to follow when debugging issues with the DataDrivenWebSite Web application that you built in Chapter 7.

▓ **Note**   IntelliTrace is available only with Visual Studio 2012 Ultimate Edition.

TRY IT OUT: TRACE EXECUTION HISTORY AND DEBUG ISSUES WITH INTELLITRACE

For the purpose of this exercise, you will modify the DataDrivenWebSite Web application project to introduce a bug deliberately that can be captured by IntelliTrace. To do that, open the DataDrivenWebSite application in your instance of Visual Studio 2012 Ultimate Edition and modify the OrderController class Create action to change the "*Name*" parameter to "*Names*," as shown in Figure 12-3.

```
public ActionResult Create()
{
    ViewBag.ContactID = new SelectList(db.Contacts, "ID", "Names");
    return View();
}
```

Figure 12-3. *Introducing a bug in code*

This simulates a typographic error in the application code. Now you are all set to debug the application using IntelliTrace. Follow these steps:

1. Compile and run the application in *Debug* mode. While the application is running, go back to your Visual Studio window. You will see the IntelliTrace pane, as shown in Figure 12-4. You will also notice that there is a *Break All* option available to break the execution and to see the trace log as it is captured.

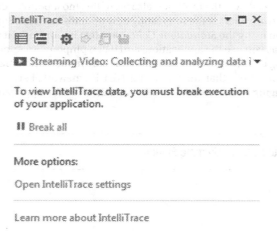

Figure 12-4. *IntelliTrace capturing log*

2. You can go to the Settings option from the IntelliTrace pane to change trace log settings, such as deciding whether to capture call information along with IntelliTrace events. This is shown in Figure 12-5.

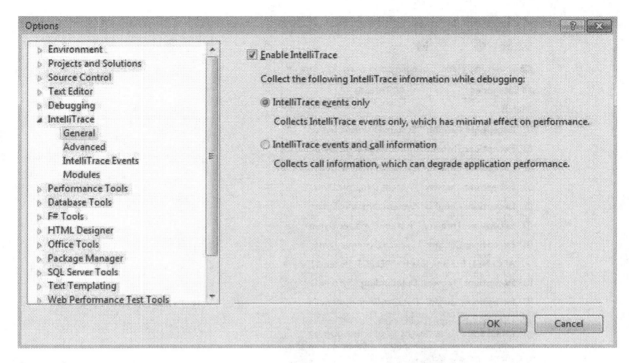

Figure 12-5. *IntelliTrace settings*

3. Navigate to the *Order* view and click *Create New.* An exception will occur, and you will see IntelliTrace reporting a *Live Event,* which is an exception caught by the debugger, as shown in Figure 12-6.

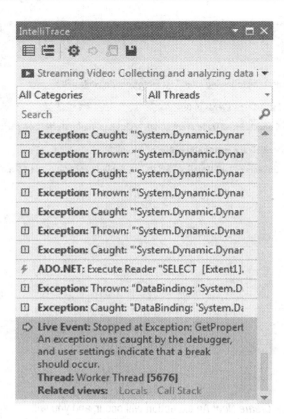

Figure 12-6. IntelliTrace capturing exception

4. At this point, click the save icon on the IntelliTrace pane to save the trace log. Go back to the OrderController and fix the issue, since you already know what the problem is from the debugger. Build and run the solution. Order creation works fine.

5. Open the trace log file (.iTrace) by double-clicking it. It opens in Visual Studio. You will find a bunch of Call Stack and Exception Data information, as shown in Figure 12-7.

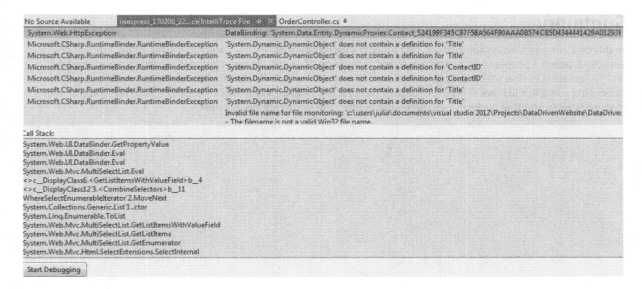

Figure 12-7. *Captured IntelliTrace log*

6. From the exception data, find the `HttpWebException` and click the *Start Debugging* button. You will notice that it points to the location where the exception occurred, even though the source has since changed and the fix was made, as shown in Figure 12-8.

```
<fieldset>
    <legend>Order</legend>

    <div class="editor-label">
        @Html.LabelFor(model => model.ContactID, "Contact")
    </div>
    <div class="editor-field">
        @Html.DropDownList("ContactID", String.Empty)
        @Html.ValidationMessageFor(model => model.ContactID)
    </div>

    <div class="editor-label">
        @Html.LabelFor(model => model.Quantity)
    </div>
    <div class="editor-field">
        @Html.EditorFor(model => model.Quantity)
        @Html.ValidationMessageFor(model => model.Quantity)
    </div>
```

Figure 12-8. *Historical debugging with IntelliTrace*

You have successfully debugged an issue that occurred in the past that couldn't be reproduced by your local debugger. This is very powerful. You can no longer claim that a bug cannot be reproduced. If the code is not in sync in different environments, team members can share trace logs to figure out which parts of the code caused bugs, even if they are historical.

Summary

In this chapter, you learned some of the best practices for building data-driven websites using Entity Framework. You also learned a couple of data access patterns in the form of repository and Unit of Work. You then studied the techniques used to deal with issues like concurrency and transaction. Finally, you learned how to perform historical debugging using IntelliTrace. These techniques and practices will go a long way in helping you to build applications that are reliable and that perform well within the defined infrastructure boundaries.

CHAPTER 13

■ ■ ■

Application Lifecycle Management

Every enterprise-scale software program goes through a life cycle of planning, development, testing, and deployment in iterations, allowing customers to see what is being developed along the way and to provide feedback that effectively drives the quality of the software to their satisfaction. As a developer, you don't just write code—you do many things in addition to writing code that align software development business needs. This is collectively called *Application Lifecycle Management (ALM), and it includes the following tasks*:

1. Participating in product planning.

2. Analyzing requirements to understand the conditions of customer satisfaction and breaking them down into deliverable tasks with specific estimates.

3. Architecting the software in different layers and modules that interact with each other.

4. Setting up environments for source control, build, and deployment.

5. Managing source code to ensure that correct versions are released according to the plan.

6. Writing unit tests to ensure that your portion of the work exhibits the desired behavior.

7. Analyzing code for best practices on performance and maintenance through Code Analysis, performance counters, and code reviews.

8. Building and deploying versions of the software for testing and feedback.

9. Instrumenting code to trace issues and to debug the code.

10. Communicating status and demonstrating progress.

The preceding list is not complete by any means. However, it is unlikely that all aspects listed will require your involvement. It truly depends on the dynamics of the team. Larger teams often have dedicated *DevOps (Development Operations)* team members to take care of build and deployment. However, it is still your responsibility as a developer to ensure that the piece of code that you write works and doesn't impact the code written by other members in an adverse fashion. Actual responsibilities are often defined in a *Degree of Completion* list that defines the "what-is-done" criteria for the team. Here is a good article on the subject: www.scrumalliance.org/articles/106-definition-of-done-a-reference.

In this chapter, we will explore some aspects of ALM that impact you as a developer building data-driven ASP. NET web applications. In particular, you will learn the following:

- How to use Visual Studio for Architecture.

- How Visual Studio can enhance your productivity as a developer.

- How to unit test and debug your data-driven ASP.NET application.

- The best practices for building and releasing software.

In the sections that follow, you will learn how VS 2012 along with *Team Foundation Server* (TFS) 2012 can help you be effective as a developer and facilitate the process of designing, deploying, and monitoring ASP.NET applications under the constraints of nonfunctional requirements. The instruction will be limited to features of TFS that are relevant to building modern ASP.NET applications and not TFS in general, since this is a topic for greater discussion and outside the scope of this book.

Architecting the Enterprise

Architecting the enterprise is a multifaceted approach to developing one or more applications operating independently or in conjunction with one another. In addition, these applications may need to interact with applications that are already part of the enterprise. There are two major activities that you do as part of architecting that precede development:

1. Requirements leading to the functional aspects of the application(s) require you to understand the various use cases as part of the problem domain, and then use them to model the different layers in the solution domain. You can use several tools for this purpose. The preferred option is to use the Visual Studio 2012 Ultimate edition, which features many capabilities that help you model the application layers. The architectural capabilities in Visual Studio 2012 support UML 2.0 specifications. UML stands for *Unified Modeling Language,* and it is the language of choice for application design. The Object Management Group's website is the most authoritative source for learning UML (www.uml.org/).

■ **Note**   Although modeling functional requirements occurs quite a bit before the actual development begins, it is a continuous process and it evolves as requirements change with the development of the application.

2. Requirements leading to nonfunctional aspects drive the constraints under which applications must function. The solution chosen for building data-driven ASP.NET applications relies heavily on the nonfunctional aspects, and it determines whether the application and data will live on-premise, in the cloud, or in a hybrid environment.

Designing New Applications

Visual Studio 2012 features several capabilities for architecting and designing applications as well as helping to monitor and analyze the constraints under which the applications must run. These capabilities are in addition to the data modeling features supported by Entity Framework that you have learned about throughout this book.

■ **Note**   Architectural capabilities are limited to the Ultimate edition of Visual Studio 2012, and a lot of diagnostic and debugging capabilities for managing the constraints are available only in the Ultimate or Premium editions. You can learn more about the capabilities in different versions of Visual Studio 2012 at www.microsoft.com/visualstudio/eng/products/compare.

The architectural capabilities are listed under the ARCHITECTURE tab in Visual Studio 2012, as shown in Figure 13-1.

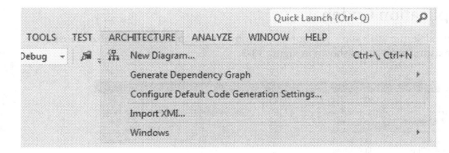

Figure 13-1. *Visual Studio 2012 architectural capabilities*

You can use the "*New Diagram . . .*" option to create a new model using the UML specifications. You have the option of creating class, sequence, use case, activity, component, and layer diagrams, as shown in Figure 13-2.

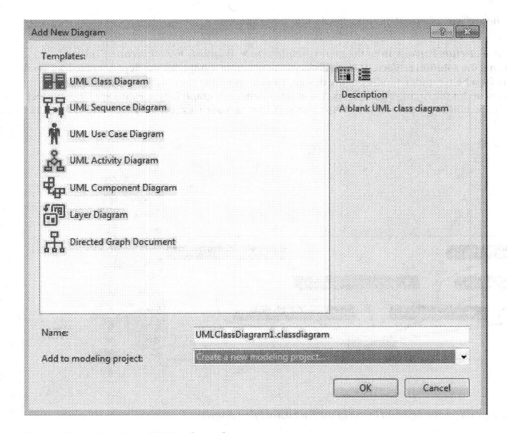

Figure 13-2. *Creating a UML or layer diagram*

▪ **Note** You can create a modeling project for your design work by selecting the "*Create a new modeling project...*" option in the *Add to modeling project* drop-down.

Analyzing Existing Application Codebase

The architectural capabilities in Visual Studio 2012 allow you not only to model your application but also to inspect the architecture and code base of existing projects, as shown in Figure 13-3.

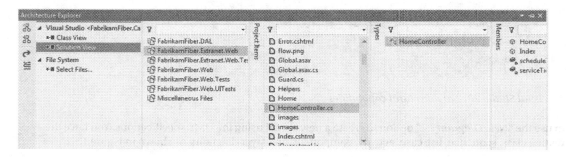

Figure 13-3. Exploring the artifacts of a solution using the Architecture Explorer

You can launch the *Architecture Explorer* from the menu *Architecture* ➤ *Windows* ➤ *Architecture Explorer*.

In addition to exploring the solution artifacts, it also allows you to generate a graph for the dependencies between objects in different layers for a better understanding of the design. You can generate the graph using the "*Generate Dependency Graph*" option under the Architecture menu. A sample dependency graph for the Fabrikam Fiber project is shown in Figure 13-4. It is available for download at http://vsarguidance.codeplex.com/downloads/get/379895.

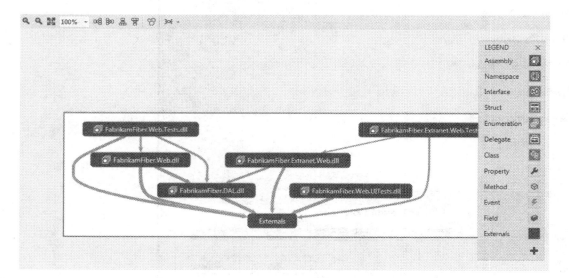

Figure 13-4. Dependency graph for the different layers of the Fabrikam Fiber project

Next, you will explore features of Visual Studio 2012 that can help you enhance your productivity as a developer of ASP.NET applications.

Enhance Your Productivity

As part of your daily routine, you perform a wide variety of tasks using your favorite *Integrated Development Environment* (IDE) Visual Studio, stretching it to its limits. Often, issues with the IDE hinder your productivity. In VS 2012, every operation in the IDE is asynchronous, so you no longer have to wait for any operation to complete (like loading the solution) before you can work on the next operation (like reviewing a build failure). In addition to the enhancements in IDE, we will now address a number of new features that can enhance your productivity as a developer.

Better Access to Files and Code

Search is now present everywhere in the IDE, and nearly all of the panes support search. *Solution Explorer* is one of the heavily used panes in the IDE, and it supports fuzzy search not only for files but also for artifacts like resources, classes, methods, and properties, as shown in Figure 13-5. In addition, Solution Explorer also allows you to preview resource files, such as images and documents, from within the Explorer so that you can quickly identify the resources you want to use.

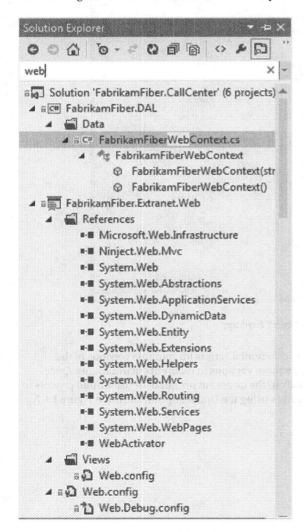

Figure 13-5. *Searching for artifacts in the Solution Explorer*

■ **Note**   Interestingly, Solution Explorer also doubles as the Object Explorer.

Accessing Data

Visual Studio 2012 features extensive support for data access. It doubles as the Database Object Explorer with the SQL Server Object Explorer pane that you can launch from the View menu. It displays the LocalDB databases associated with the project, and you have the option of connecting to any instance of SQL Server. Once connected, you can do multiple things. You can run queries and create a Database project directly from the database, as shown in Figure 13-6.

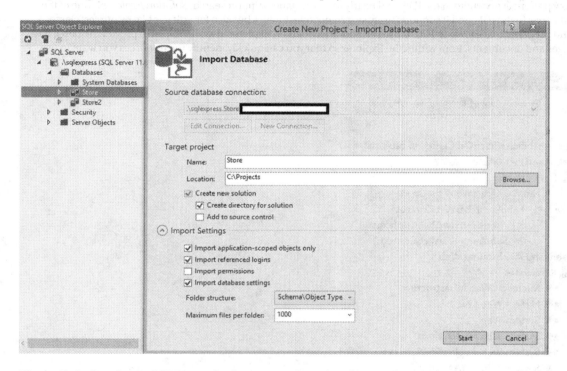

Figure 13-6. *Creating an SQL Server database project from the Object Explorer*

In addition, you can also run a schema compare to generate differential scripts for multiple versions of the database, as shown in Figure 13-7. This is useful for upgrading database versions in different environments. Once the differential script is generated, you can store it to run manually in the target environment or use a build process to the target database. Alternatively, you can directly apply the changes using the Update option shown in Figure 13-7.

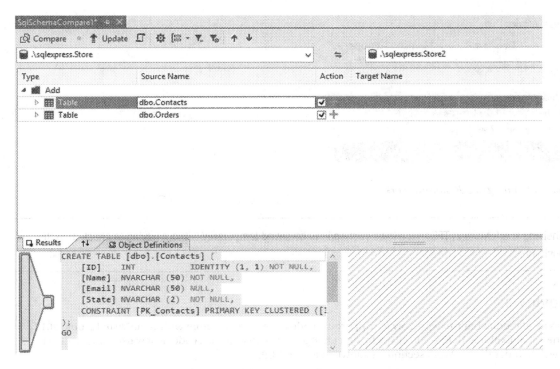

Figure 13-7. *Comparing different versions of the Store Database*

■ **Note** Visual Studio also has an SQL menu for quick access to some of the features of the SQL Server Explorer.

Suspend and Resume

Let's say that you are working on a new feature of an application and suddenly you are assigned a high-priority bug for quick resolution. What should you do? What happens to the enhancement on which you were working with all checked out files and half-completed changes? You definitely don't want to lose them. The Team Explorer in Visual Studio provides a Suspend feature that allows you to suspend your current work. All your changes will be shelved, and the Workspace cleaned (all opened files closed) for the new work to start. You can then work on the high-priority bug and, once you are done, you may use the Resume option to resume work on your enhancement. The Resume option will unshelve the changes and restore the workspace back to the state it was in when you left. Cool, isn't it? This feature is shown in Figure 13-8.

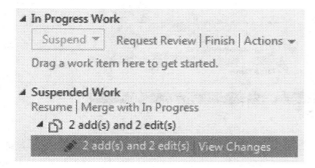

Figure 13-8. *Suspending and Resuming work*

___

■ **Note**   Shelving is a feature in TFS that allows your code to be saved temporarily without having to check in to the primary repository.

___

Code Reviews

TFS 2012 has an elaborate built-in workflow to support the code review process from within the Visual Studio 2012 IDE using the Team Explorer. Before you check in your changes, you can request a code review using the Request Code Review link under the My Work section, as shown in Figure 13-9.

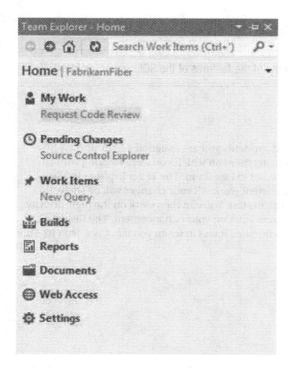

Figure 13-9. *Requesting Code Review*

In the New Code Review request screen, you can specify the person whom you want to perform the review, a subject for the review, and a description of the review request, as shown in Figure 13-10.

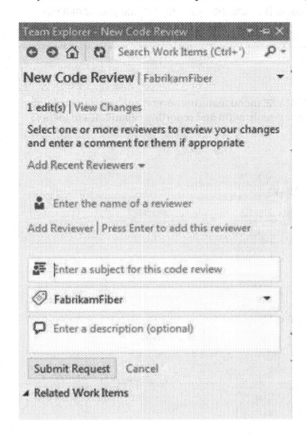

Figure 13-10. *Adding details about the review*

The assigned reviewer can accept the code review request in the Team Explorer and send feedback. The feedback options are shown in Figure 13-11.

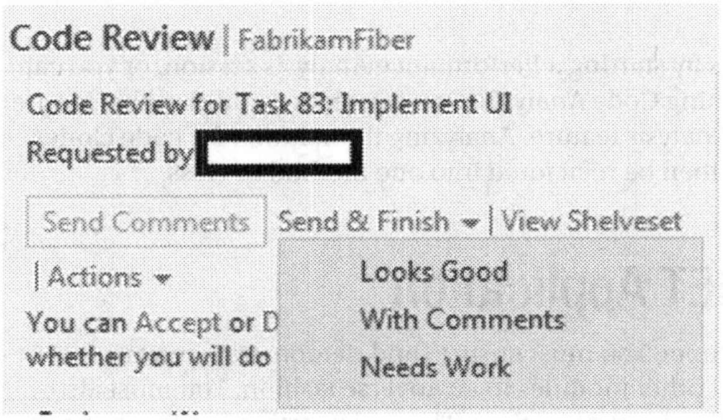

Code Review | FabrikamFiber

Code Review for Task 83: Implement UI
Requested by ███████████

| Send Comments | Send & Finish ▾ | View Shelveset |

| Actions ▾
You can Accept or D   Looks Good
whether you will do   With Comments
                             Needs Work

Figure 13-11. *Code Review feedback*

■ **Note** As a reviewer, you can see the list of files requested to review. You can click the file in your Team Explorer to compare the changes using the enhanced differential compare tool in TFS, and then you may provide your comments about each file reviewed.

Analyze and Profile Your Application

Visual Studio 2012 Premium and Ultimate editions sport an ANALYZE menu featuring several analysis and profiling tools, as illustrated in Figure 13-12. All of the tools have enhanced visualization and reporting capabilities to identify issues with code and profile performance bottlenecks.

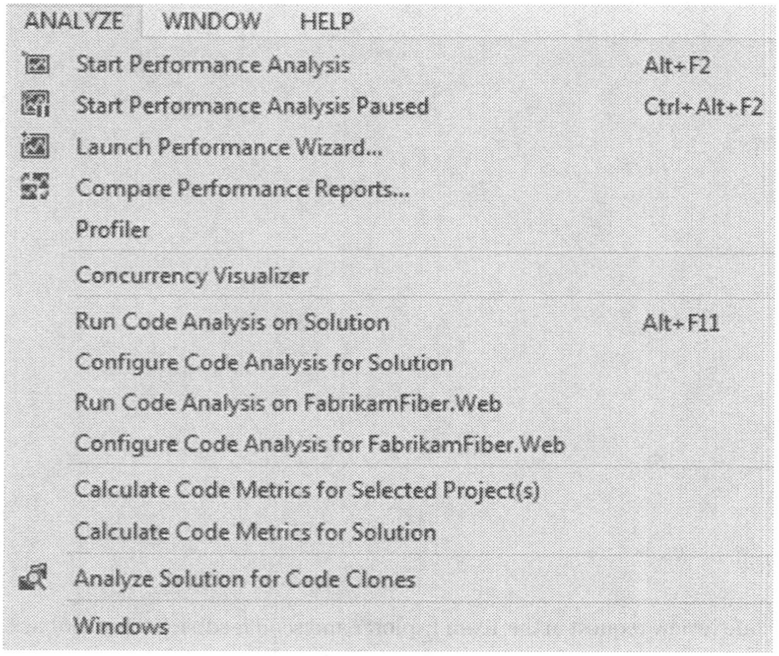

Figure 13-12. Visual Studio analysis and profiling capabilities

You could profile your application for performance issues by starting a Performance Analysis session, or you can review your application code for framework violations by running Code Analysis. One interesting addition that is sure to save you several hours refactoring code is the Code Clone Analysis feature. Analyzing the solution for code clones reports similar code blocks across the application, which can then be refactored into one method or class.

Testing and Debugging Your ASP.NET Application

Testability is an important criterion for completion for a developer. You must ensure (and demonstrate to your peers) that the code in your module works and doesn't impact other modules in an adverse fashion. You must also demonstrate that your code successfully achieves the desired business objectives. The real question is: How do you demonstrate that your code works? The answer is through *unit testing*.

Unit Testing

You can write a unit test for your block of code to demonstrate to your colleagues that it works. Both VS 2012 and TFS 2012 have extensive support for unit tests. While Visual Studio provides the platform to create and execute unit tests, TFS provides the means to ensure that builds are verified for their authenticity by validating against these tests.

Testability has been one of the key endeavors of the ASP.NET MVC team, and to support this they have provided out-of-box features for unit testing in the ASP.NET MVC 4 Project Template. In Chapter 7, you learned how to create a data-driven ASP.NET MVC 4 application using Entity Framework and how to unit test your Controllers. You also learned how to isolate code under test using Microsoft Fakes. In the following section "Build and Deployment," you will learn how to associate your unit tests with TFS Team Builds for asserting the quality of the build.

Historical Debugging with IntelliTrace

You learned how to use IntelliTrace in the Chapter 12 exercise "Try It Out: Capturing and Debugging Exceptions with IntelliTrace." In addition to testing, debugging has also been simplified in Visual Studio 2012 with new tools like IntelliTrace. While IntelliTrace was initially introduced in Visual Studio 2010, it has been further enhanced in Visual Studio 2012. IntelliTrace lets you record events as they occur in your application, and then it allows you to inspect the code, local data, and the call stack. You can store the logs for future reference and historical debugging. You can capture IntelliTrace data outside Visual Studio using the Standalone IntelliTrace Collector tool (`intellitracecollector.exe`), making it one of the most powerful tools for tracing issues in environments where Visual Studio cannot be installed, like staging and production. The following MSDN article provides a step-by-step explanation to setting up the standalone collector and debugging your application using the trace logs collected by the tool: `http://msdn.microsoft.com/en-us/library/vstudio/hh398365.aspx`.

Build and Deployment

Enterprises present different levels of maturity when it comes to releasing software in a predictable fashion. Organizations with the highest levels of maturity are able to achieve a state called *Ideal State Deployment Pipeline*, where releases are fully automated and orchestrated with builds to release software according to a predefined plan. The vision behind Team Foundation was to provide a one-stop shop for all of the ALM needs of an organization, and that includes the ability to integrate code continuously and to do automated deployments. TFS has evolved tremendously in this area, and it now supports Windows Workflow Foundation–based workflows and a number of activities to support build and deployment. The workflows are customizable templates, and they are available in the BuildTemplates folder under your Team project, as illustrated in Figure 13-13.

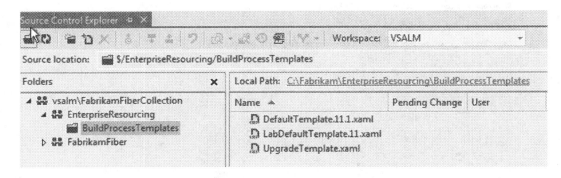

Figure 13-13. *Default Team Build Workflow Templates*

■ **Note**   TFS 2012 introduces additional workflows for deploying applications in Windows Azure.

Team Build Definition

You can create a new Team Build from the Builds section in your Team Explorer. Table 13-1 illustrates the builds that you should consider provisioning in your project:

Table 13-1. *Team Build Definitions to Consider in Your ASP.NET Web Application Project*

Build Type	Definition
CI (Continuous Integration) Build	A CI build compiles the associated solution, and it is executed at every check-in made by the developer. A bare minimum of one CI build should be associated with each Development Team. Unit test projects must be associated with the CI build as a measure of quality.
Scheduled Nightly Build	A build associated with unit tests that runs daily at a scheduled time, typically when the team is not working, can be configured. As a bare minimum, this should be configured for Development and quality assurance (QA) environments. Nightly builds should be configured to deploy the output in appropriate environments.
Release Build	On-demand deployment to a staging environment.
Gated Build	Prevents breaking changes and unit test violations from getting checked in TFS.

Team Build Definition Triggers

You can set a trigger for the build definition depending on the type of build you want to create. For example, Figure 13-14 illustrates setting up a CI trigger for a Continuous Integration build for the Development environment.

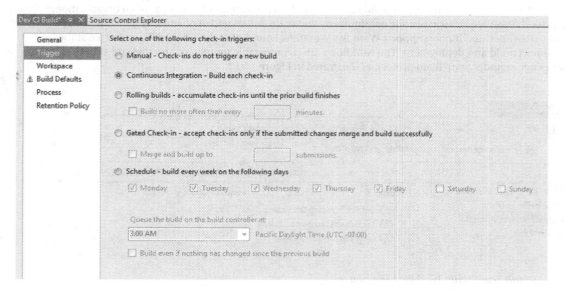

Figure 13-14. *Setting up a CI Team Build*

In a similar fashion, select the Gated check-in option for the build trigger if you want to enable gated check-in for your source control branch.

Team Build Process

With a TFS Team Build, you can do much more than just compiling the configured solution to check if there are any breaking changes. You can also associate unit tests with the build and configure it to fail if the tests don't pass during the run. Additionally, you can set rules for the build to analyze code for framework design violations by setting the Code Analysis property on the Build Template to true. This is illustrated in Figure 13-15.

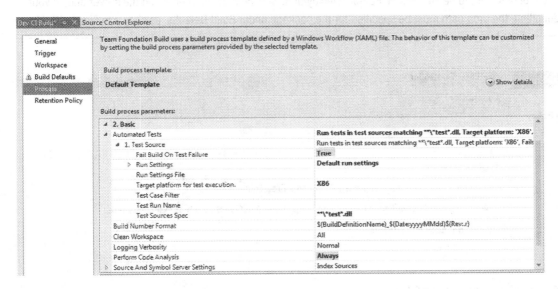

Figure 13-15. *Setting up Team Build properties for unit tests and Code Analysis*

Deploy Using Team Build

Web packages for ASP.NET 4.5 Web and MVC 4 applications created using the TFS Team Build can be deployed automatically using the Web Deployment Service. Web Deployment Service is part of Microsoft's Web Platform Installer, which can be downloaded from www.microsoft.com/web/downloads/platform.aspx. It allows remote deployment of web packages using MS Build Arguments specified under the Advanced section of a new Team Build, as shown in Figure 13-16.

3. Advanced	
Agent Settings	Use agent where Name=* and Tags is empty; Max Wait Time: 04:00:00
Analyze Test Impact	True
Associate Changesets and Work Items	True
Copy Outputs to Drop Folder	True
Create Work Item on Failure	True
Disable Tests	False
Get Version	
Label Sources	True
MSBuild Arguments	/p:DeployOnBuild=True /p:DeployTarget=MsDeployPublish /p:MSDeployPublishMethod=RemoteAgen
MSBuild Platform	Auto
Private Drop Location	

Figure 13-16. *Automated deployment of web packages using Team Build*

The command expands, as shown in the following code sample.

```
/p:DeployOnBuild=True /p:DeployTarget=MsDeployPublish /p:MSDeployPublishMethod=RemoteAgent
/p:CreatePackageOnPublish=True /p:DeployIisAppPath="Default Web Site/<Web Application Name>"
/p:MsDeployServiceUrl=http://<remote server address>/msdeployagentservice /p:username=<user name>
/p:password=<password>
```

The /p:DeployOnBuild switch triggers a remote deployment if the build is successful.

▨ **Note** For the deployment to be successful, Remote Deployment Service must be running on the server and, in your Team Build definition, the drop path must be specified for the package under Build Defaults, as shown in Figure 13-17.

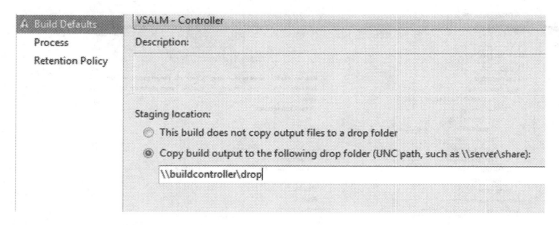

Figure 13-17. *Specifying a Build Drop folder*

In addition to deploying on premise, TFS 2012 also features built-in templates to deploy your application automatically in cloud. This article elaborates the steps in detail: www.windowsazure.com/en-us/develop/net/common-tasks/publishing-with-tfs/.

Deploying SQL Server Databases

In the section "Accessing Data" under "Enhance Your Productivity," you learned how to create a Database project from an SQL Server database. Database projects can also be deployed automatically using TFS. You can create a TFS Team Build to deploy a database using MS Build commands for SQL Server Data-Tier Applications supported by SQL Server Data Tools (SSDT). You can learn more about SSDT at http://msdn.microsoft.com/en-us/data/tools.aspx.

To create a database deployment build, first you need to create a published profile for the environment where you want the database deployed. You can create this by right-clicking the database project and then clicking Publish. The dialog to do this is displayed in Figure 13-18. Make sure to check the *Add profile to project* checkbox in the Publish dialog.

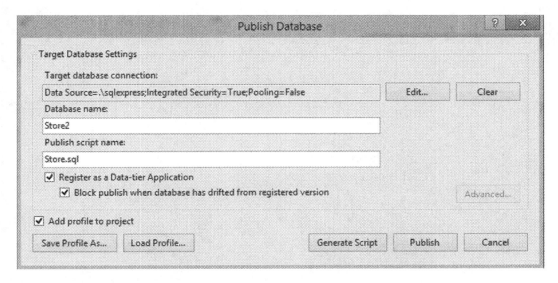

Figure 13-18. *Publishing profile for database projects*

You can then use the following MS Build commands in your TFS Team Build definition to deploy the following database: /t:Build /t:Publish /p:SqlPublishProfilePath=Store.publish.xml.

Summary

This chapter provided an overview of application lifecycle management and the associated tools used in the process of building data-driven web applications. You learned how to use Team Foundation effectively, and you also studied some of the Visual Studio 2012 features that can enhance your productivity as a developer.

Index

■ E, F, G, H

■ I, J, K

■ L

▨ W, X, Y, Z